Paul Richardson has written on Spanish cultural themes for publications such as *Harpers*, the *Sunday Times*, the *Observer* and *Attitude*. He is the author of *Not Part of the Package: A Year in Ibiza* and a gastronomic tour of Britain, *Cornucopia*.

Also by Paul Richardson

Not Part of the Package: A Year in Ibiza
Cornucopia

Our Lady
of the Sewers

And Other Adventures in Deep Spain

PAUL RICHARDSON

An *Abacus* Book

First published in Great Britain by
Little, Brown and Company 1998
This edition published by Abacus 1999
Reprinted 2000

A CIP catalogue record for this book is
available from the British Library.

ISBN 0 349 10857 9

Typeset in Baskerville and Centaur by M Rules
Printed and bound in Great Britain by
Clays Ltd, St Ives plc

Abacus
A Division of
Little, Brown and Company (UK)
Brettenham House
Lancaster Place
London WC2E 7EN

In memory of Susie Gautier-Smith
(1963–96), *la más cachonda*

Contents

Acknowledgements

A ffectionate thanks to all those friends who lent me their ears, beds, and moral support, including: Julian Alexander and Kirstan Romano, Adrian Arnold, Gerardo Barahona, Michael Blackman and Anney Weiner, Richard Beswick, Jasone Camara, Roger Clarke and Simon Su, Carol Downie and Julian Griffiths, Katy Emck, Jane and Susan Ferguson, Lisa Freedman, Felicity Hawkins and all at Classic FM, Carlos de las Heras, Ian Irvine and Laura Tennant, Rocío López de Diego, Emma Mahony and Adam Barker, Piluca Molina, Fernando Monge and Estrella, Carlos Monge and family, Hazel Morgan, Sandy Pratt, Manuel Ramírez and Susana, Simon Richardson and Sarah Whitehead, Derek Richardson, Sasha Schoenfeld, Marlena Spieler and Alan McLaughlan, Sally Stein, Marc Taeger, Edwina Taeger, Lola Trives, Isabel Trives and Juanjo, Enrique Trives and Concha, Robert Turnbull, Merle and Rodger Woodhams . . .

And thanks to Juan Ignacio for still being there.

OUR LADY
OF THE SEWERS

Preface

> 'As it seems to me the past develops, continuous, and is alive
> in Spain; like a seed still promising good things, whereas in
> so much of the West the seeds have perished.'
>
> (Hilaire Belloc, *Many Cities*)

Modernity has wiped most of Europe squeaky clean, removing most of the bugs and the grime and a good deal of the colour and emotion.

No one writes travel books about Europe any more. This is because life in any one part of the continent more and more resembles life in all the others. We exist, most of us 300 million, in such a well-kept, well-upholstered society – the sitting-room of the world, where the only barriers between one armchair and another are linguistic and monetary, and neither of those things will be coming between us for much longer. We have more and more in common. We all wear Levis, eat pizza/burgers/kebabs/Chinese, use the same toothpastes, watch the same game shows under different names (*Blind Date* in Germany makes an Englishman long for Cilla Black), get cash out of the wall if our cards are working, drive to the hypermarket on Saturday mornings and hanker after holidays in southern Europe or, if we happen to live in the south, in the north.

What attracted me to Spain, as a northern European, was the Spanish defiance of this antiseptic newness. I was fascinated by the way the country seemed to harbour pockets of eccentric loyalty to something far odder and more elemental than the shrink-wrapped sameness of modern European life. Just under the surface of the culture I saw a rough concatenation of fire, water, air and earth. Spain seemed to be waging an unconscious war against twenty-first-century blandness and conformity. Though in the cities it has practically lost this war, out in the countryside it is still fighting a rearguard action. Spain is still different. Just.

I am not the first to notice the difference, nor the obstinate resistance to change. Mrs William Pitt Byrne, a mid-nineteenth-century chronicler of Hispanic manners and morals whose travels in Spain are a catalogue of Victorian fault-finding and snobbery, disapproved of both factors, equating them with a repulsive sort of primitivism in the Spanish soul. 'Whenever the Spaniard is civilized, it will be in spite of himself. If the self-satisfied denizens of the Peninsula (a word which seems to imply disconnection from the civilized world) have submitted to the partial inroad of rail and steam, it is because the novelty has been thrust upon them by foreign enterprise,' she wrote, pursing her lips so tightly it must have caused her some pain.

Other observers also picked up on the backward-looking, inward-looking aspects of Spanish life, but wrote about them, instead, with mouths open and tongues hanging out. In a letter to his sister Sarah in 1830, Benjamin Disraeli described the country thus: 'The alfresco life of the inhabitants induces a variety of the most picturesque manners, their semi-savageness making each district retain with barbarous jealousy their own customs and their own costumes. Oh! Wonderful Spain! I thought that enthusiasm was dead within me and nothing could be new . . .'

As customs and costumes began their disappearance, towards the end of the first half of the twentieth century, hispanophiles who had settled in this charmingly primitive world began to complain of its destruction and replacement with the very thing they had fled. What they found hard to accept, of course, was that the erosion of 'their' Spain by tourism, improved communications, increased wealth and so on, was not only a consummation devoutly to be wished for the Spanish people, but was also in some measure the logical result of their own presence and writings.

Gerald Brenan, having spent the pre-war years in a village in the Alpujarras where witchcraft was still practised, snail-gatherers sang ancient charming songs in the fields and incest was believed to be a cure for madness, was surprised to discover on a return visit in 1955 that Yegen now had schools, sanitation and a regular bus link with Granada.

By the 1960s, as the tourist boom kicked in, the complaints became shriller. From his 'unspoiled' fastness in Mallorca, Robert Graves railed against the economic revolution that was polluting local culture with 'flamenco strumming by pretended gypsies' and killing off age-old agricultural methods. 'At Deyà we now import gypsies from Andalucia, at huge expense, to get in the olive harvest. Last year some farmers let it rot on the ground . . . Once all the trees are cut down we will have to erect plastic ones for the tourists to admire from their coach windows. Fallen terraces are no longer rebuilt,' he wrote sadly. Laurie Lee, Norman Lewis, and others, produced variations on the same theme. Penelope Chetwode, who made a trek on a mule across a wild stretch of southern Spain in 1961, appreciated the deliciousness of pot-holed roads and unglazed windows in the *posadas*, but detested the modern tableware, radios and *objets d'art* she noticed adorning peasant homes. 'Blast and damn all plastic consumer goods seeping in to spoil the virgin beauty of Tiscar,' she raged.

It was hardly a very penetrating or a very sympathetic analysis of social change. But if we disregard the patronising touch of noble-savagery, the jealousy of the pioneer for those that come after, of course the horrified hispanophiles were basically right. By the time of the tourist boom in the early 1960s, the traditional rural life of Spain, the rich confluence of economy and technology and spirituality that had dominated country life for a thousand years, encompassing the arts and sciences of animal husbandry, sustainable small-scale agriculture, milling and bread-making, architecture, hunting, fishing, wine-making, weaving, basket-making, artisan pottery, regional cookery, herbalism and medicine, song and dance, super-stition, ritual magic, astronomy/astrology, weather lore, sport and games, sayings, and *fiesta*, all of it intimately related to the climate and geology of its particular surroundings, was on the point of saying its Nunc Dimittis.

The traditional life, with its quiet continuity and concurrence with nature, died out in most of Europe during the nineteenth cen-tury with the rise of technology and the beginning of mass mobility. Britain, for example, where the change happened soonest and was most far-reaching, quickly became an impoverished culture with no folk music or dance to speak of, almost nothing in the way of regional cuisine, and a yawning gulf between urban and what remained of rural society.

Things happen more slowly in the south, and in Spain the old ways still haven't quite stuttered out their final words. In spite of everything – massive industrialisation, the growth of the cities at the expense of the villages, vastly improved systems of communica-tion, education, and government, not to mention a tourist industry that brings in 45 million foreigners a year, with the consequent ero-sion of the indigenous and handed-down – Spain still harbours perhaps the richest variety of traditional feasts, rites and casts of mind of any country in western Europe.

Why the variety, and why the obstinate endurance? Because Spain is an enormous country where regionalism still counts far more than centralism and local 'popular' culture far more than official 'high' culture. Because the landscapes and climates of Spain, jagged mountains, desolate plains, wind-lashed coastlines, savage cold and merciless heat, have conspired to keep thousands of smaller com-munities off the beaten track. Also, no doubt, because of the proudly anarchical, stubborn character of the Spanish, their innate understanding that if something ain't completely broke there's no sense in fixing it, that if a particular herbal remedy for headaches or houseflies was used successfully by their grandparents and their great-grandparents, to give just one trivial example, it might very well work for themselves.

I began this book in the spirit of an enquiry into a country's relationship with its past, wanting to sift out the ancient, the perverse and eccentric from the new, nice and normal. I deliberately made my journeys between the months of September and April, partly because intense heat plays havoc with my northern constitution and partly because I know that in autumn, winter and spring, after and before the tourist invasion, Spain relaxes, turns in on itself a little, and discreetly, occasionally, reveals a far more intriguing face. I soon realised that deep Spain is not completely assimilable to traditional culture pure and simple – it also hides under its cloak a fabulous hoard of other kinds of defiantly maverick behaviour, all of it flying in the face of modern laws of economy and hygiene.

Often the traditions were long since dead, or by the time I found them had been forced into strange mutations by powerful new forces like tourism, the New Age, nationalism, religious fundamentalism. Often it was hard, particularly in the drunken madness of a village *fiesta*, to tease out the old ways from the twisted, matted fibres of social reality. What deep Spain began to seem, as much as an exaltation of antiquity, was simply a celebration of vibrant, sometimes brutish individuality.

Getting the measure of something by nature so rare and random will always be a near-impossibility. Sometimes it happens when you half-expected it might. In some mud-spattered hamlet in the mountains, where children go barefoot, as in India, and pigs run in the street. More often than not it's in the last place you'd think of looking; bubbling up like a spring in the waste land. From the window of a tower-block apartment in a suburb of Madrid, a gypsy woman proudly hangs out the sheets from her daughter's wedding night. In another apartment in another city, a working-class couple find the Sacred Heart of Jesus appearing in blood on the grille of their gas heater. In a suburb of Barcelona, a teenage goatherd leads his flock across a rubbish-dump. In a tourist resort in the off-season a family kills its fattened pig, transforming it into sausages and hams and lard and *panceta* that will last until the foreigners return with their fistfuls of currency.

Deep Spain is odd, precarious and precious; and it is still there, down among the roots of things. We should hunt it out, hold it up to the light, study it briefly and delightedly, before we let it go for ever.

1

A Pig-out in Murcia

'It is astonishing how rapidly they thrive on their sweet food;
indeed it is the whole duty of a good pig – animal propter
convivia natum – to get fat as soon as he can, and then die
for the good of his country'

(Richard Ford, *A Handbook for Travellers in Spain*, 1845)

O n Saturday mornings in the flat I shared in south London I
used to be woken by rumblings of lorries and shouts in the
delivery yard of the Sainsbury's across the way. In rural Spain in
wintertime the main annoyance for liers-in is pigs, squealing the
high-octane squeal they give when they know their time is up. It happens early, at eight or nine o'clock. The blood-curdling noise lasts
for a minute or two, as the animal is dragged from its hovel and
hoisted on to a table and stabbed in the neck. When the dark hot
gush of blood begins, the neighbours can go back to sleep and for
the pig-killers there begins a long day of complicated ceremony, of
hard work, of harder eating and drinking, of *fiesta*.

It occurs to me that western society has a strange relationship with
the pig. The sheep, a much stupider and duller animal, we like to
think is fluffily attractive. Our idea of the pig is far more ambiguous.
On one hand, there is nothing cuter or more huggable than a *Babe*-
ish piglet, pink and playful. A few months older, and it becomes a

byword for all that is loathsome, greedy and gross. (Pigs in their post-*Babe* stage are popularly supposed to be filthy by nature, which is one of the great lies of all time.)

Yet no animal produces so much for man in such a short time; no other domestic animal is as economical. The Spanish know this, and respect the pig for the *chorizos*, the hams, the various sausages and lard and ears and feet and the other items of the national cuisine it makes available to them, even as they are sharpening the sacrificial knife. But then the Spanish have always understood the apparent paradox that respect for an animal and the necessity for it to die are two sides of the same coin. Look at the bullfight.

The *matanza* is a relic of the rural Europe of the past, when families depended for food on what they could produce from their own land by the sweat of their brow and there was no out-of-town superstore when you ran out. *De cerdo, hasta los pelos*, runs the old refrain: of a pig, even the hairs. The pig was a kind of living larder of good things. It still is.

What happened to the annual pig-killing in England? In how many households will you still see home-made English sausages and brine-cured hams hanging from the kitchen ceiling? It seems to me to be a custom long since dead, like putting wet clothes through the mangle or dancing round the maypole on the village green. Our folk culture is so remote from us that we can't even tell what we've lost – but since we are mostly unaware of our own impoverishment we don't much care about it either way. Instead of folksongs, we have pop songs. Instead of *fiestas* we have Bank Holidays.

Benizar is a village high in the hills of the Sierra de la Muela, northeastern Murcia, where a few miles further north you are suddenly in Castilla La Mancha and a few miles east the road signs, suddenly all in Catalan, indicate that you have arrived in the former kingdom (now Community) of Valencia. If Murcia as a whole is an unjustly neglected region of Spain, the *sierras* of the north are little known even within Murcia itself; and little Benizar is so totally ignored that it doesn't appear even on the big floppy road maps, the ones that travelling salesmen carry with them on the back seat. Yet it's a sizeable village with a population of 600, and makes a reasonable living from its olive and almond trees, its plantations of cereals, vegetables and pulses.

I drove through a series of diminishing *pueblos* – Cehegín, Caravaca, Moratalla – and wound up on a tiny road meandering over a great plain ringed with mountains. I flew through Tazona, a single street of tumbledown cottages, apparently inhabited only by three staring brown-faced children. It was the first village of Castile, and I wondered if Benizar had passed me by. But the road wandered meekly back into Murcia, and there it was, an unassuming but not insignificant village that seems to have grown up around what, for this part of the world, is a priceless natural jewel: a spring that bubbles out of the rock all the year round, even in the murderous heat of summer, and waters the terraces of half the valley. Beside the spring, beneath a giant crag, is the ancient watermill, now converted into an eccentric little place to stay. There the mountain water once turned the wheel to grind the flour that made the heavy roundel of dense bread that lasts for two weeks out of the fridge. Now it simply rushes past the old mill-run, lulling you to sleep.

The Arabs and their religion lingered on in Murcia long after they had been purged from the rest of the country by the Jesus army of Ferdinand and Isabella. One historian has it that the Murcianos were still quietly worshipping Allah as late as the first few decades of the seventeenth century. At the watermill the heritage of the Arabs is a visible fact – a ruined tower above the spring, a citadel on a nearby mountain – but the connection is subtle enough to be described as spiritual. They must have loved this place, because they always loved the sight and sound of running water, and there comes a point where pleasure and utility combine and a new sensation, you could call it a sense of the sacred, forms above the physical world like a cloud of vapour.

The windmill is owned and run by Juan and Paca Moreno. But it is Paca, as the Spanish expression goes, who has the singing voice. She is a countrywoman of fire, soul and delicious good humour, with a short frizz of mousy hair and a recently shaven moustache. She is small, trim and ceaselessly energetic, forever running and fetching, on all sides of you at once, telling stories, organising, explaining, a human *perpetuum mobile*. On a chill January night she gave me two bowls of something she calls *caldo caliente* – hot soup – made with potatoes and eggs stirred about in thin broth boiled with a lump of salt cod and a thin skein of sweet pepper.

'Is that all you want, *ná' má'*?' she said, removing the ends of her words in the Southern style. But it was so simple and good that I needed nothing else, and I told her so. She nodded, unsurprised. 'Everything I make comes out well, because everything is from the farm, nothing comes from outside, and it's all natural, all good. My potatoes aren't the same as other potatoes.' She pronounced it '*pa-ta-ta*', dropping the s. 'The eggs from my chickens don't taste the same as other eggs from other chickens. Aren't I right? Taste it and see if I'm right.' I tasted it again; she was right.

Paca's husband Juan is a white-haired mahogany-faced small sloping man, his fingers surgically attached to his high-tar cigarette. The rigorous sexism of rural life requires that the female look after the chickens and the cooking and the male the plough and the vines. He brought out a couple of plastic containers, one full of a fruity *rosado*, the other of a powerful dry red – he called them 'sweet' and 'lean'. 'I make these myself. No chemicals or any industrial shit in my wines, just the grapes I grow here in the village. The lean one's got up to 18 per cent,' he boasted. That put it in the same league as port and vermouth. The wine was strong and good, but this sounded very like alcoholic machismo.

There were watery sounds, sploshes and gurgles and bubbling laughter, from the kitchen. Paca ushered me in to a scene from a low-budget splatter movie: tubs of entrails, beige and custard-yellow, lay about the floor, emitting a strong sweet sickly smell of pig.

Behind the fridge door a pig's head stared out vacantly from a plastic bucket. The *chino*, as it's known in Murcia, had been killed that morning in a local slaughterhouse. It was a sign of the times. For a *matanza* to be legal under Spanish law, the vet must be present and the flesh of the pig be checked for foreign bodies. Easier to get all that out of the way in advance, in a white-walled place where children's ears could be protected from the panic-scream of the doomed pig.

I set to washing the entrails under the tap, learning from Paca's daughter how to turn the slimy tubes inside out with the force of the water. She told me she was a receptionist in a hotel in Benidorm, but had roared down the coast on the new E15 motorway that afternoon, knowing her old mum could do with a helping hand. Her sister was married in the nearby town of Calasparra, which was the furthest Paca would consider going for a family visit. Benidorm, observed the first daughter ruefully as she plucked another intestine from the aluminium vat, was for when her mother won the lottery.

Pig-killing needs a chilly day, a bright winter day, not too humid, not too hot. A Saturday in late January would do nicely, if the spot were high and dry. If there were plenty of good wine and the village band could be persuaded to leave their afternoon brandies and provide some jangle and oom-pah-pah, so much the better.

The other pig-killers were all city-dwellers from the coast who had ventured into the mountains of their own Community to remind themselves how life used to be lived in it. This was one of a series of days out in northern Murcia in which visitors are invited to help make bread, wine, herbal essences, honey, cheese and, last but not least, the piggy cornucopia of the *matanza*, each for the modest price of 2,500 pesetas. The scheme is run by Pepe Fuentes and his wife Lola, both Murcianos and proud of it, who count on the support of the European Union Cohesion Fund to further their labour of introducing rural ways to those unfamiliar with them. It is a brilliant idea that may however have come too late to save these precious traditions, which are vanishing as fast as ethnologists can write papers on them. Pepe sees his scheme as a way for the city to learn to love the country, for the country to reassert itself and, in so doing, for both to repair the woeful imbalance that exists between them. He is bearded, voluble, clever; moves and talks with the passion of idealist and entrepreneur.

I helped him carry the carcass, cold as lead, from the van. We dumped it on a table set up in an open space – the old threshing floor for the grain, airy and exposed, like a circular stage – and Paca's father, a perky old person in a houndstooth cap, approached it with a great grey knife, like a sculptor contemplating his first incision in a block of wood. First to fall away were the thick white slabs of *tocino* (lard) and the *panceta* with its inner stripes of pink that I began to cut into rashers for frying. Then came the ranks of *costillas*, the ribs, traditionally set aside to be marinated in wine and spices, dried and used as required at the times of year when fresh meat is less easy to come by. The primal virtue of country living, and maybe also its best lesson for the cities, is resourcefulness.

More people were arriving every five minutes: a young tall glam couple from Alicante, she in perfect make-up and designer jeans, he with his black hair slicked back like a banker. They had brought freshly-ironed frilly aprons which they tied round their waists, only to untie them equally unsullied at the end of the day. A family of dark-skinned little people with two or three grubby kids and a bouncy dog tied with a length of string to the bumper of their battered Ford Escort. A large lady from the north, married to a Murciano, who agreed with me that Murcian cooking was a fine thing but argued, without any bias whatever, that Pamplona was the gastronomic capital of the world. 'There you eat . . . like God,' she said dreamily, kissing a fat bunch of fingertips.

Most of these people hadn't been to a pig-killing since they were children, if ever. But for everyone it seemed to hold the same nostalgic charge. In the collective Spanish subconscious the *matanza* still represents abundance. Before abundance became the rule rather than the exception, it was one day in the year, possibly the only day, when you were sure to eat as much rich and delicious food as you could fill your belly with. And something in you needed to give thanks for that. The nearest Anglo-Saxon culture, sad and spiritually deep-frozen as it is, can get to this grateful consecration of plenty is the Anglican Harvest Festival, with all those tins of Campbell's soup and bananas from the supermarket.

Blue plastic bowls were laid out along the trestle tables, a fire was made and a giant metal pot, the *caldera*, set above it to cook the pig's head. Into an old-fashioned mincer went the boiled onions, then the pale slabs of *tocino*, then the leaner meat and finally the cooked meat from the head. While she worked at the bowls, stirring the pinkish mass with her hands, Lola told me about the *matanza* in her slow, warm Southern voice. She has a wide, generous face and ties up her long black hair in a printed shawl, and there is something about the way she looks and talks, a modesty mingled with confidence and also with sensuality, that summons up distant echoes of her Moorish ancestors.

The hams from the *matanza* are cured in their salt wash when the moon is waning, and put up to dry when it is waxing. But the crescent moon mustn't be the one that comes in March, because then the ham will be rancid. Curiously, though, the killing itself should take place under a waning moon, according to Gabriel Alonso de Herrera in his 1513 treatise on agriculture. At such a time, he writes, 'the flesh shall not be open to corruption nor harm, as is that which is killed in a waxing moon.'

The most notorious superstition relating to the *matanza* is that a woman having her period is taboo and may not touch the meat, for she will make the blood curdle. This is a tricky one. But the fact is that, as Laura Esquivel reminds us in *Like Water for Chocolate*, cooking is an exchange of energies and any kind of inner turmoil will probably hinder rather than help the process. 'In the end it makes no difference what people say about it either way,' mused Lola as she poured a slosh of slick red pig-blood into the sausage mixture. 'At the beginning, someone says, "Now, ladies, if there's anyone here . . ." And you do feel that if you were having your period you wouldn't go ahead, even if you knew it was a foolish thing to think. You would feel a kind of negative feeling which you wouldn't want to communicate to the food.'

Lola has come across superstitious disapproval once before, when she tried to sow wheat on her land during Holy Week. In the eyes of her neighbours it was a double offence. Not only was she, a woman, usurping the male role of ploughman – 'the man opens the earth, the woman casts the seed,' it's said – but she had the blasphemous insolence to be going about an act of creation and renewal while Our Lord was already treading the tortuous path that led to His destruction.

There is indeed a powerful religious charge in the *matanza*, which at its heart is a kind of mystery of death and new life. The pig dies so that we might live. To people who prefer not to see their meat until it is a plastic-wrapped chop in a supermarket cabinet, this idea might be shocking, but that only shows the extent to which we have all grown away from the natural process. Vegetarians have a right to protest, but anyone who eats meat should have as their ideal a love for the animal, whether alive, at the moment of death, or afterwards. There is a practical side, too, which has to do with the quality and flavour of the food. One should know what the animal has eaten, where and how it has lived, and how and by whom the meat was prepared. All these things are laid bare in the gnosis of the *matanza*.

Lola tried a spoonful of the raw and bloody *morcilla* mixture, then spat it out. Elsewhere a little of the mixture is cooked up in a small frying-pan, but some say you can taste it better raw. These *morcillas* would need more oregano and much more black pepper, the favoured condiment at *matanzas* around these parts. 'There are people who put in a little more cinnamon, a little more clove, a bit more this, a bit more that.' The principal flavours of the *chorizo* are clove, a little cinnamon, garlic, white wine and plenty of spicy red pepper – the *pimiento choricero* specially grown for the purpose. The *envuelto*, a fat pale sausage with a base of head-meat and *tocino*, has parsley, eggs and breadcrumbs, cinnamon, ground red pepper or *pimentón*, and a liberal dusting of black pepper. Each mixture is then fed into an old-fashioned machine with a handle that is turned to push the meat along a screw and into the scrupulously washed pig's entrails. It is a delicate art, because the sausage must be smooth and even all along its length and the casing mustn't be filled too tightly, otherwise it may burst in the cooking. A production line develops, with one person turning the handle and topping up the machine, another holding the guts and checking for perfection of form and a third tying the ends of the sausages with thick thread.

I took a break from the action and walked up towards the spring, my head full of the sweet excremental smell of pig. The splatter movie was reaching its gore-soaked climax: people with blood-covered hands, spattered with gobs of the stuff, wandered among slabs of pink flesh and tubs of shining, squelching, scarlet gunk. White-haired Juan followed me up, wheezing from his cigarette, to take me on a tour of the property, pointing out the walnut tree with the lamp hung from its trunk where on summer nights the young people go 'to touch each other under here'. He pointed graphically at his groin, just in case I didn't get the message. 'Tonight you go down to the disco with my son, and see what happens and what you come back with. A lovely Murciana. Which would you like, a brunette or a blonde?' If it came to it, I said, a brunette, and he roared with goatish laughter and forced his creaky hips into a pelvic thrust, to reinforce the point.

We reached a pool where the stream had been dammed and the water fell from the rock above through a curtain of moss and fertile greenery. José Maria, a smart young guy from the village, had come back for the weekend from the coastal city of Cartagena, where he worked as a waiter. He and his mates were sitting by the waterfall with glasses of Juan's wine, looking out over the *sierra*. You could see the edge of the village, the shells of new houses in red brick and grey concrete creeping round the hillside. José took a big slug of wine and sighed the bittersweet sigh of the returning exile. It was a damn fine place, didn't I think so? It was the best, most beautiful place in all Spain. If he didn't have to make a living he would set himself up here and raise a family on the land his forefathers trod. Drunkenly he spread his arms to take in the view; it was a gesture of possessiveness and tenderness. There was an abandoned farm beyond the village, just beyond the green stripe of the pine forest. José Maria knew the owner, and thought I could rent it cheaply, if I really thought that a tumbledown wreck was preferable to one of the smart new Lego houses that were beginning to turn the almond orchards into New Benizar.

Back at the scene of the crime, the first of the *matanza*'s waves of pork-based edibles was arriving on the tables: thick slices of fatty *tocino*, fried to a crisp with plenty of salt, and thicker slices of Paca's own bread to catch the drippings. The village band, a Murcian *cuadrilla*, had now turned up in their van; perfect examples of the species *Homo antiquus hispanicus*, wearing smart black shoes and cardigans around their bellies and chewing on toothpicks. They unzipped from black cases a series of strange local instruments, some with twelve strings, others with six, one a kind of mandolin with baroque flourishes at the neck, the *bandurria*; another a quarter-sized guitar as tiny as a child's toy.

The lunch-break at *matanzas* happens even later than the hour laid down in the already leisurely schedule of Spanish meal times. The sky was going off-colour at the edges and the pinkish tubes of raw sausage lay in slippery heaps on the blood-stained tables. One reason for the lateness must be to keep up the ritual magic and energy of the day as long as possible before breaking its rhythm. Once, at another *matanza*, I nipped down to the village for cigarettes and the newspaper, and got back to find that the spell was broken. But the main reason is that most *matanza* meals are so heavy with fat and protein that you are incapable of movement

afterwards. In the south and west the menu might be *migas*
(crumbs), a fearful classic of Spanish rural cuisine. Breadcrumbs or
similarly sized balls of flour-and-water dough are fried in copious
amounts of pork fat and olive oil, and the *migas* are eaten with
tocino, sausage filling, chopped liver and kidney, or, but preferably
and, any other piggy by-product there may be around. All, needless
to say, fried. For the purpose of tossing the *migas* in the boiling oil
there exists a special pan with a long handle reinforced with struts,
to prevent the pan literally flying off the handle during a particularly energetic toss.

The pig's head had been pulled out of the cauldron and delved
into for its meat, which is the main ingredient of the *envuelto*. Taking
its place in the foamy water were the fresh *morcillas* and *butifarras*,
which bobbed and glistened in there for an hour, looking like
bloated amputated limbs. The *migas* had reached halfway stage in
their progress from a solid mass of dough to a mountain of golden
crumbs – now they looked like small doughnuts – and the village
band struck up a scratchy little dance in three-time and Paca and I
leapt around a bit in the dusty car-park. There were holes in her
mouse-brown tights.

A long trestle table was laid and we gorged on the golden *migas*,
scooping them straight from the pan along with fried strips of crisp
tocino, fried liver and kidney, and forkfuls of brown spicy greasy *morcilla* filling. It was disgustingly delicious, and there were groans of
pleasure from around the table. But as the meal went on there
came a strange transformation. Faces were drained of their colour
and lost their party smiles. The large lady from the north, whose
cackles of mirth had been the sound-track of the day, put down
her fork with a clatter and gave a loud moan of discomfort. A shiv-
ery evening wind seemed to howl around the table. One by one the
digestively challenged pig-killers left the table, limping like
wounded animals towards the watermill, where at least they could
nurse their stomachs with coffee and brandies around the fireplace.
I stayed in my place till I could stand it no more, contemplating with

glazed eyes the fat-coated plates and smeary wine-glasses and the sun as it set, colouring the mountain sky pig-pink.

That night I lay in my room in the old mill listening to the white water in its channel beside the house. It was midnight. I had slept since six and the *migas* had only just gone down. The heating had broken the night before and Paca hadn't had time to fix it, what with all those entrails to clean and supper to make and all those people coming the next day, so the air was freezing cold. I felt the ache of unaccustomed physical labour, mingled with the dull hammer-blows of Juan's eighteen-degree wine.

There was a knock on the door, a clearing of a throat, and a young voice that said: 'Well, are you coming out dancing or what?'

I moaned inwardly – it would be village kids on Ecstasy, a sweaty basement, tacky Spanish techno and having to chat up a local brunette to keep Juan happy. I wasn't on for that. I wasn't on for anything. 'No,' I said croakily, muffling my mouth with the duvet. 'Not now, Juanito, I'm knackered. Another day,' and I could hear the boy slope off with an adolescent's scuffing steps, probably thinking it was just what he'd expected, no staying power, typical of these foreigners, always chatting up the old women about the boring antiquated crap they know about and getting off on the killing of poor defenceless animals. Then, when the time comes to hit the town, they wimp out on you. Pathetic.

Short Stories

HOLY WEEK NOTEBOOK

Wednesday night. A bad time to arrive. The train, packed with rumbustious military service kids on their way to Cádiz/San Fernando/Badajóz, crawled in from Albacete at 9.30 pm. All roads to the centre blocked off by passing processions. The taxi overcharges me, leaves me at the Puerta de Jerez with my grandfather's old leather case. Women clicking by in black high heels, black-suited señoritos on their arms. Some wear *mantillas*, those high-on-the-head delicate traceries of lace with a long thin train tumbling down the back, worn with a little black dress and, if the wearer is extra pious, a rosary twisted among the fingers.

First gulps of the olfactory cocktail, proper to Holy Week, that includes wax, incense, horseshit, garlic, frying oil. I force my way round to the Plaza Virgen de los Reyes, clinging to the walls of the Reales Alcázares. Fall on Millie's doorbell. Gone out. Sit on the doorstep, finish the bottle of wine I'd started on the train, then discover I've been pressing the wrong doorbell. Millie shows me upstairs with a torch, explains she's had to smash the light at the top of the stairs so as not to pay for the electricity. She laughs uproariously, comparing herself with the blind Audrey Hepburn in *When Darkness Falls*, lashing out wildly at the offending lamp.

Millie on her sofa-bed, drinking rum and Cokes, munching crackers. 'I wouldn't go down there if you paid me. It used to be wonderful. It's total hell now.' She plans to stay in bed till Monday, watching old movies and sending me out for food. Out on Millie's balcony, there is the Giralda, rocketing in billows skyward, bats darting about its summit in an aura of floodlight.

Thursday morning, the city hot. Crossed the river to see the Cigarrera. A biblical scene, the scourging of Christ, beads on the cat-o'-nine-tails slapping against each other as the float moved along. The *costaleros* or float-carriers, strapping lads, wearing a white headpiece like a very large inside-out sock, thickly padded round the head and at the neck. White T-shirt, dark black-blue cotton trousers, *alpargatas*. Families crowd around the floats when they stop, excitedly locate their sons/brothers/cousins under the thick skirts of the float and offer them mineral water and encouragement. One fat red-faced *costalero* sits on the steps, so puffed he's unable to tell his friend he's feeling better now. Reaction of people lining the route: varies according to fame of image and degree of devotion it arouses. Upturned faces, half-unconscious self-crossings. The occasional tear in the occasional eye. Sevillano appreciation of the expressions on these, to the untrained eye, very similar figures. Virgen del Cachorro (of the puppy). 'She's so *maternal*, isn't She?' said a housewife to her friend. Virgen de la O. (Because the first thing the Virgin said when She gave birth was 'Oh'.) Purple tunics, red candles. Two little girls taking the piss, tugging at Her skirts, are reprimanded by a nearby trumpet-player. 'Now girls, there are some things in life that are serious, and you've got to respect them a little.' La Exaltación. Gold chain around Christ's neck, clanking in rhythm. Quavery trumpet solo over drums, sounds like Herb Alpert.

Sevilla and Triana = Buda and Pest = San Francisco and Oakland. Cities often lumped together but actually distinct (and separated by water).

Thursday night and Friday morning together make up the *madrugá*. Great night of suffering and extremes of pain – and it wasn't very nice for Jesus either. Moving around the city is nearly impossible. The crush is unbelievable. Hard to keep your mind on sacred matters when rubbish bins are overflowing, cans cover the streets and it is physically impossible to move left, right, forward or back. 'Now, you've got to be Sevillano to get to Campana in the *madrugá*,' someone says. Being Sevillano is a kind of fundamentalism, the object of worship being . . . Seville.

Get to the Basilica of the Macarena at midnight. People scaling railings, trees, walls. A mad girl from Lepe, falling about, swearing, embarrassingly trying out the Virgin's special cry of adoration ('*Guapa! Guapa! Guapa!*'). Kids, grandparents with *bocadillos* in tinfoil and bottles of water. 'She won't be long now; this is the last of them,' parents tell sulky children as the hooded horrors stream out of the church. The Brotherhood is 2,500-strong. An endless slow line of cones, peering expressionless eyes through slits, and wand-like candles. Do they all fit in there, or do some have to wait out the back? Between the doors opening and the final appearance of Our Lady, two hours. A cynic would say the result justifies the wait. A Sevillano would say two hours isn't long to wait for such transporting loveliness. When She finally comes out, it's what Sevillano journalists call '*un momento apoteósico*'. A tiny girlish face, almost on the point of breaking down in tears (littlest girl in the playground), loaded with all these trappings, this gold crown in a gigantic halo around Her head, immense heavy cloak slathered with gold thread. The capacity to invest an image with such power is something we (White Anglo-Saxon Protestants) have lost. The apologia for adoration of the Virgin in Holy Week is that through Her you're contemplating the death of Her son. No, it's a glorification of *Her*, the Eternal Feminine, the Earth Mother, on Her precious throne of light.

They say it rained on the *madrugá*, a thin almost imperceptible trickle, more like dew, for half an hour. This meant that the great Virgin of Hope of Triana had to be delayed or diverted, and accordingly came face to face with Her great rival, the Virgin of Hope of the Macarena, in an alley. First time this has ever happened. I wonder what they said to each other . . . 'What the hell are you doing here?'

Through the glutinous mass of bodies up the long Calle Feria, along the Alameda de Hercules. Found a place in Placentines, outside the restaurant Casa Robles, clinging on to the trunk of an orange tree. The blossom just coming. Past comes El Silencio: total austerity, only music a weedy trio of bassoon, oboe, clarinet. Then Jesus the Great Power. No great power left: abject weakness, total dejection, absolute suffering. Five a.m., and the crowds show no sign of diminishing. 'This is a little bit heavy, eh?' says a voice from beneath my armpit. People sitting on rubbish bins among the cans and scrunched-up tinfoil, beers passed over our heads. By the bins a few girls have cleared a little space by force and are already dancing a naughty *sevillana*. General disapproval: very much too soon. *Sevillanas* are for that great big frilly rave, the April Fair — not for now, when Jesus is half-way through dying.

I am half-way through dying. Limp home at six, feet in agony, to watch the rest on Giralda TV. Since the main action in the Plaza Virgen de los Reyes is only a few steps away, I feel less bad, inexplicably. Find ice-cold loquats in Millie's fridge, watch forest of black cones emerging from cathedral's fug of incense and candlelight. Flick to chat-show about the *mantilla*. Seems to be back in fashion: 'The *mantilla* shows off a woman marvellously. But the gentleman must be able to set off the beauty he has at his side.' Out on the terrace, grey light of dawn, and it's still groaning on. Shrieking cornets, hammering drums, permanent roar of crowds.

Good Friday afternoon. Children run among the *nazarenos*, fumes of frying *churros* on the Puente de Isabel II. Greasy, sleepless faces feeding themselves with more grease, sugar and chocolate. The streets are perilous with congealed pools of wax; grey, purple, dirty red. A woman wheels her mini-*nazareno* baby in a red pushchair, holding his hood in her hand along with his cup of Coke. People relating their horror-stories of the *madrugá*. 'I was caught in the crush at Campana, couldn't move one way or the other for an hour and a half, etc.'

Little by little the city comes to its senses, cheering up as it's clearing up. On Saturday afternoon nobody takes much notice of the processions. Feels like a proper *fiesta* day, munching fresh coconut and peanuts and caramelised almonds and those odd cold slippery yellow beans (actually lupin seeds). In the Parque María Luisa in the warm evening, breeze coming like a cool mist through the greenery and old *azulejos*. Eyes tired and headachey. Millie stirs from her bed, now that the coast is clear, and ventures out into the street to buy food and fags. We have a rum and Coke and watch *Some Like it Hot*.

2

Off to See the Wizard

'Caves, hermitages, megaliths, cloisters, remote sanctuaries,
cults of impossible saints, faith healers, magic mountains,
occultist chapels, alchemical capitals, paintings with unusual
symbolism, holy mummies, memories of incredible wonders,
stories of vampires and wolf men, miraculous seers and
mythical legends are still, if not exactly our daily bread, then
the salt of another reality that sprinkles our peninsula with
the marks of a strange universe, incomprehensible and all
the more disquieting as we succeed in penetrating its
essence, so distinct from the logical discourse of our dirty
days in the city.'

(Juan G. Atienza, *Guía de la España Mágica*)

Ask a Spaniard in the street what he knows about Galicia, and the
first thing he'll remark on, probably, is its reputation for rain.
'Ah, Galicia – it never stops raining up there,' he will say, half in
amusement and half, depending whether or not his part of the country is currently suffering from drought, in envy. A second thing that
might occur to him is the Galician fondness for eating octopus. 'Oh
yes, the Gallegos, they love their octopus,' he might say, less admiringly, explaining how the slithery beast is presented in chewy white
slices on a wooden plate – *a feira*, in the style of the town fair – and
eaten in quantities and with a relish that are frankly unbelievable.

This Spanish Everyman might then go on to tell you something
vaguely ominous about witches and ghosts and/or strange rituals

and miraculous cures and curses on whole families; in short, something about the rich pagan spirituality of the people of Galicia.
Cleverer conversants might even fire a Gallego proverb at you –
possibly the famous one that says that if you don't make the pilgrimage to San Andrés de Teixido, spiritual G-spot of the whole
community, while alive, you'll be forced to go when you're dead – in
order to point up the supposed continuance of popular belief in
spirits, hauntings and visitations from beyond the grave.

The roots of Galicia lie in Celtic civilisation, and the Celts had
their ways with magic. To that extent it makes sense, the side of
Galicia that makes room for such a wealth of superstition, ritual
and myth. It adds up pretty convincingly when you're there, anyway,
in this damp corner of north-west Spain, pointing like a green arrow
into the dark Atlantic. The weather here is proverbially wet and
unstable, prone to sudden chills and mists that sweep in from the
sea, giving rise to mysterious shapes and lugubrious shadows. (The
Mediterranean is all light and openness and simple, blazing truths;
the Atlantic is shifting certainties, multiple realities.) If the people of
Galicia were in some way quixotic, changeable and interested in
the worlds that lie beyond the hard, bright world of appearances,
you feel as you travel across the land, peering through the weather
at the variegated landscape, it would hardly come as a surprise. So
much of culture is climatology.

Galicia is often cited as one of the last outposts of traditional
Spain, a place that bad communications, remoteness and poverty
have conspired to keep several steps behind the rest of the country.
To an extent this is true, but only to the same extent that anything
is true here, in this oddly ungraspable world. In the countryside,
farmers still work their tiny plots with a horse, or oxen, pulling an
old-fashioned iron plough. Harvesting is still often done with the
scythe.

But with Manuel Fraga at the helm (Fraga was ex-minister of
tourism under the dictatorship, and one of the few Franco hench-
men to have flourished equally in the new democracy), Galicia has

begun a 'Great Leap Forward' that is gradually bringing this eccentric straggler into line. Roads, dams, hospitals, 'centres' of one kind or another, are what come first. The fishing villages of the south-west have succumbed to construction fever, and the stuff going up is mostly dull, four-square, cheap modern rubbish. Galicia's premier beach resort of Sanxenxo is almost as nasty as Fuengirola. Inland, huge tracts of ancient forest of chestnut and oak have been replanted with a rapacious kind of eucalyptus which grows at a metre a year, to the delight of the local cellulose industry. Nothing can grow under or around the eucalyptus, thanks to a toxin contained in its leaves and bark. No undergrowth; no animal life; no ecosystem.

Fernando Sánchez Dragó, writing in the late 1970s – ancient history for the New Spain – writes about fiestas in the town of Viana del Bollo where the men and boys howl at the full moon all night long, and of bizarre marriage customs in San Félix de Donis, near Lugo, in which the groom sleeps with the best man and the bride with the best woman, and of special cakes baked to ward off werewolves, of spells to find buried treasure, of Celtic magic still in use in modern homes. 'For whatever reason', he writes with effusive admiration, 'the skyscraper never took hold in the Galician city, gangs of workers never cut open the bends of the roads, Ribeiro wine was never served in Duralex glasses, and lorry-drivers never got used to having lunch in cafés where the dishes had numbers instead of names.'

Twenty years later these things are part of life, here as much as anywhere. Modernity is doing its work with the same unsmiling efficiency as it's exhibited everywhere else. If there is still another Galicia, magical and strange and reeling from the shock of the new, the time to look for it must be now.

I took the night train from Barcelona to Vigo, because it seemed like a good idea to travel from coast to coast, feeling the change from one ocean, one way of being, to another. It was cramped, cheap and uncomfortable – Spaniards call the service 'El Shanghai', presumably in mocking allusion to Chinese squalor and unpleasantness – but people shared out their picnic food and talked, as they do on all the most tedious Spanish trains, and a bottle of cheap Catalan red made sleep a possibility. Opposite me in the compartment was a sociologist from Madrid who had lived in the US for years. 'This country has changed beyond belief, oh yeah,' he said as he pulled off his socks, showing off a perfect 'I've lived in America' status-symbol accent. 'But if you want my opinion, I don't think the changes have been fully . . . how would you say that? . . . *digested* yet.' I knew what he meant and it was a good way of putting it; as though modernity were a big Sunday lunch of three courses and wine which Spain has still not found a way of working off.

Outside the window, next morning, the mist lifted to reveal hillsides, fields, a riverbank, all decked out in the deciduous colours of the northern autumn: chestnut, holm oak, ash, each at its particular point in the spectrum of yellow, red, brown, green. The farming land, squeezed in between the river and the mountain, was fragmented into miniature *parcelas*, each one neatly ringed by stone walls. They seemed joke-sized, too small to be for real, like a child's drawing of fields. In every one of three or four, cabbages tottered head-high on thick stalks: Gallegos pluck the new leaves from beneath the crown, shred them for their famous cabbage soup, the *caldo gallego*, and leave the plant to grow.

Vigo is a rough-edged Atlantic port city, scruffy, dank and briny. Wandering its melancholy streets in the early morning rain, I felt a strange culture shock, so brusque was the change from shiny happy po-mo Barcelona to this rusty, musty, sad old town. All provincial cities have it, this sense of being perpetually five years, or ten or fifteen, behind the rushing current of the metropolis, away from the main stream, among the sluggish eddies and stagnant pools of fashion. In a street market, rain pummelling the makeshift polythene roof, there hung ranks of women's drawers and corsets, of a design and colour – a hideous shade of pinkish orange, best described as 'dirty flesh' – long since banished by Marks & Spencer. Bookshops were forbidding places where you asked for the book you wanted and the staff, long-faced gentlemen in specs, climbed stepladders to find it for you. Browsing seemed a new-fangled thing, a dangerous liberty. Knowing no other Gallego authors than Rosalia de Castro, the nineteenth-century poet whose fervent hymns to her native land fuelled dreams of an independent Galicia, I blurted out her name and was presented with *Cantares Galegos*, a paperback collection of her most passionately nationalistic work.

On the little ferry north across the *ría*, I sat on a bench on deck as the sun came out and sparkled on the water. The coast around Vigo is often nicknamed 'the hand-print of God', and now I saw why. Five slender estuaries, the *rías*, feel their way inland past islands that fend off the fury of the Atlantic. The air is sweet. Figs and lemons, peach trees and vines grow in the gardens along the water, buoyed up by the mild climate. Everywhere are sandy beaches that would hardly be out of place in the Caribbean, when the sun's on them and people are not. I read in one of Rosalia's rapturous songs:

> *'Lugar máis hermoso*
> *non houbo na terra*
> *que aquél que eu miraba*
> *que aquél que me dera',*

'A lovelier place/There was never on earth/Than the one I saw/Than the one that gave birth to me.'

In a village on the other side of the *ría* I slept on a sitting-room floor, ate microwaved lasagne and cheesecake and watched Disney movies on the video. The house was a newish apartment block, one of many built to house the middle-class overspill from Vigo. From the window I could see the neighbours' orchard – apple trees, a lemon, and a patch of absurd, towering cabbages – with the backdrop of headland and quiet water, covered in the mornings with a thick layer of rolling mist.

Cándido and Ana were a couple of young Basques, dragged unwillingly westwards by Cándido's job as a geologist with a cement company. For anyone into stone and the possibilities of stone, Galicia is paradise, and Cándido drove around the countryside in his big four-wheel drive marvelling at post-Devonian schist and Kimmeridgeian clay deposits. Meanwhile Ana, at home with the baby all day, ground her teeth with boredom, claiming that the locals were cold and cliquey, and missing her friends, Basque cooking and the big-city chic of Bilbao. 'My idea of a perfect day is to go out for lunch with friends, then go to a movie in the afternoon. How am I ever going to do that in Vigo?' she moaned.

They were modern urban people, light years from the old worlds of magic. But in the days that I spent with them, I saw occasional signs of something far less anodine. A few miles up the road, I heard one day while buying my bread in the baker's, was the village of Coiro, once a known haven of witches and still a byword for pagan goings-on. The witches would meet on the beach near Áreas Gordas, at midnight on the night of Saint John, the most magical night of the Spanish ritual year, and do the things that witches do. The Inquisition had a field-day in Coiro, sending in a special squad of interrogators from Toledo to break up the coven. Among those arrested and put to death was a poor old dear called María Solina, who clearly had no idea what day of the week it was, let alone being able to say the Lord's Prayer backwards. Anyway, according to my source at the bakery, people who have beach houses at Áreas Gordas say they've sometimes heard things, whoopings and wailings at odd hours of the night, and in the morning they've gone out walking with their dogs on the beach and found the charred and smouldering remains of bonfires.

It was mid-October, and the final remains of a long, hot summer had been swept away with the last autumn leaves. It rained for a day, a night and another morning, pummelling the roof of the fish-markets where the women shouted at each other over the crates of glimmering hake and tuna, as if in answer to the rain. People seemed reassured, relieved almost, by this relentless soaking. They crowded in twos and threes under flimsy umbrellas. Women with provincial hair-dos, as neat and round as cabbages, huddled giggling at the bus stop. Green, sodden Galicia: old veg and moss. My clothes, permanently damp, began to smell, and dogs followed me into churches.

In the car-hire shop, I asked about *meigas*. In Galicia's complex spiritual universe the *meiga voladora* is the woman who has a close relationship with the Devil and can fly through the air at will, the *aquelarre* is the witches' moot or meeting (often held on Friday nights, and always on the Night of Saint John), and the *estadea* the airborne procession or fly-past – though Galician witches seem not to favour the broomstick as a means of travel. The young lady at the desk, dark-haired and moustachioed, was tapping away at a computer. '*Meigas?*,' she said with a smile, incredibly unfazed by the question. 'Well, I do know people who've seen them, but I've never seen one myself. When I see a *meiga* with my own eyes I'll believe in them, but not till then. Can I have the number of your driving licence?'

Her father, sitting next to her, gazed admiringly at the screen. The technology had arrived from Head Office a year ago, and they were still getting used to it. As my contract emerged from the printer, he grabbed it and brandished it in front of me. 'Look. You can write all this on a piece of paper, put it in that machine there' – he cast a glance at the fax – 'and it'll come out in Santiago in a second!' He opened his eyes wide and shook his hand loosely on his wrist, in the Spanish gesture of incredulity.

Computers, faxes, credit cards: this is the benign, impressive witchcraft of the modern world. But the old man noted my interest in the odd ways of the occult, and willingly backtracked into the rougher magic of his forebears. He took up the theme of *curandeiros*, the witch doctors and quacks that were once rife throughout

Galicia in the days before there were doctors, and still linger on in many rural villages, and in cities where the New Age has dawned, as a kind of refuge or retreat from technological medicine. 'The difference between the *curandeiro* and the doctor,' he declared, 'is that if, say, you've got a bad finger, or if it's broken' (he showed me a finger: 'but this isn't broken'), 'the *curandeiro* will cure it and not use a bandage, but the doctor has to use a bandage. People in Galicia go to the doctor first, and if he can't do it, they try the *curandeiro*. That way, if they die, they can say they've done all they can.'

He knew of a famous one, in a hamlet outside Ourense, and got out a map to show me where. 'He's been on the TV, this man; people come from all over to see him. A clever man, but he didn't get anything from reading books. They say he learned it all from his father, in the village where he grew up.' The village was called A Pena. *Pena* in Spanish is pain, grief, anxiety. So the doctor's nickname is therefore resoundingly inappropriate. They call him 'O Bruixo da Pena' – The Wizard of Pain.

I told Ana, the thoroughly modern Basque girl, about this and she laughed at first, as she prepared a piece of hake for the microwave. Then she thought for a moment, and remembered that her grandmother had been an expert on herbs, and that when her mother was dying from kidney disease, she had fixed up a session with a healer. 'It was when she'd tried everything else; she was desperate. As a matter of fact they were two young guys. Their technique was a sort of herbalism, the kind of thing my grandmother knew about. But it was all mixed up with Christian signs and symbols. They mashed up the herbs into a compress and laid it on her skin in the sign of the cross.

Of course it didn't work. What did you expect? But the strangest thing about it was that she bothered going at all, an educated woman like her. I wouldn't have.'

Ana stabbed contemptuously at the buttons on the microwave; three minutes on High, and it wheezed quietly into life.

*

In my rented car, I drove slowly across a deep brown waterlogged plain littered with shreds of mist. By the side of the road, a woman hacked at something with a scythe. A team of heavy horses, yoked together with a great wooden beam, hauled its way across the earth, and bowed people, collecting potatoes, formed dark shapes like twisted tree-trunks. I felt as though I'd been beamed down into a Constable painting, one of those heavily painted, densely-textured ones where even the air looks as thick as Brown Windsor soup.

Cortegada, Folgoso, Trandeiras; a string of villages with their vines and cabbage-patches. Almost every house had its own *hórreo*, the granite storehouse on mushroom pillars (to confuse the rats) that has become almost as much a symbol of Galicia, to other Spaniards, as octopus and rain.

The wizard lived in a big modern grey granite house with a grey concrete forecourt, on a little hill just beyond the village of A Pena. It was by far the biggest house in the area, and its size and newness seemed to suggest that the *curandeiro* had done rather well out of his prayers and potions. When I arrived, in the darkening chill of an autumn afternoon, there were already two or three of his patients sitting on a wall. The first in the queue, a miserable-looking woman who had cycled there with her son from Folgoso, said she'd already rung the bell but there was no answer. I tried it myself. This time there were confused shouts from within, and in a few minutes the door opened and a small dog came hurtling out yapping into the yard.

'Perlita! Perlita! Stop that! Come here!' came a shout, and the small dog's mistress, a tiny, dumpy woman with bright button eyes and one of the loudest speaking voices I've ever heard (the peasantier the people, the louder they talk). Mr Eladio was still taking his after-lunch nap and would be down in half an hour. She barked at the queue in raucous Gallego and disappeared inside again, leaving Perlita to sniff around the terrace.

We were an odd lot, the patients sitting on that grey wall with its soggy view of potato fields and vineyards. The woman behind me was a large and bossy Galician matron with a face like a shark, who had been coming to the local *curandeiro* ever since she was first married. 'That was forty-four years ago now, if memory serves,' she said, stealing a glance at her thin and somewhat faded husband, who made a face as if to say it was forty-four years too long. 'In those days he used to see people only on Sunday mornings, after Mass. This time I'm here only for the blessing, I'll be in and out in a minute. Is it your first time? Because if it's your first time you're bound to take an hour or so, and I've got to be up tomorrow for the Potato Festival in Cortegada so you won't mind if I just nip in before you. I've known Mr Eladio for years, of course. I've had people telling me I'm *tonta*, that someone of my standing ought to be seeing the doctor in Ourense, not some country quack, but I always say to them, "Let people do what they want."'

'Or what they can,' broke in the sad-faced younger woman, tired of the matron's rantings. She wore a black sweatshirt with pink-and-purple spangly bits, black leggings and a pair of fake Reeboks. Her son, who sat sullenly on the concrete floor playing with the dog, looked like any ordinary pre-adolescent European child, probably wishing he was back in his bedroom playing Tetris, or out and about on the mountain bike. His mother wouldn't say exactly what was wrong with him, but by the way she shook her head and wrung her hands it was something pretty major. To me he looked not so much ill as bored. They had tried *everything*, she said, and seen *everyone*, before giving up on big-city medicine for good. Being from Folgoso, a couple of villages back down the road, she'd been off to see the wizard countless times. Her mother first brought her at the age of eight – a little younger than her son was now. So she was merely falling in with family tradition.

'I've tried everything, too. I've been to doctors all over Galicia, but nothing's ever worked,' sighed a woman with a limp and a pained expression who had just arrived with her husband. Another malingering wife, another long-suffering husband. 'And what's wrong with you, then, that you've come so far to see the *curandeiro*?' she asked me mildly.

'I'd rather not talk about it, if you don't mind. I find my problem rather . . . difficult to explain,' I vacillated. The sad-faced woman nodded, as if she understood. But the shark-faced matron had swivelled her suspicious gaze on me, and I now felt I was in the spotlight.

'Come now, tell me what's wrong with you and I tell you what's wrong with me,' said the woman with the limp, brightening up visibly at this welcome chance to discuss her symptoms. 'Does it make you want to cry, sometimes, when things get really bad? It does? And does it make you want to lie in bed all day, like you're no good for anything?' She nodded in satisfaction. 'Well, that's what I've got, too.' She wasn't sure that Eladio would work for her, but she felt it was worth a try. 'I don't know. I've heard he's done some great things, miraculous things. But until I've seen with my own eyes what he does I can't say for sure. I still haven't looked him in the face, so how can I be sure what to think?'

There was something richly Galician, it struck me, about her defiant scepticism. According to a hoary old Spanish saying, if you meet a Gallego on the stairs you will never know whether he is going up or down. It's a bit of a racist slur, intended to imply that Gallegos are shifty and cunning; but what it really means is that life in Galicia, more even than life in general, is an equivocal business, full of shifting certainties, and one should never be too hasty to come to conclusions.

On one side of the forecourt where we sat was a jerry-built warehouse that might once have been used for storing potatoes. Its metal door clanged open, and out stomped the bustling wizard's wife again, shouting something in her corncrake voice. The mother and son were first. (They emerged half an hour later clutching a plastic bag full of medicines. '*Cosas del campo*,' 'things from the country', said the boy.) Next came the matron, who was here only for the blessing. And then it was my turn.

I was ushered through the factory door. The interior was a cold, cheerless space with high ceilings and a concrete floor. As my eyes adjusted to the grey gloom, rows of chairs, a small stage with a desk and chair, placards, crosses, slogans, signs, sprang into view. The warehouse was unlit except for a desk lamp to the far left, where a portly elderly man sat wearing a heavy tweed jacket and waistcoat. The first thing I noticed when I sat down in front of him was a scrap of paper on the desk, on which were scribbled columns of numbers. They were four-figure numbers, apparently referring to large amounts of pesetas.

I had spent my last half-hour on the wall spinning my story, which had now to be told. It was inspired by an article I had noticed the day before in the local paper, about a woman tried for the murder of her husband and a female friend of them both. She had been motivated, she said in court, by jealousy.

My disease, then, would be one that shows no physical signs, but can eat up your soul just as much as any cancer. I was jealous of my girlfriend – so intensely, all-encompassingly jealous that I was becoming fearful of the dark violent thing inside me. I felt I might do someone, or myself, serious harm if the corruption went unchecked. It was almost as if an evil *meiga voladora* had put her spell on me. (I edited this last bit out in the telling, thinking it too outrageously gothick even for this corner of old Galicia.) I was dry-mouthed and nervous as I told my tale, but the old man swivelled his desk lamp on to my face and listened with furrow-browed concentration.

'How old are you?' asked the great *curandeiro* when I was done, and I lied a few years younger than the truth, knowing I must look scared and confused and innocent under the spotlight of his lamp. 'Now let me tell you this. I've been working here for forty-four years, and my wife with me, and what we are dealing with most of the time are major illnesses.' He sounded brusque and angry, and I braced myself for my dismissal as a tiresome timewaster. 'Here in Spain most of us are Catholics. In Asia they're Buddhists, and in America you can choose the religion you want. I don't know how it is in England, but in Spain there are Ten Commandments. What are they? What are those Ten Commandments?'

My mind went into a flat spin. What was he getting at – something about not coveting your neighbour's wife? I struggled with the three-way intellectual task of resurrecting my school Divinity, translating it into Spanish and then into Gallego. Wasn't the first Commandment the one about not recognising any other God than me? Good. We were getting somewhere. Now the second. I couldn't bring it to mind. My vision wandered for a second to the shelves behind the desk, which glinted with glass and coloured boxes.

'*Ama el teu prósimo com a ti mesmo,*' he said solemnly, with a note of sternness in his voice. 'Love thy neighbour as thyself.' Of course. 'Now, you and this *muchacha* have this problem. But I want you to remember that second Commandment, because it's the only way you'll ever feel normal again. Say it to yourself in your head, ten or twenty times a day. Now, do you smoke? Well, that's a fault in you. I want you just to say "Yes" if what I say is true. Do you suffer from tiredness?' Yes. 'Depression?' Yes. 'Do you feel weak at certain times of the day?' Yes. 'Do you have problems of the stomach – wind and constipation?' Very occasionally. 'Ah-ha.'

There was no doubt about it: this was a very strange visit to the doctor. But I had brought it on myself, and my bad faith was as bad as can be. Eladio offered to write me out a prescription, but I said there was no need. Thanks to the miracle of his healing powers, I was almost feeling better already.

Mrs E, bright-eyed and bushy-tailed, came stomping up to the desk and enquired how the consultation had gone. She took my arm and saw me out. 'It's true what he says, you know, dear,' she said affectionately. 'We must all love each other like brothers, and never do each other any harm. If you remember that, life will always be good to you. So, you're on your way now, are you? To England, is it? Blessings on you, *filliño meu*, and may God relieve you of your trouble.'

I slunk out of the room and into the dark like a guilty soul.

*

The city of Lugo is normally a well-mannered sort of place that verges on the sleepy, but when I passed through there on a Saturday night in October the town was partying in honour of its patron Saint Froilán, and was therefore in higher spirits than usual. The authentic smell of a Galician *festa*, a combination of the fishy/meaty reek of stewing octopus, cigar-smoke and frying oil, filled the streets. In the park between the town and the river Miño the *pulpeiras* – octopus stalls – had taken up residence. In makeshift canteens lit by neon strip-lamps, men and women dressed in white were sweating over giant copper cauldrons containing a purple and flesh-coloured rubbery mass that gyred and gimbled under the wooden spoons of the cooks. At the simpler stalls it is a question of taking your wooden plate spread with octopus chunks and scoffing it somewhere near, squatting on a wall or standing up. At the grander ones there are white-clothed tables under big marquees, and unlabelled bottles of cool cloudy Ribeiro wine to drink. Backstage at one of them I saw five country girls in white headscarves peeling potatoes in the half-dark.

The octopus isn't yet an endangered species, but if it ever becomes one, much of the blame will have to fall on Galicia. Gallegos are suckers for it. Official figures for annual *per capita* consumption of octopus in the region are hard to come by, but you only have to register the two or three permanent *pulpeiras*, bright with formica like English chip shops, in every little town, the great copper vats bubbling away on weekly market days and the fact that practically every restaurant and bar the length and breadth of Galicia serves *pulpo* in some form or other, and you can see we're talking kilos rather than grammes.

It is strange, the process by which something becomes a delicacy, and strange too that it remains one, bearing in mind that the dish in question might be eaten thousands of times in the lifetime of a given individual. *Pulpo a feira* used to be eaten mostly in the interior of Galicia, where it was made with dried octopus, not with fresh. Now it's served up with relish wherever two or three Gallegos are gathered together.

The national dish, which is what *pulpo a feira* surely is, is something you can never get tired of because it's part of your identity, something that marks you out as belonging to a particular social group. The queues of people at the *pulpeiras* on a party night in Lugo aren't there just out of hunger. They're there because something clicks pleasantly in the mind as they take their first forkful from the wooden plate and their teeth come down on the tender chunks of octopus flesh, so perfectly seasoned with olive oil, salt and *pimentón*. A tiny voice, fainter even than the voice of conscience, whispers to them what it always whispers on these occasions: 'I eat octopus, therefore I am Galician.'

The *fiestas* had filled up all the hotels in Lugo with farmers and their families from the villages, and I went south again in search of a bed. I settled on Sarria, service town for the so-called 'French' route of the Way of Saint James, and stayed there a couple of days. It turned out to be a good move, because in the verdant pastoral countryside between Sarria and Triacastela I met an alchemist, a worker with natural ingredients and spiritual forces, a modern magician with medieval roots. He was born on the Way of Saint James, in the hamlet of Lousada de Samos, and lives there still, drinking from the deepest wells of arcane philosophy.

Galicia has always had a deep understanding of the physical and spiritual properties of stone. Architects, stonemasons, sculptors have always flourished here – men such as Antonio Palacios, known as the Gallego Gaudí; Maestro Mateo, genius behind the romanesque Pórtico de la Gloria in Santiago cathedral; and the anonymous builders of Galicia's thousands of neolithic dolmens, menhirs and hilltop fortresses. A geological chocolate box, it attracts mining companies and drillers for things and experts like my Basque friend Cándido.

Magical stones, healing stones, stones of power and influence, are vital elements in the spiritual hardware of the place. Santiago

Lorenzo, author of a book called *Galicia Mágica* and also owner, somewhat disappointingly, of a massage parlour in downtown Vigo, writes about famous stones like the *camas do santo* (beds of the saint) on which childless couples queued up to make love under a waxing moon. Pilgrims on the famous *romería* of San Andrés de Teixido still pick up pebbles from the road and toss them on ancient heaps called *milladoiros*. The gesture has no very clear meaning, but may be a cultural memory of pre-Roman times when travellers offered stones to the god of the road.

At the windswept sanctuary of the Virgin of the Boat, on the coast at Muxia, you can walk down from the church to the 'miracle stones' which are supposed to have healing powers. Within the church itself are votive offerings from people who claim their lives were saved by the Virgin. A small boat hangs from the ceiling – the gift of a crew of grateful sailors. But the stones outside represent a far older and deeper-rooted cult than Christianity. It's arguable, too, whether the stones are not a bigger attraction for the thousands of pilgrims at Muxia's big September *romería* than the Virgin of the Boat herself. The most famous of the three great rocks has one flat surface tipped steeply sideways so that you can walk underneath one of its edges. Gallegos have used it for centuries as a cure for rheumatism and kidney problems. Why those diseases should be the ones it cures, and not cancer and AIDS, is anyone's guess. If you pass under the overhanging rock, and you have faith, they say you'll be free of them for life. It was a grisly, lonely day when I was there, and the sea and the perilous rocks made it easy to see why this is known as the Coast of Death. But I nipped under the overhanging stone, just to be on the safe side, and lay on top for a few seconds for extra effect, and felt that, yes, I was now slightly less likely to suffer from rheumatism and/or kidney problems than I would otherwise have been.

The sign said 'Exhibition', beside a geometric design built up of beige, black and rust-red stones. An arrow pointed off the road and on to a track through a tunnel of trees. The woods were lush, deep green and dark and the chestnuts were ripe and littering the ground in their prickly cases. I peeled and ate one as I walked. It had a childhood taste, crisp and creamy, edged with tannin from the bitter inner skin.

Antonio Bello López was up a tree collecting bayleaves. As he saw me arrive he shinned down with a big bunch under his arm and came to greet me, the smell of the green bay on his hands as pungent as cologne. A skeletal full moon in the afternoon sky augured well for this wild harvest. He would strew the leaves around the house and the place would be filled with the resiny-spicy scent of the bay, like the scent of freshly-painted varnish on old wood.

Antonio is bearded, compactly built and sinewy, with the Old Testament look of a man who is used to undergoing trials of his physical and spiritual strength. He lives with his old mum, a gentle countrywoman, in a grey stone house with a slate roof and chickens in a kind of shed built into the ground floor, as is traditional and still common in the countryside of northern Spain. He was born and grew up in this house, but ran away to see the world when he was seventeen, as the 1960s sputtered into life. He lived in San Sebastián, Madrid, Barcelona, Málaga, Norway, Africa. On the island of Lanzarote he worked with the architect César Manrique, who noted the young man's creativity and aptitude for stone. On the island of Fuerteventura he had one of the 'moments' experienced by all self-respecting mystics: a vision, a blinding aureole of bright golden light, and coming out of the light, a cross. 'After that, my friends said I was going crazy. And in a way I was, a little, no?' he said amusedly, stroking his silver beard.

After the vision he moved back to his old house on the Way of Saint James. He felt unconnected and alone. He spent whole days meditating on hilltops, among the rocks and stones. He was sitting cross-legged in a *castro* one afternoon and felt a disagreeable pull to return home. 'I resisted it for a while, then I had to give in. When I got back to the house, there were two men impatiently waiting. They said they'd come from Malta especially to see me. Only one of them spoke. He didn't speak, so much as give commands that had to be obeyed. He said, "Wash your feet." So I washed them, with a stone in the water. Then he said, "Now we must eat." So I prepared something. Finally he told me that in three days' time things would start to change. "You'll see." My life would change; people would start to arrive. And he was right.'

Antonio Bello López began to study alchemy; he began to peer into the *grimoires* of medieval sages who must once have walked past his house on the Way of Saint James; timidly he felt his way along the corridors of ancient science. And visitors – psychologists, chemists, historians, astrologers and astronomers – began to arrive in a steady trickle along the Way. The strangest visit by far was from two NASA scientists, charged by their employers with a mission to look back into the treasure-house of pre-technological wisdom and see if there was anything High Technology had missed.

It wasn't long before Antonio found his first Talismanic Stone. He discovered it as he has all succeeding stones, by picking up on its texture and mass and colour and the magnetic vibrations it seemed to emit. It was a heavy rock weighing perhaps three kilos, with the form of a rough spiral rising to a triple peak that to some eyes seems to represent a mountain. He developed an uncanny relationship with this stone, and the connection grew more and more powerful the more he revered it. The stone sat there on the table; he would feel his hand move automatically towards it. Sometimes, annoyed by its control over him, he would move it out of his way or even throw it in the rubbish. But it would always reappear in odd places; on top of the fridge, or under the bed. This was his favourite stone at one time. Others have since taken its place.

Antonio showed me upstairs to the gallery he has made on a long landing running from one side of the house to the other. A delicious autumn breeze blew through the room, bringing the smell of fresh pasture and chestnut woods. He brought out a simple brown, round, flattish pebble from his bedroom where he keeps it by his bed at night. It was extraordinarily smooth and warm under the hand. 'I love the touch of it.'

At the centre of the stone's flat surface was a tiny pattern, barely discernible to the untrained untuned eye, of a nose and eyes. Looking up I saw the same pattern, a primitive staring face, in one of the paintings that hung on the wall; paintings with a difference, made entirely from crushed coloured stone, meticulously poured and sprinkled in abstract patterns. This I imagined was the way the alchemist made his living. Too much of it was clichéd hippy art, but there was one piece that interested me, bearing in mind the vision in the Canaries. It was a cloud of signs and symbols surrounding a bulbous organic cross in black stone. Floating above the cross was a circular patch of much lighter colour, perhaps representing the flash of light on Fuerteventura. I also liked the spider on the web, which was inspired by a real-life spider on the door to a cupboard in the artist's kitchen. Every time he opened the door to take out a plate, the spider's work was destroyed, so Antonio made this piece as a tribute, a repayment for the damage and inconvenience caused.

Then he led me through to his laboratory. It was not one of the public rooms, he rarely let people see it, and our voices took on a reverent hush as we entered. The room was dark and dirty, the beams black with soot. Up among the rafters hung a spindly frame with spokes, where the *chorizos* used to hang. It was, all things considered, an unusual laboratory. Around the walls, all over the table, everywhere you looked, were white plastic cups filled with coloured powders. Antonio finds stones in riverbeds, on hillsides, in the prehistoric castles that litter Galicia, and grinds them up in a pestle and mortar. There are good times to find them, and not so good. 'Sundays are often good for working. I feel my spirit lift.'

On the slate rooftop beyond the window was a collection of glass demijohns. Mysterious liquids bubbled within them. My mind was dizzy with resonances, zapping from 1950s monster movies to the esoteric tracts of the Elizabethans and back to Mary Shelley's *Frankenstein*. Antonio goes out at dawn and collects litres of dew from the leaves of plants and trees, and steeps the ground stones in the water. Some of these jars had been up on the roof for years. 'See that one with the orange stains up the side? That's been cooking for eighteen months,' he said. Another was filled with a thick black sludge of more recent vintage. This he thought more promising. To ask him why it was promising and what exactly it promised, though, I felt would be a crass intrusion on this nebulous world.

The man's love of stone runs to extremes that most of us would find hard to swallow. And swallow he does: stones crushed and mixed with water. '*Da igual lo que me haga*' ('I don't care what it does to me'), he said. 'Sometimes eating stones makes me feel radiant, full of energy.' Geological Ecstasy, or poison on the rocks? 'I often don't eat for a day or so and just drink spring water. Food dampens down my energies. I once met an old man from China who told me that in his country chickens are fed crushed quartz, and when you eat the meat, it prevents syphilis. I have taken no pills for years, not even aspirin. The stones keep me healthy.' The old man from China pops up from time to time in one of his waking visions, which are arguably not unconnected with the regular ingestion of crushed stone and the avoidance of normal food. There is a fountain that seems to be filled with light, rising in a great swell and falling in spirals. And beside the fountain stands the Chinaman.

Gallegos, possessors of the pan-Celtic blarney of the Irish and Welsh, are great tellers of tales and makers of myth. Before I leave Antonio tells me another story, and it's a good one. In a field near his house is a natural spring known in the village as the Bishop's Spring and believed to have miraculous powers. The belief is connected to the legend of a priest, walking the Way of Saint James, who was passing the spring at some point in the Middle Ages and struck up conversation with a former leper. The leper had been cured of his affliction by drinking the water of this spring. A year later the priest came by again. Either miraculously or by a bureaucratic process, he had been turned into a bishop. Hence the name.

Antonio's grandmother, who was a wise old bird, knew this story. So when her grandson contracted some childhood disease, I think whooping-cough, she avoided the doctor and took him to the Bishop's Spring. She bathed the child's head and hands in the sparkling water, and he was cured. And, ever since then, Antonio Bello López has stuck to the stone and the water, and ever since then he's been a picture of sinewy, hermitical health.

It is just possible that he may be slightly mad, but this seems to me an unprofitably reductive way of looking at things. I would prefer to see in him a facet of the Galician character taken to an extreme: I mean the interest in signs and wonders and the numinous powers at work behind the safety curtain of reality and the mysterious connections that bind one experience to another; the spiritual perceptiveness that Wordsworth in *Tintern Abbey* called 'a sense of something far more deeply interfused'.

'I am the Way,' said Christ. The important thing was never the arrival, but the journey. I think this is what Antonio would have said, or something like it, if I'd got round to asking him what it was all in aid of, what it was all *for*, for heaven's sake, the mystical business with the stones and the dew. His answer might have emphasised the importance of process, development, change, and the secondary importance of aims, and goals, and endings. He might have said something, also, about the Way of Saint James being a palimpsest, a magical interweaving of past and present, a continuum of knowledge and Galician-ness which he and his curious experiments are helping to maintain.

Short Stories

THE LITTLE TRAIN

On the little narrow-gauge railway that creeps along the coast from Alicante to Denia and back, skirting the concrete wonderland of the resorts, pushing through suburban lemon groves and abandoned terraces where the fruit trees, denied the water that now goes directly to the tourists, rattle in the breeze like skeletons. Alicantinos, even the majority that don't speak Catalan, fondly apply the Catalan diminutive when they call this *el trenet*: the little train. It always reminds me of Proust's *petit train*, the 'little crawler' that chugged romantically along the coast from Doncières to Hermenonville and Saint-Pierre des Ifs. It has old-fashioned luggage-racks up near the roof, dark plastic seats that stick to your skin in the heat, short curtains of rough dark fabric that flap wildly beside the open window, and a self-important toot-toot as it pulls into tiny stations that consist of no more than a platform and a bench. To your left are stark mountains, toothed and jagged. Along the track are fences thickly lined with bougainvillaea, sweet purple and sherbetty orange.

At a country stop outside La Vila Joiosa, 'the joyful town', an old lady gets on. Her hair, which was perhaps once jet black, is now badger-grey and hauled back into a bun. It's June, but she's still wearing a black cardigan. She pulls it round herself, at the same time opening a fan and working it energetically over her face. And, just before the little train moves on towards Benidorm, she stops her fanning and crosses herself.

3

Strange Sport

On the desk in front of me is one of my favourite photographs of all time. It's a black and white portrait of an old man with scraggy old man's arms held behind his back so that the sinews show, like the wings on an old chicken. He is standing to attention with a long pole upright beside him, barefoot on what looks like black sand, wearing a sheepskin dress-thing without seams or buttons or joins. On his head he wears an extraordinary hat, a kind of primitive fluffy bearskin that makes up nearly a quarter of the old man's total height.

Having absorbed all this information in a few seconds, the viewer thinks lazily, 'Third World tribesperson snapped *Last of the Mohicans* style by early camera', and glances down at the caption to have his hunch confirmed. 'Participant in the ceremony of The Apparition of the Virgin of Candelaria to the Guanches, held in Candelaria in the year 1928,' it reads. The Guanches were the original inhabitants of the Canary Islands before the Spanish conquest, and the Virgin really did appear to a few of them on a famous occasion in Tenerife in 1390. So this old man was dressing up as a Guanche tribesman for a folklore celebration of the Apparition. That's OK, then. But when you look back at his face, you see that it's remarkable, proud and hooded-eyed and hieratic. He looks like the witch doctor of some African tribe. You focus on his enormous crescent-moon moustache and his long white beard, which isn't curly but falls in a thick single lock straight down over his fur tabard almost to the level of his elbows. If this is a fake beard, it's a very convincing one for the late 1920s on an island off the coast of Africa. And if it's not, where does that facial hairstyle come from? Because it certainly doesn't belong in twentieth-century Europe.

The hundreds of thousands of tourists who make their way to Tenerife each year must all have their reasons for going there. My reason was this photograph and the trip switch it flicked in my mind, the suggestion that even on these aggressively colonised tourist islands the historical past might be better represented in the present, closer by far to the surface of life than I'd ever imagined.

Some places tell you where they are in the world. They say: this is where I belong, this is my latitude and longitude. Others are harder to pin down. Sometimes it seems they deliberately set out to confuse you, either because they can't make up their own mind which continent and century they're in, or because they rather enjoy the sense of your not being sure.

Just when you thought it was safe to think this was more or less European, more or less familiar to senses conditioned by Spain and Italy, the Canary Islands suddenly throw at you a landscape that is starkly, soulfully African, or a Cuban accent, a Venezuelan dish, a piece of Berber culture, or a palm-grove and waterfall straight out of the West Indies. By the same token, get on to the motorway and roar into Playa de las Américas, Tenerife's savagely single-minded tourist resort, and you'll think this is total modernity, a twenty-first-century paradise/inferno like hundreds of others across southern Europe. Push in a little deeper and you'll begin to see the ancient strangenesses of a place that emerged from prehistory only 500 years ago.

Even the expected thing, the supercharged tourist industry that has given these volcanic lumps stranded off the coast of Africa their reputation and *raison d'être*, can come as a shock if you're not mentally prepared. One dark day in March I took a cheap flight from Gatwick, one of the airborne chain of cattle-wagons that pick up winter-wasted Britons and dump them in the sun, and woke up next morning in Las Galletas, a just-add-water holiday town that was so new, so lacking in antecedents or history, that it seemed as surprised to be there as I was. There had, however, been a minuscule fishing port here once, and somewhere under the avalanche of apartment blocks was still a tiny core of whitewashed huts. On the doorsteps of these huts it was good to see grannies grouping to gossip and complain about prices, as grannies have done ever since the dawn of time.

Las Galletas means 'The Biscuits'. As I wandered along the prom, past cafés full of lobster-pink tourists, the place did have a crumbly insubstantial quality about it, like a plate of Rich Teas left outside overnight and nibbled by mice. There was another connection with baking to be made: the purplish-brown-black volcanic sand on the beach, so outrageous to the common-sense view that says that sand should be yellow, was precisely the colour of Oreo cookies – the kind, remember, that Americans compared to Jesse Jackson because he, too, was black on the outside, white on the inside. Elderly German and English bodies were laid out pale, like corpses, on the black sand, or shuffled along the esplanade. There is no off-season here; the machine of tourism grinds on through the northern winter for the retired people and kicks back into top gear in May or June for the families and singles. Even at its lowest point, hotel occupation on Tenerife never falls below 80 per cent, and, or rather because, the temperature never falls below 18 degrees.

I crept along the south coast of the island, progressively more dazed by what I saw. Los Cristianos, another fine example of the Spanish paradigm that consists of a fishing village turning into a tourist conurbation within twenty years, was a mass of bad building surrounded by a post-apocalyptic wilderness of volcanic rock and rubble. In this treeless landscape it is impossible to disguise or beautify anything with recourse to nature. Half-built apartment blocks, their façades properly concreted and whitewashed, back and sides a shameless wall of grey breeze-blocks barely humanised by washing-lines and sun-shades, looked like ships stranded in the desert when the sea had retreated after some ecological catastrophe. The whole area west of the airport, where charter flights roared in every five minutes from Hamburg, Helsinki or Hull, was christened by the Spanish conquerors La Costa del Silencio – 'The Coast of Silence'. Now the name just seems like a joke.

The hot sun began to burn off a thick mist, and little by little the Teide, the great volcanic peak of Tenerife and at 4,000 metres the highest point in Spanish territory, emerged gleaming white into the tropical morning. The sheer size of the Teide is ridiculous. Mont Blanc in the French Alps is only a few hundred metres higher, and this is the centre point of an island you can drive around easily in half a day. Even the look of it, conical and smooth-sided like a picture-book mountain, is somehow implausible. The Teide doesn't have quite the star quality of other ex-volcanoes like Mount Fuji and Kilimanjaro, but like them it produces affection and admiration and even a vague sort of spiritual yearning in those who live around it. The Guanches regarded the mountain as their most sacred symbol. Any animist tribe worthy of the name would have done as much. Islanders today still gaze up at it in bleary-eyed curiosity as they venture out on to their balconies in the morning, which is as close as most people get to worshipping anything these days.

I stopped by a public phone and rang my contact, a journalist on a local paper who has carved out a niche reporting on the traditional sports and games of the Canary Islands. His byline was in that day's edition, previewing an important session of Canarian wrestling that same day in the village of Tegueste, on the north-eastern side of the mountain.

The universe of Canarian sport includes some fourteen or fifteen different activities, said Luis. Canarian wrestling is only the most popular and best organised of them. Beyond that are *palo canario*, Canarian stick-fighting, and its similar-but-different form *garrote*. At the wilder end of things, where 'sport' shades over into 'game' or 'pastime', are *salto del pastor* (shepherd's jump), *arrastre de ganado* (cattle-dragging) and *lanzamiento y esquive* (literally 'throwing and dodging'. One player throws stones, or oranges or lumps of clay, and the other dodges them, or doesn't, as the case may be). As Luis tried vainly to describe the odder ones, my mind began to wander towards the Monty Python sketch that cruelly takes the piss out of absurd and marginal folklore: 'Zis was ze Trondheim Hammer Dance, in which ze old ladies are struck about ze head with wooden sticks or knödels . . .'

I was to be there that evening in Tegueste, at the sandpit/stadium where Canarian wrestlers traditionally do their thing. I arrived after nightfall and the *terrero*, a square sandy-floored ring with raked concrete seats on all four sides, was filling up with small dark people in sombre country clothes. Most of the audience appeared to sport bushy Zapata moustaches. So did some of their husbands. There was a heated murmurous atmosphere of agricultural folk having a good time. The air smelt of a combination of farm animals and energetically applied Palmolive soap.

Out on to the sand came two young men, squatly built and barefoot, wearing white shorts whose hems had been rolled up to form a thick band around the upper thigh. They shook hands, bent down towards each other as in a deep bow, and locked into a human arch, shoulder to shoulder, each grabbing the other's rolled-up shorts for extra support. The point of the sport is to topple the other guy by jostling and grabbing him, hooking his leg from under him or pushing him out beyond the whitewashed circles in the sand. The wrestlers spend long seconds motionless, looking for a movement that will unbalance their rival, then resume their strange double stagger round the ring.

These men were anorexic compared to any sumo wrestler, but fat
looked like being an issue here as well. A big porky person from the
home team of Tegueste waddled on and found himself interlocked
with a relative thinny from the visiting village, El Rosario. The fatty
grunted and groaned, pulled hard on the other man's trouser-roll
and there was a terrible ripping sound. You could imagine his
mother thinking of the expense. Within seconds the thinny was on
the sand, clutching his right ear. It's like a miniature rugby scrum;
your ears rub painfully. But the victor, far from punching the air in
a gesture of triumph, did something surprising. He pulled up the
loser from the sand, shook his hand and ruffled his hair as the two
made their way out of the ring. Luis said this was a fine example of
the moral delicacy, the essential nobility of Canarian wrestling,
which still puts a high value on sportsmanship and fair play while
other Johnny-come-lately sports, like football, have been brutalised
by their own (thoroughly unjustified, in his opinion) success.

When the freezing concrete seating had almost put paid for ever
to the circulation in my legs, I hobbled up through the crowd and
wandered around an exhibition of old photographs laid out around
the *terrero*'s upper gallery. They were pictures of rural scenes from
the villages of northern Tenerife featuring weddings, *fiestas*, banana
harvest-homes, family singalongs. The subjects all had the wide-
eyed, slightly blurry awkwardness of people unused to the
mysterious workings of the box camera. Above each set of pictures
was a printed slogan, repeated like a mantra: 'Not all past time was
better, but we remember it with the happiness of nostalgia.'

Canarians have a close relationship with their islands' history,
simply because big chunks of it happened not all that long ago, and
so remain vividly close to them. It must be an interesting experience
for Europeans (the Canaries aren't really Europe, but they form
part of a European state) to be just five centuries away from a tribal
past. Three of the photos in that exhibition, all taken in the village
of Valle de Guerra on the north coast, gave an idea of how it must
feel. One showed an arched two-floored house with Andalusian-style

window bars. 'The dwellings of the inhabitants of Valle de Guerra have evolved over time, until today when we admire this magnificent *chalet*, built with all the most up-to-date devices for living in complete comfort.' Another picture showed a typical *pajal*, a straw-roofed Tenerife peasant house inhabited in until the early 1930s. And a third showed the mouth of a cave, perhaps three or four metres deep, the former home of 'Guanche aborigines' in the same village of Valle de Guerra. The cave would probably have been occupied until 1495, when the Spanish finally conquered the last of the local rulers and the Guanches, an ancient people with Berber roots, were taken into slavery either as farmhands or in aristocratic households on the mainland.

Before the disaster befell them they had been shepherds and arable farmers, dressing in sheep- and goat-skins and living mainly on *gofio*, a ground toasted meal mixed with honey, milk or lard. It seems there was no metal anywhere on the islands; if there was, the Guanches had no use for it. It's become a Kevin Costnerish cliché of pre-colonial peoples, but they do seem to have been peace loving and well behaved more often than they were whooping savages who shrank heads in their spare time. Even the Spanish were impressed by their sense of honour, their generosity towards prisoners of war, the way they leapt to their deaths from the clifftops in defeat, and other qualities appealing to Castilian notions of virtue. Fifteenth-century Guanche society wasn't a classless society, but it was a remarkably fluid and flexible one. Nobility was gained, not born into, and anyone could reach a position in high society following a brief Civil-Service-type investigation into his character. There was a kind of questionnaire: Had the candidate ever a) been seen killing or milking goats? b) prepared food with his hands? c) stolen food in peace-time or d) been dishonest with anyone, particularly a woman? If the answer to all these questions was No, it was up, up, and away into the social stratosphere.

These people got a big kick out of physical recreation. The main Guanche *fiesta* of Beñesmen, in celebration of the grain harvest, was

'It's a Knockout' meets the Flintstones, with tribespeople locked in physical combat, fencing with sticks, lifting stones and jumping rocks. The Spanish missionary Father Espinosa, author of an account of the famous appearance of Our Lady to the Guanches in 1390, attended one of these sports day/harvest festivals. 'During the year (which they counted by the moon) they would make many general gatherings,' he recorded. 'And he who was king and governed at the time, would offer them board and expense of heads of cattle, *gofio*, milk and lard . . . and each would show his bravery, making a display of his gifts in jumping, running, dancing, fighting, and in the other things they understood.'

The *terrero* was an outdoor patch of rough ground, and fighters wore a skimpy G-string affair of rush fibre and leather strips on each side, all the better for combatants to grab each other with. Rolled-up shorts fulfil the same function nowadays. Otherwise, Canarian wrestling seems to have changed little from the days of these tribal romps. It's hard to think of another sport that has clung so tenaciously to its historical origins, unless it were one of the half-dozen other Guanche games that still have Canarians wielding sticks and lifting stones all over the archipelago.

The greater part of the Guanches' modest way of life was swept away by the new broom of Spain's imperial dreams, but fragments of it escaped the purge and lived on, as it were, in holes in the wall and behind the sofa. Back in 'The Biscuits', I went to the supermarket opposite the apartment to stock up on basic items like milk and bread and coffee and pasta. Beneath the milk was a whole shelf of *gofio*; toasted ground wheat, maize and barley in various combinations; pastel-yellow and pinkish-grey powders in transparent plastic packages. The pinkish-grey ones looked like bags of cement. I knew it still formed a part of the Canarian diet, but to see *gofio* in such a context, packed up for sale to housewives along with the milk and bread and coffee and pasta, sent me into a pleasant Proustian daydream. I examined the packages, concentrating on their various cheap designs and obvious brand-names – 'El Teide', 'El Guanche' –

and eventually chose a small packet with a picture of a squatting figure in a loincloth grinding corn in a small stone mill.

Canarian friends of mine had warned me it was vile, and it is. Mixed with milk, it forms a thick sludge that sticks to your palate and has to be removed by increasingly desperate movements of the tongue. It would be like eating wallpaper paste, except that the cloying pale purée is partly redeemed by a toasty malty taste that could be kindly described as 'comforting'. On the whole, though, *gofio* is one local speciality I would cross the street to avoid, along with Tibetan yak-butter tea and jellied eels.

I had promised its organisers I would record for posterity that the First Conference on Indigenous Sports and Traditional Games of the Canary Islands took place during the week of 18 March 1996 in the grand salon of the Cabildo de Tenerife, the headquarters of the island government. The conference consisted of a series of talks by experts, and since these experts were either sportsmen or bureaucrats or both, the room hardly echoed with hilarious laughter. A fug of officialdom hung over the proceedings, smelling of statistics and reports and committees and the whole sluggish machinery of local politics.

Some of the talks were amusing in spite of themselves. One man was an expert on stone-lifting and plough-lifting, and lamented the fact that young Canarians seemed to have passed over these two cornerstones of their identity in favour of foreign sports, imported mostly from the Peninsula (hisssss!), like *fútbol* and *basket*. They were essentially trials of strength, he explained, used by the Guanches to prove their manliness to themselves and their friends on the feast day of Beñesmen. Particular stones were selected for a combination of weight and ease of handling, and over time these stones came to acquire an almost magical importance. (There was one in the conference room, part of a small display of Canarian sports equipment. A grey volcanic lump, it sat glumly on the purple carpet, perhaps wondering what this new-fangled 'football' had that it didn't.) As for plough-lifting, this was apparently a later development, since the Guanches used goats' horns to scratch a furrow in the earth, and something so light and delicate wouldn't provide much of a challenge to the weight-lifter. In the rural context, at least, the plough would simply have been one of the heaviest domestic objects around, and therefore irresistible to any Canarian anxious to show off his muscles.

'Our traditional games have always been pursued by the phantom of their disappearance,' the man said sadly. In the case of stone-lifting and plough-lifting, though one sympathised with his sadness, one felt that it was no surprise. The modern world could not put up with something so brutally honest in its implications. If you lifted the stone, you were a hero. If you failed to lift it, you were a pathetic weakling who deserved to spend the days grinding *gofio* with the women.

Customs, like species, have their own reasons for becoming extinct. Adelto Fernández Álvarez, from the small verdant island of La Palma, had come to talk about his and the island's speciality, which happens to be one of the most charming and purest sports in the world. It is also one of the daftest, and over the last fifty years or so this fact has contrived to keep it in something very like total obscurity. Adelto had brought with him from La Palma a long pole with a round utensil, a kind of scoop with a 12-litre capacity, attached to the end. The *calabazo* would once have been made from a hollowed-out pumpkin, but this one began life as a biscuit tin. It reminded me of the helmet on a medieval suit of armour.

La Palma is blessed with a wealth of natural springs. The springs flow into canals, and before there were electric pumps the water had to be brought from lower, wetter terraces to higher, drier ones. So the *calabazo* came into being, and with it the *calabacero* whose job it was to shift water from place to place with his copious scoop. We were shown a video of a *calabacero* at his work beside a stone tank, framed by tropical greenery. He was a sinewy-looking middle-aged man with a fag clamped in his mouth who sat and stood in time with the up-and-down movements of the pole and scoop as he filled it in the canal below and emptied it with a satisfying *sloosh* in the tank above. Five minutes of this, and the man ground to a halt and removed the fag from his mouth, huffing and puffing from the effort. Adelto put the video on freeze-frame and explained that *calabazo* puts a terrible unequal strain on the back muscles, to say nothing of the insalubrious effects of long periods of hard physical effort in such damp conditions.

Even in the days when this activity fulfilled an important function, when it was a job like any other, there was a ludic aspect to *calabazo*. Bets would be taken on how much water participants could move in a certain time, or how long they could last before presumably collapsing from a combination of exhaustion and chronic back pain. The sheer tension, the edge-of-your-seat exhilaration of it all must have been nearly unbearable. Following the inevitable conversion of country pursuits into urban trends, *calabazo* has smartened itself up a bit and is busily trying to sell itself as a real sport with proper rules and regulations and people who are actually better at the thing than others. The video showed water being removed from a school swimming-pool as part of a demonstration that goes round teaching the children of La Palma about this little-known facet of their cultural heritage. There have been *calabazo* shows at country fairs on the island, but the problem at these events has always been that the tanks take five minutes to refill between each participant, so that there is more standing around than actual sporting action.

The previous month had seen La Palma's first-ever *calabazo* championship. It was a small step for mankind, but a giant leap for manual water transportation. It had been a tremendous affair, said Adelto. After an impressive struggle for supremacy, the eventual winner had been Ramón Papa Chola (crazy name, crazy guy) with no less than 800 litres of water pumpkinned in three minutes. (I made a quick calculation on the back of my notebook: 800 litres in 3 minutes is 266 litres a minute, which means 22 ups and downs of the scoop every minute.) Overnight Ramón had become *calabazo*'s first and greatest star, its Cantona, its Indurain, and an instant role model for local youth. Before long he'd be on bedroom walls all over the island, kids would be begging their parents for a *calabazo* for Christmas, and another Spanish tradition would have been brought from the edge of extinction into a bright new future.

The wrestlers turned up in dribs and drabs, from school and office and building site, wearing shellsuits and tracksuits and business suits. The range of age and size was wide: there were callow adolescents with thin white arms and floppy fringes, and scarily huge middle-aged men with beer bellies and legs like tree-trunks. All of them joshed manfully with each other, irrespective of size, and there was much scornful talk of *maricones* (poofters).

Jesús María Delgado Gonzalez, 'Susi', the twenty-six-year-old trainer of the Canarian wrestling team Brisas del Teide (Breezes of the Teide), had been at the conference on indigenous sports out of loyalty to one of them and curiosity about the others. His team had a training session that evening, and he wondered whether I'd like to sit in. Susi was born in Holland of Spanish parents who returned to Tenerife when he was ten. His roots are in the southern village of Fasnia, one of the places on the island where the wrestling tradition runs deepest, so no one was very much surprised when he took it up at twelve. 'My father fought as a young man. They used to have matches between bachelors and married men, between the hill and the mountain. There are still a lot of wrestlers around, but the village tradition is dying out. Most of the younger guys are going to Santa Cruz. We've got jobs to do and, anyway, the wrestling facilities are much better here,' said Susi as we drove along the sea-front, past a whitewashed mission church in a state of peeling disrepair.

The sport has changed since Susi's father's time; whether for better or for worse is a moot point. What was once a hobby for rural *aficionados* is now organised, professional, commercialised. Teams have a league table and depend for their existence on the support of supermarkets, DIY companies, even local branches of McDonald's. (The Brisas are sponsored by Pepsi.) There is money in Canarian wrestling. Not only do many fighters make their living from it, but the most successful fighters can make up to six million pesetas, more than £30,000 a year. There's now a star system, headed by the *numero uno* of the moment, a six foot six giant from the tiny western island of El Hierro. Pollito de la Frontera – real name: Francisco Pérez, nickname: 'little chicken' – makes Canarian girls go weak at the knees and fills the hearts of young Canarian males with virile admiration.

We were at a rough-and-ready open-air *terrero*, fenced in and floodlit like a basketball pitch in the Bronx, in a tower-block district on the outskirts of Santa Cruz. A few local kids were kicking a football around. A dog had been tied up behind the shut-up boardings of an open-air bar. It yelped endlessly and desolately.

Susi ordered the team on their warm-up run round the block, and fifteen minutes later they returned one by one, in order of size. Last back to the sandpit was a fat little boy with a red face. It occurred to me then that Pepsi was not perhaps the ideal team sponsor, unless of course it was the Diet variety. Plainly Susi had been thinking along the same lines as he watched the boy struggle up to the ring. There was an important match coming up, he told me under his breath, and the team wasn't exactly on perfect form.

'Diego, you know in two weeks' time you've got to be able to get around as fast as the others,' he said to the boy with friendly crossness, turning his features an even brighter shade of pink.

'That belly's not going to go down fast enough,' put in an older team-member as he pulled off his tracksuit and pulled on wrestling shorts.

'No, not if he doesn't go easy on the burgers and the hot dogs,' said Susi. 'How many times a week do you eat chips, Diego?'

'I don't eat them.'

'What about *bocadillos*?'

'I eat *them*, yes. But not much, once or twice a week. With cheese and tomato, never with ham or *chorizo*.'

'And how big's the bread – *this* big?' Susi opened his arms wide, and both of them laughed, the trainer and the trained, at the silliness of the idea.

It was time for the team collectively to roll up its shorts and get into the classic Canarian-wrestling interlock position, which it did in all possible combinations of fat and thin, young and old, weedy and tough. For the first time I had a close-up view of the complicated gesture that begins the bout. Let me see if I can describe it. The wrestlers stand head-to-head with each other, or rather ear-to-ear. While the left hand seeks out the trouser hem and grips on to it for dear life, the right hangs down vertically, finds itself alongside another right hand and, approaching from the opposite side, like that party game of Dead Man's Finger where you end up with a fist made of two sets of digits, sort of intertwines with it. The two right hands then drop gently downwards together, and when they touch the sand, the fight begins. It sounds absurdly complex, but the whole procedure takes no more than a second or two.

The sandpit was suddenly alive with grunts and groans. Susi had told the team they were to concentrate on a particular tactic, the leg-hook. So there they all were, trying to hook their heel round their opponent's leg while he tried desperately to do the same. It was a bizarre sight: a colony of crabs doing Jane Fonda on the sea-bed. My little fat friend Diego was paired with a monster, a road-drill operator three times his size who looked as if he could cheerfully slice the fat boy into rashers and eat him between two slices of bread as a mid-morning snack.

When the right arms of this odd couple intertwined, it was like a mature sequoia intertwining with a bean sprout. When the leg-hooking began, however, it was clear the contest was much more evenly balanced than it first appeared. In spite of his wobbly little thighs, the fat kid's feet were getting into places the construction worker's couldn't reach. They scuttled around the *terrero* in a surreally awkward waltz. Then, just as it seemed the big guy was getting the upper hand, the little guy chipped in a foot behind his shinbone and sent him toppling – slowly; a cooling tower being demolished by an expert steeplejack – and he landed with a resounding, painful-sounding *thwock* in the sand behind him. It was just like a song they sing in the Canary Islands, laughed Susi. There's a line in it that goes: '*El grande pierde, el pequeño gana*' ('The big one loses, the little one wins'). He hummed a snatch of melody, and ran into the sand to give Goliath a helping hand.

Next morning I left my crumbly biscuit-tin town, planning to look for oddities and oldness among the breeze-block conurbations. Along the road out of Las Galletas a team of small dark men were making their way to the banana plantations, sacks slung over their backs. (The plantations – domesticated jungles – are visible from air and sea as great shimmering slabs of stone-coloured nylon.) They had moustachioed, sun-baked faces, wide and expressive as Andean Indians'. Was this the Guanche strain, or the legacy of recent waves of immigration from other ex-colonies like Cuba and Venezuela? When Canarian peasants arrived in South America they were frequently mistaken for Indian half-castes, such was the facial similarity.

I headed north-east, making for the mountain. From the plane, I'd seen the Teide burst through its cloud-cover, a black solitary island in its own white sea. Now I was pushing up into that sea from underneath; the air was drenched with humidity; the chilly mist blew around the drifts. In Villaflor, the highest village in Spain – it's hard to believe, the place is so sober-seeming and colonially bourgeois, all sash windows and racing-green paintwork – I stopped and ate *papas arrugás con mojo picón*, literally 'wrinkly potatoes with spicy wet stuff', in a restaurant with a panoramic view of cloudy nothingness. Further up, streams rushed down through the sub-tropical greenery. The water was melted snow, as winter gave way to spring up there.

Around the mountain's peak is the great circling toothed volcanic crater, and within it the lava plain, a flat bald place carpeted with pumice stone where nothing grows. From as near to the snowy summit as you can reach without spiky boots and a stiff drink, I looked down at a landscape of jagged rust-red crags straight out of a *National Geographic* photo-essay on Utah or Northern Australia. Down on the lava plain, I built a snowman and sat him on a tiny hill looking out portentously over the desert; stout Cortes on his peak in Darien.

There was a place on the map called Taganana. A Guanche name, like most of the hundreds of others in the Canaries that begin with Ta, Te, Ti, Ar, Er, A, Gua. Arguayo, Erques, Artenara, Tazo, Tetir, Tinajo, Agaete, Tegueste, Guarazoca. The written form of the Guanche language looks like I imagine Phoenician or Mesopotamian to have looked. When it is transliterated into Latin characters there are odder resemblances, between Guanche and Basque, Guanche and Breton and, believe it or not, between Guanche and Welsh. Here's an example. *Punapal* in Guanche means 'son by first marriage or principal wife'. *Pen-appill* in Welsh means 'main descendant'. *Guanche* itself may have meant 'white', because the Berber tribes of the Canaries were pale compared to mainland Africans. And the Welsh for white is *gwyn*. Preposterous coincidence? Quite possibly. But Taganana: it sounded resonantly exotic. The map showed it as a lonely spot on the far north coast, hemmed in by mountains and deep volcanic valleys.

The road to the village was a noble piece of late-twentieth-century engineering, endlessly switch-backing along razor-sharp ridges that plunged on either side into Byronic chasms. Every corner was a reason to stop and stare at plants I'd only ever seen in the hothouse of some botanical garden, their flowers acid yellow, blue and shocking pink. There were whole fields-full of *tunera* cactus, its paddles studded with bright orange prickly pears. When, in about 1845, these cacti became infested with parasitic *cochinilla* beetles, a lot of Canarian farmers got very rich very quickly. For thirty years the islands were a major supplier of the red food colouring called in English cochineal; but in 1875 a much cheaper artificial equivalent was discovered, and the boom turned to bust and bankruptcy.

On one of the hairpin corners I had to stop, sit on the crash-barrier and light up a cigarette, resting my eyes on the deep valley that swept down in a stately curve towards the blue Atlantic. It was lined with ranks of terraces, stacked up as steeply as cheap seats at the opera, that made you wonder how farmers round here could possibly work their land without a cable-car and/or a good head for heights.

On the terrace below me sat a goatherd in a baseball cap, looking out over the same view, though understandably without quite such a pronounced sense of wonder. Andrés Ribero has lived most of his seventy-eight years in the valley, though he was born a few miles away in the mountains of Anaga. 'I've not been here long,' he shouted up to me as he pointed out his little dominion, a cluster of newish farmhouses with flat roofs painted green and red.

Andrés' favourite topic of conversation turned out to be the familiar Spanish countryman's complaint: that the countryside is not what it was, that young people aren't interested in the land, that tourism is the priority now and what's tourism ever done for me? Look at these terraces, for example – the way the walls are crumbling, the fruit trees dying, the ground un-tilled. He chuntered away quietly, while far below us a long line of brown goats meandered across the fields towards the dairy. Andrés' own herd was grazing high up on the rocks above the road, nibbling busily among the cactus.

In his right hand the old man held a stick, a length of cane as thick as a child's wrist. This was what he used for prodding the undergrowth, for pushing past the painful spines of cactus leaves, and for leaning on to get his breath back when the going got tough in this tough-going topography. When he was younger and nimbler, he said, he used to nip down the terraces with the aid of a long

pole – not this common-or-garden length of bamboo, but a special
stick as tall as himself that is now gathering dust in a storeroom in
his house. 'With that stick sometimes I could jump, ooh, a good
eight or ten metres down the mountain,' he said, his voice taking on
the retrospective pride of a grandfather recounting youthful
exploits.

Talking to Andrés, I felt the mixture of euphoria and awe that I
always feel when tradition seems to unfurl itself like a richly-
coloured carpet in the plain white room of the present. I'd been
curious about the terrace-hopping tradition of the Canaries – the
indigenous sports brigade now calls it *salto del pastor*, 'shepherd's
jump' – and here it was in front of me, suffering from a severe lack
of teeth but otherwise alive and well. *Salto* is an example of what
happens when a rural pursuit that responds to a particular practical
problem – in this case, how to get down steep hills quickly and easily
(getting up them is another story) – begins to lose its roots in the
country, its practical *raison d'être*, and has to look for other ways to
survive.

(NB: Don't go to Taganana unless you like to eat *Fisch, Kartoffeln
und Salat* and drink *Taganana-Wein* with a busload of tourist lobsters. Surprised by the nastiness of the cheap buildings strung
along the sea-front, I ate my sulky picnic in a car park among
ranks of tourist buses. The Atlantic looked cold and angry now.
I watched a herd of plump pensioners teetering along a cause-
way leading to a giant windswept rock. Perhaps one of them
would fall off . . .)

Fran and Adán were students at the University of La Laguna.
Physically they were very different: Fran was tall and rangy, with a
scruffy honey-coloured beard; Adán was smaller, wider, with a black
beard and black ponytail. But both had the earnestness and mental
energy that people who have been students in the past can only

look back on with nostalgia. Medicine and physics, respectively, are what Fran and Adán spend their intellectual brain-power on, but their passion is the martial art of Canarian stick-fighting, in the version of it known as *garrote*. In an anteroom of the government building they brought out their weapons: great poles as high as your head, made from wild olive, eucalyptus, bay or quince wood. The straightness of the pole is important; so is its flexibility. Tradition dictates that the wood should be cut under a waning moon and left outside for several days and nights, dried and hardened in the fire and treated with pig fat, vinegar, wax or dung (tradition is a little vague on the latter point).

One of the major studies of Canarian culture, Juan Bethencourt Alonso's *History of the Guanche People*, says *garrote* was played at the Beñesmen celebrations in summer and was hugely popular before the conquest, but has since fallen from favour. 'In our youth there were many of us who knew this manly sport, totally lost today.'

This is an exaggeration, and Fran and Adán are the proof. The two of them belong to a group of twenty-two stick-waving *garrote* enthusiasts, probably the only such group in Tenerife. Their guru and teacher Jorge Domínguez, from the next-door island of Gran Canaria which has a little more deeply-rooted *garrote* tradition, went around his home island interviewing shepherds about their fighting memories. He even went to Cuba, where the sport is better known than in the Canaries thanks to mass Canarian immigration in the nineteenth and early twentieth centuries. As a manifestation of ethnic culture, traditional sports like this were frowned on by the Franco régime and for many years after the Civil War they were kept alive mainly by individual families, who passed down the ancestral skills from parent to child.

Domínguez's eager students absorbed all this information and set to work learning the rules of the game and its peculiar technical terms. *Punta* means one end of the stick, *trozo* the other and something else which I've now forgotten for the bit in between. As in Eastern martial arts, the physical language of *garrote* has its roots in aggression – the Guanche shepherd needed to protect flocks and pastures, his most valuable resource, against attack – but has settled into a peaceful exercise in defensive skills. Guessing that how you react to a heavy blow with the stick would be one of those skills, the first thing Fran and Adán did was take a few classes in Canarian wrestling. They went down to the black beach to practise the important art of falling painlessly. Four years later, with a regular training session of four hours a week, they were experts in their archaic art. When I asked them, half as a joke, if they saw *garrote* as an important manifestation of their identity as Canary islanders, they both went a bit solemn and Adán said firmly, 'Yes.' Fran turned down the corners of his mouth and said: 'Oh yes. Definitely.'

Fran, the group's suavest, most lethal fighter, its Bruce Lee, gave me a crash course. The combatants stand face to face, one foot forward, one foot back, holding the stick like a sword. The hands grip the stick so that its length and weight are perfectly balanced and a flick of the wrist can send it spinning towards a delicate part of your opponent's anatomy. Classic movements include the sideways swipe to the head that leaves the victim in a daze but draws no blood, or the upward thrust between the legs. The blunt end of the stick can also come in handy when the aim is to inflict a particularly large amount of pain. In practice, friendly fighters tend to avoid the violent stuff. In theory, one fighter, whether student or sheep-farmer, could wipe out his opponent with a single well-placed blow.

He told me that women are more and more attracted to the sport. It seemed an unlikely thesis until a young girl, small-framed, bright-eyed, darkly pretty, came into the room with her lecture notes under her arm. She turns out to be another medical student, a friend of the boys and a demon with the pole. I retire from the action and watch her and Fran do their worst.

Now it really looks like primitive sword-fighting, though I know they wouldn't thank me for saying so. Someone said good stickmanship was all about *el juego de muñecas*, the play of wrists. The wrist-twisting and the delicate footwork make the thick stick swing this way and that, frequently threatening to trap bits of body in its path. Movements are stealthy and elegant, a ballet of violence, and the battle takes place in silence apart from the musical knocking of wood on wood.

They stopped, and I clapped my hands in genuine appreciation, and Adán made a little speech and awarded me a T-shirt with the name of their club and an image of two *garrote* fighters going at each other hammer and tongs. I had nothing to give them, and preferred to take: a picture of Fran standing to attention with his trusty stick. I adjusted the exposure and looked at him for a second in the viewfinder, tall and lanky and strong and scruffy-bearded, posing with the stick as high as his head. He reminded me of something. What? The black and white photo I keep on the desk in front of me. Give him another forty years and a fur coat, I said to myself as I swivelled the focus, and the boy could almost be that old tribesman on his way to the Beñesmen games.

Ker-chunk.

The Whistler's Mother

La Gomera is a small island an hour and a half from Tenerife by boat. There are two important things to know about it:

1. It is serenely beautiful, quiet and unpolluted.
2. It has no airport.

It doesn't take long to work out that the second point is the reason for the first. La Gomera has never had an airport, not, presumably, because it didn't want one – it's the ambition of all islands – but because there is simply no flat space on the island large enough to incorporate the kind of runway on which a charter flight can land with its load of lobsters. For thirty years the Gomeros have stood by and watched the brutal uglification wreaked on neighbouring islands as a direct consequence of the tourist industry, and one would hope that they realise how lucky they are. (In fact I'm not entirely sure they do.)

The ferry leaves Los Cristianos, which is a former fishing hamlet turned tourist conurbation, and arrives in San Sebastián de la Gomera, which isn't. As the boat docks, you look at the straggly little town cowering under a pile of volcano-cloud, and wonder whether this can really be your destination, or if the boat has simply stopped off en route to let a few more passengers on board. A noughts-and-crosses collection of streets made up mostly of low two-storey colonial houses with roughly tiled roofs and English-style sash windows, a comic-book towerette made of cream and purple volcanic rocks in a patch of parkland near the port, and a Portuguese-Gothic parish church of the Assumption with two palms outside it and a plaque commemorating Christopher Columbus and his final stopover in the Old World before striking out for the New World, are all there is to see in San Sebastián.

According to one historian with an over-active imagination, Columbus stocked up for his voyage on some of the local cheese. Remembering this, I bought some – it was fresh and cool, made the day before – also bread, oranges, chocolate, cigarettes and a resiny red wine from Tenerife. Then I set forth on the mountain road that circles the island, crossing each of the great *barrancos*, the ravines that emerge like the arms of a starfish from the central volcano of Garajonay.

An hour later I was sitting on a rock in a palm-grove with my feet in a waterfall, feeling that after years of research I had at last found the perfect and truly Platonic picnic site. The name of this place was Vallehermoso, 'lovely valley', and for once it was no exaggeration. The walls of this steep valley were terraced right up to the sky and tides of vegetation tumbled down them into the *barranco*, while a little road wound among the plantations. There were cacti and succulents that people in northern cities have to pot and pet and feed special food merely to keep them alive, but here they were flowering joyously in huge clumps, purple, red and yellow, by the roadside.

There were figs, vines, prickly pear and fruit trees all in blossom; loquat, plum and peach. The landscape was exotic and familiar at the same time. The basic colours were clear blue, deep green, white and brown, but it was as though someone had turned up the Brightness knob. It was the Mediterranean on hallucinogens.

La Gomera has little in the way of high culture, and you get the feeling its 18,000 inhabitants aren't too worried about that. But they have their own dances, like the African-influenced *tajaraste* or drum dance, and certain dishes and types of pottery, like the squat round bowls that are made by two or three women in the village of El Cercado and have exactly the same forms and decoration as bowls I have seen in Berber communities in Algeria. And they have something wonderful and weird that is all their own: a whistling language that was used by the ancient Gomerans to communicate over long distances – a kind of oral telegraph – and has somehow found its way down to the present day. At least, that's what they say in the guidebooks. In practice, *silbo* has lost ground drastically over the last thirty years as communications on the island have improved, and when mobile telephones finally get here, it'll surely be killed off for good.

Is anyone still whistling out there? After lunch, I set off to find out, armed with a 'linguistic analysis' of *silbo* by the local expert Professor Ramón Trujillo. There are two bookshops in San Sebastián, and this was the only thing on the subject in either of them. Ramón Trujillo says, in his scornful professorial way, that 'it would be puerile to establish a direct relationship between the communication difficulties posed by the island's geography and the invention of *silbo*.' (To me, it seems a perfectly intelligent suggestion.) According to the professor's researches in the 1970s, when he chatted to the pre-eminent whistlers of the day, *silbo* has no grammar or syntax of its own but acts as a form of sign language, like Morse code or handwriting. To form a sentence, the whistler translates word by word from Guanche or Spanish into code, whistles away, and the receiver on the other side of the valley puts the process in reverse.

I drove around aimlessly for a while, wondering where to start, until I came to a village of little houses in the local style, which had whitewashed walls prettily inlaid with flat blue-grey stones. There were palm-trees among the terraces, and a warm wind blew up from the sea. A stream rushed through the village, watering vines and orchards. Below the road was a washing-place where the water fell into a stone tank and drained away down the hill. A woman stood at one of the stone washboards, beating the understains out of an enormous pile of wet clothes, probably dreaming of a washing machine.

By the roadside two old men played with a puppy. I stopped and asked them if they knew how to whistle. They said there was only one man left in the village of Chipude who did. His name was Antonio Torres, and he was standing over there, next to that house with the falling-down terracotta roof-tiles, cleaning a butcher's knife in the street.

'Oh no, I can't do that any more. I used to, but not any more,' said Antonio. He was in his sixties, and had a week's growth of white beard. He seemed, not sorry, so much as shy, as if what he meant to say was, 'What do you want to know about that old nonsense for?'

'Can't you even remember a single word?'

'Not a word. I've forgotten it all.'

'What a shame. Don't you think it's a shame?'

He shrugged silently, testing the sun's reflections on his shiny knife. '*Cosas de la vida*. Things of life. Sometimes old things die, but new things are born. And *silbo* isn't dead yet. Francisco, come over here and show the foreigner some of your whistling.'

A little boy, grubby-kneed and tousle-haired – his nephew – skittered up to us. He said he was eleven years old and went to Chipude village school, where one of the teachers gave the children *silbo* lessons after school hours. He'd been whistling for two years, and knew a lot of words.

'OK, then, what's *silbo* for "house"?'

Francisco opened his mouth delicately, like a cat, and inserted the knuckle of a forefinger so that his tongue slid back and doubled up into the mouth. His other hand seemed to act as a resonator, modulating and amplifying the sound. '"House", OK. Here goes.'

It was surprisingly loud, the noise he produced. Written down in graph form it might look something like this:

The sound echoed round the valley. It was both louder than ordinary whistling, and more intense. It had a kind of up-and-down, cantabile quality to it, like the old children's TV programme 'The Clangers', whose protagonists were space creatures that conversed in melancholy hootings.

'And how do you say . . . I don't know, "pesetas"?'

Again the boy made the complex instrument of mouth and fingers, and this is what came out:

He whistled me the words for sheep, palm tree, school, uncle, nephew, village, love.

'And what's "It's time for lunch?"'

He made a longer series of falling and rising tones, almost a melody. And then something marvellous happened; the kind of moment anthropologists must dream about. From across the road, at a distance of a few hundred metres, came another whistle. A deeper, more sonorous whistle – the voice, you might say, of experience. And Francisco answered it in his higher-pitched, impertinently piping note.

'What was that?'

'That was my mother calling me. She said, "Lunch is ready. Come," and I said, "I'm on my way."'

He pointed out his house, and I could see a black-clad figure on the flat roof. It wasn't far away, but it would have been too far to shout, and a bore to walk. By far the easiest, cheapest and funniest way for this woman to tell her son to come and eat was the domestic language they both understood. Who needs mobile phones when you can whistle?

Hearing all this *silbo* in practical use seemed to jog the uncle's memory, and cautiously he put his knuckle in his mouth and blew, and little by little he seemed to get back into the swing of things. Antonio's delivery was a little slower than Francisco's, and the sounds he made were deeper, rustier. They struck up a conversation, a complete exchange of *silbo*, and I have no idea what it was about because I couldn't bear to interrupt. The moment and the melody were just too ridiculously beautiful.

I left them gently hooting at each other. The whistler's mother, meanwhile, hung out the clothes on the roof, one eye and an ear on her son, and her mind on the pot of *gofio*.

Short Stories

THE MOUNTAIN OF HATE

Tor, high in the Catalan Pyrenees on an outcrop of Spanish territory wedged between France and Andorra, is not the kind of place anyone would want to spend much time in, unless anyone relished the idea of cutting himself off almost completely from the chaos and comforts of the twentieth century. The village consists of a dozen more or less intact houses, all without electricity and telephone. Its population oscillates between ten or twenty in the short mountain summer, and two, three or four in the long savage winter, when the village is cut off from the outside world by 12 kilometres of snow-choked dirt track. Above the village is the mountain, and a great swath of virgin forest which, at 4,800 hectares, lays claim to be the largest area of private land in all Catalunya.

As if the remoteness of Tor weren't spooky enough, around the village and its mountain has grown up a formidable *leyenda negra*, at the heart of which is a feud that has claimed three lives in the last twenty years. The last of the deaths was on 30 July 1995, when seventy-year-old Josep Muntané, nicknamed El Sansa, was found strangled with a cable. Earlier that year Muntané had been declared owner of the mountain and its 4,800 hectares, as the only resident of Tor with any legal right to them. The judge based his decision on the statutes of a private company set up in 1896 by the thirteen families then living in the village, which require the owner of the mountain to be a resident of Tor and also the head of a family.

For certain other actors in the drama of Tor, it was a decision that carried no weight. Some said El Sansa went for years without visiting the village, that he was wrong for the job. Salvador, El Pastor, a shepherd of eighty-four who still takes his flock up and down the mountain, says he was 'a man who made enemies'. Whether made by himself or others, there's no doubt he had them, and no more so than Jordi Riba, El Palanca – his eternal rival, bitterly opposed to Muntané's long-cherished scheme of building a spa on the mountain. In 1980 two of El Palanca's employees were murdered by an unknown hand. Over the years that followed, horses and cows were found slaughtered around his land. The day after the funeral of Josep Muntané, El Palanca told a reporter: 'He'd wanted to get rid of a lot of people and now they've finished him off.'

Tor is a Spanish version of the badlands, a wild landscape that has always attracted bandits, smugglers and desperate men. The Civil War lasted several years longer in these parts, where Republican rebels fleeing their fascist conquerors were relatively safe in their mountain hideouts, than in the rest of the country. Resentment runs in the blood.

Only the handful of young hippies who have settled in the area, building log cabins with roofs pitched at eccentric angles and lined with turf for extra warmth, seem free of the feud and its ramifications. Grigori and his friends clearly don't share their neighbours' deep-rooted loathing of El Sansa. They admit he was probably the only one with any clear idea of a future for the land. They suggest it might be turned into a nature reserve, as long as it were controlled by 'someone with authority' and not left to the mercies of Tor's warring factions. Only in that way, they say, will peace ever come to the mountain of hate.

4

The Virgin in the Ash Tree

'This graven image [the Virgin of the Pillar] is at this moment the object of popular adoration, and disputes even with the worship of tobacco and money: countless are the mendicants, the halt, blind, and the lame, who cluster around her shrine, as did the equally afflicted ancients, with whom physicians were vain, around that of Minerva: and it must be confessed that the cures worked are almost incredible'

(Richard Ford, *A Handbook for Travellers in Spain*, 1845)

'You will allow me to pay homage to one that I consider to be the Universal Mother . . .'

('Rappel', *My Favourite Virgins*)

L ast week I went with my boyfriend's brother to see the Virgin. It was a Saturday, and a bright bitter day in Madrid – Madrid being the highest capital city in Europe and the one, according to its inhabitants, metaphorically as well as literally closest to heaven.

We stood in the bus queue by the triumphal arch at Moncloa and shivered. Gerardo had brought along a small guidebook called *Villages of Madrid*, and I flicked through the lurid 1970s photos while we waited. A few years before, I had been on a day-trip to El Escorial, but the place looked so bleak and terrifying, squatting on the hillside like an enormous grey toad, that I'd decided to give it a miss and make for the Valley of the Fallen instead. The Valley of the Fallen was the Generalísimo Francisco Franco's vilely overstated and oversized monument to himself, a cathedral to bad taste hollowed out of the mountainside and a far scarier piece of architecture than Philip II's monastery-dreamhome, but I wasn't to find that out until I got there.

A bus drew up at the stop and the queue shuffled forward. 'San Lorenzo del Escorial' said the sign in the windscreen. The Spanish word *escoria* means 'slag' or 'dross' (from the Greek *skoria*, refuse). El Escorial then literally means 'the slagheap'. The monastery, and by association the village, was named after Saint Lawrence because the Spanish had beaten the French in the battle of St Quentin on 10 August 1557, and 10 August happened to be the day of San Lorenzo. Why it wasn't called 'San Quintín del Escorial' is anybody's guess. Perhaps the fact that Saint Lawrence died in gruesomely pious circumstances (he was grilled to death, and not many people know that he is, for this reason, the patron saint of Spanish cooks) captured the Inquisitive imagination of the king.

'Is this the right bus for the Apparitions of the Virgin?' asked Gerardo.

I felt, Englishly, that it was an embarrassing question. But the driver took our tickets and said gruffly, automatically, as if we were football fans at an away game asking the way to the local ground, 'Yes, yes. You get off at the last stop, next to the monastery, and walk down the hill, and you'll see the Prado Nuevo. That's where the Apparitions are.'

As long as there have been devotees of the Virgin in Spain, She has taken a particular delight in appearing to them. Nearly 2000 years after the birth of Her son, She is still popping up, for some reason often in trees (there are Virgins of the Almond, of the Ash, of the Thorn, even of the Carob. Our Lady of Fátima appeared in a holm oak) but also in caves, wells, fountains, stables and boats. Visions of Virgins hovering in mid-air amid a blinding light, uttering words of comfort, healing whatever ailment the seer may be suffering from, are so commonplace that the Spanish press no longer bothers to report them. (The same is true of stigmata, foaming at the mouth, speaking in tongues, levitation and other semi-religious phenomena. The aged aunt of someone I know goes into a trance and blood pours from the palms of her hands on a regular basis. The rest of the family thinks she's a bit of a joke.)

The editor of one of Spain's legion of occult magazines, *Enigmas*, told me on the phone that there may be as many as thirty ongoing apparitions of the Virgin Mary across the country. He reeled off a list of some of the sites, which are usually forlorn provincial villages where nothing had ever happened until the Mother of God turned up in all Her splendour.

'Garabandal, Ibros, Pedrera, Avinromá, Santibañez . . . How many more do you want?' said Señor Jiménez del Oso. 'There was a new one last month in Madrid; you may have heard about it. Some couple say their sculpture of the Virgin is shedding tears. The sculpture's made of plastic, by the way. There's a lot of it about these days, you know. A *lot*. But then there always has been. It's like a survival of medieval piety.'

Before the Arabs arrived in El Escorial there was already a Virgin there. She was called the Virgin of Grace and had Her own chapel; Philip II is supposed to have prayed there while his own, somewhat larger place of worship was under construction. But, according to a seminal work on Spanish revelations of Our Lady by the Spanish occultist and seer 'Rappel', the chapel was burned by Republicans in the Civil War in 1936, the priest and sacristan were both slaughtered and the image of the Virgin shockingly profaned.

The Virgin of Grace is still revered in the village in a half-hearted sort of way but Her fame has been swept aside by a mighty rival: Our Lady of the Pains. This *parvenue* first appeared in the early 1980s in an ash tree by a roadside on the outskirts of the village, close to the municipal rubbish tip, and has created about Her a phenomenon, a spectacle, say an industry, to rival Lourdes or Fátima.

Before we deal with the Apparitions, a word about the woman to whom they appear. Her name is Luz-Amparo Cuevas, which for a

clairvoyant could hardly be more appropriate. *Luz* means 'light',
amparo is a religiously-charged word for 'shelter' or 'refuge', and
una cueva is a cave. So a possible subtext of her name could be 'she
who brings light and comfort to dark and uncomfortable places'.
Amparo, for short, was born on 13 January 1931 (13.1.31 – spookily
palindromic) in a hamlet in Albacete, and moved to Madrid with
her husband to look for work. She is a woman without natural
advantages of any kind. Uneducated and practically illiterate, she
used to suffer from a heart condition until she went to Lourdes in
1977 and had it fixed. (Perhaps she also learned something about
Catholic cults while she was there.) Her husband Nicasio, also in
poor health, is a doorman in the same block of shops and flats
where Amparo works as a shop-assistant.

For forty-nine years her life was no different from that of any
other ordinary working-class woman. The daily struggle to get by,
bringing up seven kids, going shopping, gossiping with neighbours.
She had always believed in God, but was too preoccupied with her
domestic burden to do anything much about it. But in October
1980 everything changed. She began hearing strange voices that
told her to pray for the peace of the world and the conversion of sinners, and warned her that she would soon have to go through
'painful trials'. Within a few days the trials started. She began to
bleed from the forehead, eyes, mouth, shoulders, back, side, hands,
knees, feet, either from open wounds or through the skin. A heart
appeared in blood on her chest. She had Technicolor hallucinations
starring Jesus, the Virgin Mary, Satan and a choir of Hollywood
angels. There was a delicious smell in the air whenever she went into
one of her trips. She levitated. She cured people miraculously. She
spoke in a mysterious unknown language which sounded – to those
of little faith – like nonsense but was described by her as 'the language of heaven'. She did everything people with Powers are
supposed to do, and more.

Amparo's bouts of ecstasy tended to take place at inopportune
moments. On Easter Day in 1981 she and Nicasio went to her

brother-in-law's house, as they did every year, for an *aperitivo* before dinner. They had been chatting away for a while, presumably about Amparo's recent peculiar experiences, when all at once she started having another one. Blood seeped from the palms of her hands and she frothed at the mouth. Her brother-in-law put her to bed and mopped up the blood as best he could with a handkerchief. (He has the handkerchief even today and has washed it again and again, even with bleach, but the blood refused to disappear. We're talking stubborn stains.) When the subject came to an hour and a half later, she said she'd been fully conscious throughout the whole experience. 'I was talking to Jesus,' she said.

Not content with her small domestic stage, Amparo soon started flipping out in public. One morning found her in a bakery in El Escorial village. 'She asked for five loaves, as usual,' remembers Francisca Herranz, the baker's wife. 'Then suddenly she leant on the counter and put her hand to her forehead to stop the blood that was coming from it. We took hold of her between a few of us and sat her down in an armchair. Then we saw that she was bleeding from the hands, knees and feet, and when we took her hand away from her side we saw that she had blood there as well. She was in ecstasy for two hours.' The ecstasies in the bakery started happening on a regular basis on the first Friday of every month. On Ash Wednesday she turned up to buy bread, and when the time came to pay, Francisca noticed she couldn't get her purse open for the stigmata on her hands.

Amparo and the baker's wife turned out to be soul-sisters. The two of them went on a long weekend to Lourdes – Thelma and Louise wielding rosaries in a coach – and of course Amparo had to have one of her fits on the way. Just outside Zaragoza, it happened to be; aptly, since that city is home to Spain's Virgin *numero una* and the patroness of the country, Our Lady of the Pillar.

That was what you might call the end of Phase One. The beginning of Phase Two was when she went down one morning to the patch of land Amparo and Nicasio rent from the town hall, on the outskirts of the village. It's a rough bit of semi-countryside, right next to the main road from El Escorial to Valdemorillo, and a reasonably pleasant landscape of ancient trees and a thin cover of grass. The land is called the Prado Nuevo, 'new meadow'. From the road you can just about see a large basin, a kind of drinking-trough for animals. There was Amparo that morning, by the drinking-trough, minding her own business, when all of a sudden the Virgin appears in the branches of the ash tree next to her. According to her neighbour Lolita, Our Lady told her to say her rosary every day and pray for world peace. She also let her know that from now on the water in the drinking-trough – henceforth to be known as the 'sacred spring' – would be charged with healing powers.

The Virgin in the ash tree, the spring with miraculous powers, the illiterate woman with an all-inclusive repertoire of signs and wonders: whether Amparo realised it or not, she had all the ingredients at hand for a full-scale International Cult Phenomenon. The few things she lacked were easily acquired. First, a spiritual director; no self-respecting seer of Virgins should be without one. Applications poured in, a short-list was presented to Amparo and she chose Father Alfonso María, a Carmelite monk from Madrid. He was cautious at first, quoting St John's Gospel, chapter 4, verse 1: 'Brethren, do not trust any spirit, but examine if the spirits come from God', but eventually agreed to hear her confession. As she approached the confessional box, Fray Alfonso noted a powerful scent of roses. He lent her a crucifix to meditate on while they talked, and for a day afterwards the scent of roses seemed to emanate from the crucifix. The smell even emerged from the tape-recorder when he played back the tape of one of her ecstasies. He says that's how he knew she was genuine.

Then she needed publicity, but neither was this long in coming. Before long the press were sniffing around the Prado Nuevo, where the apparitions of Our Lady of the Pains were becoming a regular occurrence. Amparo went on Spanish TV, explaining that the Virgin recommended frequent use of the rosary: 'I've seen the Santísima

Virgen Dolorosa in the meadow asking me for people to pray the holy Rosary, for people to confess, for them to take Communion, that the Lord has been forgotten, that before people take Communion they should confess their sins, because there are a lot of sacrileges being committed, and that people should pray the holy Rosary which will save the whole world from a great danger,' she burbled. During one of Her messages, the Virgin suggested it would be nice if a chapel could be built on the spot where She first appeared. Nothing was ever built, but a small shrine was wedged among the branches of the ash tree and a picture of the Virgin, painted in School of Woolworth's style according to Amparo's description, placed inside it.

Fifteen years have passed since the incident in the bakery, and the Apparitions have become the focus for a fully-fledged industry. On the first Saturday of every month the Virgin still appears at the Prado Nuevo, but nowadays Amparo makes a tape-recording of what Our Lady says and broadcasts it to the huge crowds that gather there in the afternoon. Coaches arrive from all over Spain and Portugal, bringing traffic congestion and noise and litter, irritating the sophisticated agnostic residents of El Escorial. The Beneficent Foundation of the Virgin of the Pains, the financial arm of the cult, is thought to have amassed a capital base of 500 million pesetas, £2.5 million, from the contributions of the faithful. The local government of El Escorial, determined to turn the village into a thoroughly modern bourgeois dormitory suburb of Madrid, is enraged to see itself portrayed as a haven for some of the most vulgar, archaic and unrespectable elements of Spanish society. Passions have been inflamed on either side. If the Apparitions and the whole machinery of the Prado Nuevo are fakes and Amparo Cuevas is a foolish fraud, then the Virgin in the Ash Tree is one of the biggest rip-offs of our time. Whether or not it's for real, it's an impressive testament of faith.

I phoned the Foundation earlier in the week to make sure of the time and place, and a nice girl answered on the third ring and told me yes, at around five o'clock it usually happens, on the first Saturday of every month. And how would I find my way to the Prado Nuevo? 'Well, you just walk down the hill from the monastery, past the fire station, it's a kilometre or two. I shouldn't ask anyone where it is if I were you. You see, the people of the village aren't too keen on us at the Prado Nuevo, and they might point you in the wrong direction. Best thing, if you get lost, is to ask in the Religious Objects shop half-way down the road – they'll put you on the straight and narrow.'

So we got off at the stop nearest the monastery, paid our 800 pesetas and ran around the cavernous halls of San Lorenzo de El Escorial in ten minutes flat, ticking off the library, the church, Philip II's cell and the creepy Pantheon of the Infantas, known in Spanish as El Pudridero, the 'rotting-shop', from our list of Should Be Seens. Then we followed the road down the hill in the face-aching cold, past a rococo palace-ette, the Casita del Principe, built over an old chicken-coop, and into the dull semi-detached outskirts of the village. Spanish Saturdays are even sadder than English Sundays. A woman in a headscarf scuttled by on the opposite side of the street. Could she be a devotee of the Virgin on her way to the monthly moot? We found the Religious Articles shop, already doing a roaring trade in kitschy souvenirs (best item: a mini-poster of the Virgin, either resplendent in white with fluttering cherubs or chaste in a long black cape, bearing your own photo and the legend 'Souvenir of my pilgrimage to the Prado Nuevo. I invoke the protection of Our Lady of the Pains', price 5,000 pesetas – 25 quid). If we hurried, we would just catch Her, said the gleeful lady behind the counter.

By the roundabout was a gypsy woman selling rosaries and post-cards. A few metres further on was another. Where in the village there wasn't a soul, here there were suddenly crowds, milling in and around a makeshift red-brick building that looked like a cattle barn – the basilica of Our Lady of the Pains. Outside was a rubbish-strewn car park with ranks of empty coaches with number-plates from Barcelona, Oviedo, Sevilla, Bilbao, Lisbon. One of the drivers was sprawled out asleep on the front seat, immune to the cold and the traffic of souls outside. On the hillside in the distance was the grim barracks of the monastery of San Lorenzo de El Escorial, emblem of a spirituality as different from this as Monteverdi from Mantovani.

We threaded our way through the coaches and scrambled over a grey stone wall into a wide meadow where thousands of people were standing about, transfixed in a peculiar silence. They were people of all sorts and ages; country people with lived-in faces, short stubby poor city people stuffed into cheap coats, fresh-faced young happy-clappies in dungarees, and odd one-offs like the posh woman in a puffer-jacket and pearls kneeling on a plastic bag from the ritzy department store El Corte Inglés. I asked someone the way to the Apparitions, and she whispered something in Portuguese. Another woman put her finger to her lips with a look of patronising disapproval, as though I were mentally subnormal. They were all listening to something, a low drone coming over the loudspeakers.

Then it dawned on me: the voice I was hearing was, if not the voice of the Virgin Herself, then the voice of Luz-Amparo Cuevas reciting the conversations she had had with her that very morning by the sacred ash tree. The taped Message today was a condemnation of sinners and sinning in general, punctuated with moaning and groaning and End-Is-Nigh apocalyptic clichés. At moments of extreme emotion the voice broke down into gentle sobbings and expostulations. A sample:

'My daughter, today my heart is full of suffering and pain, for the situation of the world is grave, my daughter. Men are being drawn more and more each day into iniquity and allowing themselves to be won over by the king of lies, my daughter. Begin by kissing the ground in reparation for so many sins.' (Here the entire crowd fell creakily to its knees and kissed the ground, though I noticed the posh woman in the puffer-jacket drew the line at this and, perhaps wisely, simply made a deep bow from a kneeling position.)

'Thus will the world be, my daughter, as in a desert.' (Long pause.

Prolonged sobbing over the P.A.) 'There will come great calamities on the earth, on the sea and in the air. There will be many of those who call themselves good who will die together with the bad. Alas, my daughter, for those shepherds who have been given power to govern the Church and who change the laws that Christ has made for it! Alas for those shepherds who disobey the authority of Christ! Alas for those shepherds that have dragged and continue to drag a great number of souls into the abyss!'

The Message came to an end and the crowd seemed to thaw out. They had got the serious business over with; now they could jolly around for an hour or two before getting back on the bus. There is a cheerfully Chaucerian aspect to the goings-on at the Prado Nuevo. You get a good day out, a nice gossip about illnesses and, if you're lucky, a miracle or two thrown in. A makeshift stall sold ham sandwiches in clingfilm sheaths. Two middle-aged women on the far side of the meadow climbed awkwardly over a low granite wall and squatted in the grass for a pee. Next to the enclosure marked 'Enfermos' ('Sick') a traffic-jam of wheelchairs was building up.

We had not seen the Virgin, but we had at least listened to Her, or heard Her words through the mouth of Her Spanish representative, which might be as good as we'd get. But I was curious about the ash tree, the sacred spring, and all that. Where was the shrine wedged into the branches, the drinking-trough where it was said a mere sip of the water would cure anything from duodenal ulcers to a cold in the head, if you were properly charged up with faith?

We found the *old* Prado Nuevo, not the hastily commandeered new one, on the other side of the road, behind a forbidding six-foot fence topped with barbed wire which appeared to run around the entire property but gave on to it through a single gate. We picked through the mud, among trees as grey as rocks, past beggars who composed their faces into attitudes of agony as we passed and cheered up in a flash when they thought our backs were turned. They were doing well here, with so many aspirants for the kingdom of heaven. All around, among the stones, people were hunkering down with their picnics, swaddled in coats and scarves, or struggling to open deckchairs against the chill wind of the *sierras*. There was the sacred tree, a great solid stumpy thing, its top half decked with flowers, images of the tearful Virgin and the votive offerings of Her followers. Here and there postcards, photographs, folded bits of paper had been wedged into cracks in the bark. A woman was adding to them now; stuffing a plastic flower into a knot-hole, kissing the tree, standing back and crossing herself.

A loose queue of women had formed behind her, some of them dangling rosaries from their fingers and muttering devoutly. The women seemed to be having most of the fun. Everywhere you looked around the tree, there they were, handing out the food and drink, chatting contentedly about the latest miracles, fiddling with their rosaries. The men seemed abstracted, restless, out of place. They yawned, and jingled the change in their pockets, and strolled about boredly on their own, looking at their watches, wishing they could have spent the afternoon swigging beer with their mates, watching the big match.

We sat down on a vacant rock and surveyed the scene. A small elderly lady in a sky-blue church coat was standing near us, rosary in hand, straining her eyes towards the ash tree. On the road behind us the weekenders roared by in their cars. The sky was greying and it was miserably cold, but the lady managed a smile as she turned her gentle face towards me. She reminded me of my grandmother.

I asked her whether she'd ever seen the Virgin of the Pains, and her eyes lit up. '*¡Si, si!* I saw Her, not in flesh and blood, like I see you, but sort of like a silhouette. There was a terrific light, and She came down from heaven like this.' She placed her pink little hands in an attitude of prayer.

So what did it feel like, to see Her like that, all of a sudden?

'It was something so great, so marvellous . . . It's changed my life. I'm so very happy. I've got three children. My daughter used to work in the Talbot factory, making cars, you know, and she had a

French boyfriend. But then she came to the Prado Nuevo and it changed her life as well. She gave up the job, gave up the boyfriend, and now she works in the Foundation's residence for old people. She is so happy, you know, she even enjoys cleaning the old dears' bottoms!' Her husband, retired through illness, had stayed at home that day. He wasn't a believer, but frail and in no position to argue with his wife's radiant conviction.

'I'm from Ibiza, and my friend here is from Madrid,' I told her.

She looked worried.

'Oh dear! Ibiza is a bad place. You should come away from there – there's lots of sinning, lots of naked women on the beach, lots of drugs.' It was a fair enough description. 'What a pity, to see young boys like you led into sin. The devil is clever, you know, he tricks young people into drugs and naked women. Are you Catholics?' I said No.

'Protestants, then?' Not even second best.

'Oh dear, what a shame!' She grabbed my arm in a gesture of sympathy.

'May the Virgin convert you! Here, let me give you this rosary. You can say it every day as the Virgin commands. Here, take it – I've got plenty more at home.' It was a simple string of plastic beads. I would be unlikely to use it, and it had come to me not so much out of generosity as from a sense of good Public Relations, but I was touched all the same.

Another small lady in a coat came up to join us and was excitedly introduced by the first. 'This is my friend from – where was it, dear, Salamanca? Valladolid? She's been coming here for fourteen years, haven't you, dear?'

She nodded proudly. 'That's right. I first came in July, just a month after Amparo's first vision. I was in despair, you see. My son – you two lads remind me of him. How old are you, love? Ah, well, he must be a few years younger than you. He started drinking and staying out all night and messing about with girls. For months I'd been going around the house on my knees.'

'Her kneecaps were black and blue,' the first lady chipped in brightly.

'Yes, they were, black and blue,' chorused the second. 'But then I answered Our Lady's call, and in return, you know, She did me a marvellous thing, *un favor muy especial.* My son's stopped going out, doesn't drink a drop now – nothing but a glass of red wine with lunch – and he's going to be married this summer.'

'You see! You see! It's another of Her miracles!' cried the first lady, beaming with delight.

We prised ourselves away from the pious pair and went to find the sacred spring, site of many a take-up-thy-bed-and-walk scenario in the early days of the Prado Nuevo. The 'spring' is, in fact, or was until Our Lady's first appearance in the ash tree, a drinking-trough for cattle. Ringed with barbed wire, with Coke cans bobbing in a few inches of stagnant water, it did not inspire great confidence as an alternative to conventional medicine. Worst of all, a sign next to the trough, clearly the work of the pharisees at the town hall, informed would-be partakers of holy water that the 'spring' had been officially analysed and found to be contaminated, and was therefore far more likely to cause illness than to cure it.

A peasant woman in her Sunday best gazed at the sign and shook her head at the iniquity of it all. The wind came up again and whistled past us, making the Coke cans sail Armada-like across the trough; but the woman's hair, mercilessly lacquered into a thin brown helmet, stayed exactly where she'd left it. 'It's a shame, what they've done to the sacred spring,' she told me conspiratorially, wrenching her rosary like worry-beads among sinewy fingers. She had the powerful, leather-bound hands of someone who has worked the soil all her life. 'But it won't stop the Virgin doing good in whatever way She can. We're still getting one or two miracles every time. Only last month I saw it with my own eyes, a woman went up to the ash tree on crutches, kissed the tree, and when she went away she was carrying the crutches under her arm! She even had to be told she was walking normally, *la muy tonta* – the silly thing!'

A family of four, scoffing slices of *tortilla*, were squashed on a blown-up lilo on the ground nearby. They had been at the Prado Nuevo that same day in December, and nodded their heads at the helmet-haired woman's story. But they had witnessed another marvel that day, and the father was keen to relate it. While the Virgin's message was being read, the P.A., 'the big contraption over there with the speakers', had suddenly gone dead and begun rumbling like a distant storm. Palmira from Lisbon, a regular visitor to the ash tree ever since she was cured several years before of some unspecified but dreadful illness, fell to the ground in a faint. When she came to, she told the faithful the Virgin had appeared to her in a fragrant cloud. 'My daughter, I have some important information to communicate – the names of all those present who will be saved,' she'd said. Palmira, who had all the names in her head, shrieked in Portuguese for a piece of paper and a pen. People scrabbled around in their bags in great excitement, but pen and paper is the kind of thing you can never put your hands on when you really need it, and by the time a biro and a half-crushed cigarette packet had been rustled up, the names had gone clean from her mind.

A small crowd was now gathering around me, chattering about the monthly prodigies they had seen with their own eyes, or, as was more often the case, that a friend had seen with her own eyes and told them about later.

I shushed the conference into silence and asked a question of them all: Who among them had actually seen the Virgin? And what was it like? Three or four hands went up, and I scribbled down a few of their impressions.

She was hovering in the tree.

At head height, among the branches.

Definitely a person, not just a formless dazzle.

No, a blinding light, accompanied by a strange perfume.

Una tirilla de negro, a little strip of blackness.

She appeared to me in front of the sun and climbed majestically above it, as if climbing a staircase.

It was the greatest moment of my life.

My life changed at that moment.

She was . . . maternal, loving, so very beautiful. *Guapa, guapísima.* She spoke directly to my heart. I'll never forget it as long as I live.

Back at the basilica, as the light faded, the congregation was filing out from the last prayer of the day. The sleeping coach-driver stretched in his seat. There was now a strange and horrible pseudo-Latin American muzak blaring over the sound system, and the generator that powers the building in the absence of conventional electricity – the town hall has refused to connect it – made the music waver and wobble. Supermarket samba in a wintry landscape in the Sierra de Madrid, with Franco's tomb and Philip's folly glaring down from the hillside above. I couldn't decide, still can't, whether to think of it all as desolate and depressing, a tawdry piece of manipulation, the naïve being fleeced, as usual, by the cynical; or a touchingly ramshackle manifestation of true faith. But one thing was for sure – the cold had stopped me feeling my face. I gave my rosary to an awe-struck beggar. Then we ran.

Short Stories

A MAN AND A MODEL

In deep countryside near a village in Extremadura, a shepherd boy was tending his flock on a hot summer afternoon. He wore a shepherd's straw hat and a shepherd's leather bag round his waist, and he was close to dozing as he sat under the shade of an olive tree.

What he saw next made him jump to his feet. It being a Saturday in high summer, there were tourists in the village, admiring the church, the fountain in the square that gushes out icy-cold spring water all year round, and the picturesquely run-down village houses with their cockeyed wooden balconies. But the visitors were normally middle-aged German or British couples, or parties of elderly folk from Barcelona, not the apparition of sensuality and urban glamour he saw before him. A friend of mine had come on a day trip with a friend of his, a beautiful, tall statuesque girl who makes her living as a catwalk model. She was scantily dressed in the heat, probably in some white floaty fashionably hippy thing.

'*Buenas,*' said the shepherd to the man and the model, gulping a little and fiddling with his straw hat. The visitors were enchanted with the landscape of stone walls and fruit trees, the buzzing quiet, the heavy summer smells of thyme and scorched earth. They stopped under the olive tree and exchanged a few words, mainly about the heat and the flock of sheep, which were nibbling determinedly among the dry stalks of wheat.

'But, with this dryness, how can they find enough to eat?' asked the girl.

'They get enough, don't you worry. Look at them, they're as fat as seals,' said the shepherd, overcoming his shyness.

The couple strolled on, heading back to the village square and the car with its Madrid number-plate. But after a minute or two my friend needed a pee, and he walked back a few metres into the *campo*, to see the shepherd boy lying down, now, under the same olive tree, hat pulled down over his face, giving himself a slow, dreamy, comfortable wank.

5

Old-time Religion

'The supreme emotion of Granada is Islam. Towers of a Moorish palace that seem to require the necessary complement of a muezzin in white clothing; little towers of the Albayzín, their exotic bells replacing the dreamy, plangent song of the Muslim call to prayer . . . ; ruins of mosques in the fertile valleys, among fields sown by the finest agricultural race; dusty old Korans that turn up in the attic of some ancient Moorish mansion . . . The memory of Mohammed is a powerful presence in a city that believes itself to be Christian'

(Rodolfo Gil Benumeya, *Neither East nor West: the Universe as seen from the Albayzín*)

'Even though you tie a hundred knots – the string remains one'

(Jalaluddin Rumi, d.1273)

'Not everyone's here yet. Still twenty minutes to go,' said Ahmed, removing his boots in a leisurely manner at the door of the mosque.

The imam stroked his long beard, and frowned. Gliding up to Ahmed, he laid his forefinger on his watch, tapped it twice and said, 'We did agree on two-thirty, not three, you know. Isn't it time you gave the call?'

'Oh yes, of course, I'll give the call,' said Ahmed hastily. He put on his boots again and stepped outside to a scruffy little back yard into which shone a square metre of thin afternoon sun. He raised his head slightly so that his voice would carry, causing his beard to detach itself from its normal resting-place on his chest, and out of his mouth bubbled the resonant syllables uttered by thousands of other mouths on Friday afternoons all over the Muslim world: '*Allahu akbar! Allahu akbar!* God is great! Come to prayer. Come to your salvation. I testify that God is the divinity, that there is no other god but God, and that Muhammad is his messenger. *La ilaha illa-Llah!* There is no god but God!'

In the inner courtyard, which separated the mosque from the street, was a tap running into a basin built up into a kind of shrine with white cement and a mosaic of broken tiles. Earlier I'd washed myself here, according to the requirements of the *surah* in the Koran that says: 'Believers, do not approach your prayers when you are drunk, but wait till you can grasp the meaning of your words; nor when you are polluted – unless you are travelling the road – until you have washed yourselves.' De-pollution means three rinses each of the hands, the face, the mouth, the nostrils and the feet.

Now I was sitting cross-legged on the floor along with six or seven other men, the women having retired to their own section at the back. The mosque was a modest room, designed in 'desert' style with whitewashed walls and hand-formed arches, and furnished with prayer rugs and rush mats and a few humble pots and ornaments on shelves around the simple prayer-niche in the corner. We shook each other's hands and smiled and said, '*Salaam alekum,*' and relapsed into pious silence. Some of the congregation began whispering prayers; others fingered strings of wooden beads. I was the only one in the room, apart from the women at the back, not sporting a generous growth of beard. I was also conspicuous by my lack of a colourful turban in green, blue or white, with a conical centre and a sash hanging down the back, as seen on Turkish pirates and Saracen horsemen in old-fashioned history books. I wore a pair of old black Levis, and they wore baggy Muslim trousers.

They knew the form, and I didn't. They knew how to raise their hands and let them flop down in that peculiarly Arab way, and bow, and then sink to the knees and bend the whole body forward so that the forehead rests on the floor. (Some of them even gave an authentic little groan of humility as they did so.) They had mastered the tricky art of moving, quickly and with the minimum of fuss, from a kneeling position to a standing one. They felt the rhythm of those gestures, and how to make the movements flow smoothly into each other. They knew the choreography of submissiveness, whereas I was barely able to figure out the dancer from the dance. I was an English agnostic (*a-gnosis*, without knowledge) swimming in a spiritual soup of lukewarm Anglicanism and New Age vaguenesses of peace and positivity. They, on the other hand, were Spanish Muslims, converts to a religion that held sway in their country for the best part of a thousand years; sure of its value in their own lives and quietly, but absolutely convinced of its capacity to bring about a better world.

I walked to the end of the Plaza Nueva on a hot day in November, one of those throwback days the southern Spanish climate seemingly has saved up from the summer and lobs from time to time, with careless generosity, into a chillier season; I found the Carrera del Darro, the snaking cobbled lane that follows the little river Darro along the gully that separates one of Granada's hills from another; and I spoke to myself the lovely names of the alleys that slunk catlike up the hill to my left: Calle del Aire (street of the air), de los Aceituneros (of the olive-merchants), del Bañuelo (of the little bath), del Horno de Vidrio (of the glass-kiln), del Candil (of the oil-lamp), del Horno de Oro (of the gold-kiln). Picking one more or less at random, I turned into it and began the climb up its steep stone stairs, feeling my way into the ancient and beguiling neighbourhood the Arabs called *al-bayyacin*, 'the falconers' quarter', and modern-day Granada calls the Albayzín.

The Albayzín is not just another Old Town like the old towns you find in all Spanish cities, most of which are nothing more than a few picturesque and smelly streets clustered around the cathedral. This is something else again; a square mile of labyrinthine corridors sidling between high whitewashed walls. The streets here are so narrow, wrote the fifteenth-century Austrian traveller Hieronymus Münzer, that 'one mule can't allow another to pass, unless it be in one of the more famous streets, which have a width of four or five elbows'. Behind and among these walls lies a dense web of secrets: tiny squares with a couple of trees and a fountain; *cármenes*, medieval town-houses often with their Arab arches and courtyards intact; and magical gardens rife with citrus trees, cypress, jasmine and honeysuckle, the flowers spilling voluptuously over the walls and scattering their perfume into the street. The more you wander, the more you lose your sense of direction, confusing one whitewashed wall and one fig tree with another, and the more you are sucked in and seduced by the mystery of the place. The Albayzín has very little to do with the rest of Granada, which is noisy, provincial, bourgeois, mundane, geared to the changes and chances of the recent past. It is a world apart from all that, exotic, apparently changeless, its Moorish legacy still hanging in the air like the scents that seep from its gardens.

The falconers' district was one of the many neighbourhoods in the old Granada of the Nazrid dynasty (1238–1492) whose inhabitants were characterised by their trade (embroiderers, potters, weavers), religion (Jews, Mozarabic Christians), illness (lepers), or place of origin (of Gomeres, of Zenetes). Unlike other neighbourhoods, the Albayzín had its own administration, its own magistrates and judges. This was because, though it now seems like the epitome of gentle living, it had in Moorish times a reputation for what one Spanish writer nicely describes as 'boisterousness'.

If anyone got excessively boisterous, the Albayzín had Granada's madhouse, the Maristan, built by Muhammad V in 1367 and unforgivably demolished by the town council in 1843. An estate agent

might say the area enjoyed a full range of public services. Its inhabitants could choose between twenty-seven mosques in which to say
their five-times-daily prayers; some of these were later converted
more or less thoroughly by the conquering Christians into churches
like San Juan de los Reyes, just a few steps up the hill from the
Carrera de Darro, with its minaret masquerading unconvincingly as
a bell tower. The neighbourhood also had innumerable public
baths, *aljibes* (cisterns), bridges over the Darro and gates in and out
of the *barrio*, and a good number of these things are still fulfilling
their original functions.

I bought myself a map of the Albayzín in the time of Al-Andalus.
It was a fantastically detailed piece of work compiled by the architect
Carlos Sánchez, who has a fourteenth-century Nazrid house down
by the meandering Darro. The map revealed fifty-five extant pieces
of Moorish building, and I set to wandering its maze of alleys in
search of some of them. The sound of water, trickling, dripping,
bubbling, gushing, was everywhere I went, making me think of the
promise famously made by Allah to all good Muslims, that they shall
be 'rewarded with gardens watered by running streams, where they
shall dwell for ever'.

I went to the little bath-house, called by the Arabs the Baths of the
Walnut Tree, by the river, with its domed roofs dotted with skylights
in star shapes like the star-shaped cut-outs children use for making
biscuits. At the top of the hill I found the Daralhorra, the late-fif-
teenth-century mansion once home to Fátima, mother of the
ill-fated Boabdil, Granada's last king. When the city fell in 1492, the
mansion was turned over at the Catholic kings' behest to a convent
of Franciscan nuns, but the building was more or less left alone; the
tracery of the arches and the reflecting pools of water in the patios
are still there for our own eyes and hearts. A little further to the east
was the courtyard of horseshoe arches which once belonged to the
most important mosque in the Albayzín, built in the late thirteenth
century, 'sanctified' in 1501 by Isabella's confessor Cardinal
Cisneros and demolished in 1565 to make way for the new church of

Our Saviour. The baths, palace and church are both open to the public, which is a rare luxury in the secretive Albayzín, where passionate visitors are forced to knock on doors and peer through padlocked garden gates.

Details sprang out of the blissful generalities. It was almost Saint Martin's Tide, the beginning of the pig-killing season all over Spain, and some balconies had strings of red *pimiento choricero* – the peppers for *chorizo* – hanging to dry in clumps along with the washing. A woman in an apron was cleaning her yard by the Arab method of dousing the surface with water and brushing it out through the door. The lower part of the Albayzín was chic and relatively well kept, all hand-painted *azulejo* tiles and grand, deserted gardens and *cármenes* with poetic names such as Of the Three Stars and Of Lost Love. Further up, the streets got rougher and more dogshit-strewn, there were more canaries squeaking in ranks of cages in the windows and the plants were in old oil-cans, not terracotta pots, and, it being almost lunchtime, there was a pervasive smell of chickpea stew.

Making my way slowly up the hill, I skirted a forbidding length of wall down the Carril de San Agustín, fringed along its length by clouds of jasmine, pink bignonia, passionflower and pastel-blue plumbago. Further back from the rim of the wall you could see the tops of fig and lemon trees, loquat, and persimmons loaded with plump coral-red fruit. A persimmon tree had stretched its branches right over the white wall and dropped its over-ripe fruit in sticky red splotches like squashed tomatoes on the cobbles. You could only guess at the *calme, luxe et volupté* of life behind this wall, but my map showed a huge area of garden dotted with pools, trees planted in verdant walks, and a large and probably exceptionally grand house in the middle. At the other edge of the property the map marked a solitary Moorish tower. When I rang the bell beside the garden door, it swung open and you could see a long pergola covered with an ancient grapevine, leading to a rose garden, and beyond that another tunnel of a darker green, perhaps ivy or cypress.

A doorkeeper who had been collecting persimmons in a wheel-barrow came to tell me it was more than his job was worth to let me in. He explained that the *cármen* under his charge belonged to Doña Mártir de García Alba, an elderly lady who had given him strict instructions not to allow strangers beyond the front gate – instructions issued from her modern apartment in the town, from which she made occasional sallies to her cool *cármen* in the coruscating heat of the Andalusian summer.

'But she need never know. Just let me take a turn around the garden,' I pleaded.

'But someone will see you come in, and then the entire Albayzín will know.'

Whatever happened to doorkeepers? Modernity has made them redundant by a combination of security guards and entryphones. To me there's something noble, and something resonantly Semitic, about the profession of the man or woman who keeps the door, who often lives beside or above it and is in a way the human face of the house, since theirs is the first face you see as you enter. The Albayzín seemed to be keeping the profession alive. I remember the shy gypsy girl in the Arab baths whose pot plants were gradually emerging from her lair and invading the patio; and the deaf man who leaned crossly out of a tiny window high up on a wall, and then eventually welcomed me in, gesticulating merrily, to yet another fabulous Moorish mansion. Another, a crusty querulous old chap at the Casas del Chápiz, sticks in my mind because it was he that, unwittingly, gave me first access to the corner of the Albayzín, the facet of its philosophical make-up, that I'd most been wanting to locate.

The Casas del Chápiz is a collection of houses rebuilt in late Moorish style by the Spanish Muslim Lorenzo del Chápiz in the early sixteenth century, and now the headquarters of Granada's School of Arabic Studies. When it was founded in 1932, the school must have been a pioneer bridge-builder between Christian and Islamic cultures, but now there are bridges going up all over the place – in fact the Albayzín is nothing but a great big overarching bridge between West and East, Christian and Muslim, present and past.

In the last twenty years, less than 500 after it officially departed, Islam has begun to trickle back into Granada. This time its adherents are mostly Spanish people in their thirties and forties who have lived through the counter-cultural movements of the 1970s (drugs, Eastern mindwarps, Leftist politicking) and found them all wanting. Many of them have put down roots in the Albayzín for romantic and aesthetic reasons, though they can often be heard to deny the fact. They are building mosques and opening Moroccan-style teashops, and their wives walk the narrow streets in wraparound headscarves and floor-length skirts. Their children, called not Antonio and Susana but Abdullah and Salima, go to local schools but might have extra study in the *medraza* on Fridays, as their Catholic friends have Sunday School. One estimate suggests there may be 1,000 of them in Granada at present, and 5,000 in Spain as a whole.

Yusuf Idris, the librarian at the School of Arabic Studies, lived with his wife and children in a flat on the eastern edge of the Albayzín. Entering his home was like being teleported instantly several hundred miles southwards: Yusuf motioned to me to take off my shoes, and we padded through to a study decorated with large coloured posters of the Ka'aba in Mecca and assorted famous mosques, along with verses from the Koran rendered in exquisite Arab calligraphy and then badly printed in cheap garish colour, probably in North Africa. Pinned to a cupboard door was a prayer timetable made up by some Islamic foundation in Birmingham, UK, with columns of figures indicating the correct hour and minute for Mecca-ward prostration, based on the phases of the moon and Granada's height above sea-level. There was one chair in the room, next to a desk with a small computer covered with a neat cotton shawl. We sat on the floor, which had been spread with rugs and small unyielding cushions.

The basic pattern of Yusuf's life is common to a lot of his cohab-itees in the Albayzín. He was born and raised in a Catholic family in Madrid, christened Juan José, and sent to a series of Catholic schools which left both him and them mutually unimpressed. There was no sudden conversion to anything, no blinding flash, but a process of discovery that took him slowly across a variegated, though often unsettling, spiritual landscape.

'I can't tell you when exactly the process began . . . perhaps when I was born,' he said, settling into a cross-legged position on the carpet as nonchalantly as a paterfamilias into his favourite armchair. 'There's a kind of destiny to it. The Arabs call it *fatum*. All I can say is that as a young person I suppose you want to break free from the environment that surrounds you. You're not happy, not comfort-able. You ask questions, and you want real answers.'

As he relaxes into the conversation I take my first careful look at this fascinating specimen, trying to get my head around the notion of the Spanish Muslim, which is producing a sort of mechanical glitch in my brain. Yusuf has put together his look with impeccable good taste, and in a manner that suggests neither East nor West but somewhere between the two. He wears a simple mustardy-brown jacket over a caramel sweater, baggy brown cords and an olive-green flat-topped skull-cap. His salt-and-pepper beard of uneven length, and the solemn, bookish way he speaks, seem perfectly in tune with the idea of an Islamic academic who looks askance at worldly frivo-lity. But, as is often the case with Beards, underneath the hair I perceive a more mischievous, younger person, and out of the formal manner occasionally come sparks of something much more street-wise, vivacious, vulgar. The Spanishness keeps slipping past the Muslimness.

During the last decade of Franco's dictatorship, when rebellion must have seemed almost like a duty, Juan José dipped into Marxist-Leninist activism, psychology, Hinduism, yoga and rock music. 'To me, at that time, the world was a world of magic. Magic and sex. Sex was the greatest mystery I could imagine.'

He went to England with the idea of settling there, but after two weeks a waking vision told him he was wrong to stay, and he caught the next plane home. He began instead a slow southward gravitation. The process speeded up. A scientist by training, he was taken on by the Institute of Astrophysics among the peaks of the Sierra Nevada. His latest metaphysical interest was astrology, which he now believes may have acted as a bridge to the esoteric and mystical traditions of Sufism. And before long he had come into contact with a Sufi *tariqa* and embarked on his twenty-year relationship with Islam.

At that time there were only a handful of Muslims in Andalucia. The movement had begun in Córdoba and Seville, but took form and shape in Granada. 'It's curious that Granada should have been the place,' he muses. 'It must have had something to do with the Granadino character, but this has always been a breeding-ground for all sorts of sects and cults. There's been everything: Buddhism, witchcraft, strange Catholic things. *Al-hamdu-lillah*, I'm finished with all that now.' The Arab word was beautifully pronounced in the authentically guttural accent of a fluent speaker, and without a shred of self-consciousness. 'And I do think Granada is possibly the best place in Europe, maybe in the whole world, in which to live an Islamic life.'

I remain unconvinced of the truth of this, in the light of what he subsequently tells me. His first steps as a Muslim were under the aegis of a group of converts with its base in Norwich, of all places, and a leader or *shaykh* who is Scottish, of all nationalities. The group has grown into a worldwide movement, the Granada branch of which now has its own headquarters and mosque on the western fringe of the Albayzín, in the Calle Elvira. This was where Yusuf Idris started out; but he is critical now of its cultish exclusivity, its aggressive propagandising and, most of all, the presumption of its Scots leader in applying the word *shaykh* to himself, the term being charged with implications of wisdom, experience and Koranic knowledge which some say he does not possess.

As the group grew and prospered, it grew further and further away from what some people thought a Sufi *tariqa* should'be, and inevitably there was a kind of schism, with a few dissatisfied convert rebels seeking solace in the teachings of Shaykh Muhammad Nazin al-Qubrisi al-Baggani and the *tariqa* established by his followers in Northern Cyprus. Granada's fledgling community then split into tiny entities who spent too much energy in biting each other's backs and not enough in pulling together to create a solid-based society – the notion of a stable society, of course, being at the heart of Islam.

There are several small mosques in the Albayzín but none of them is plural, open. There is still no permanent *medraza*; Muslim children are forced to attend local state schools and Koranic teaching is a makeshift affair. 'Our social situation is very bad. The community has been a failure,' concludes Yusuf. So much for Granada as a prime site for the Islamic life.

In the background, behind the door, I could hear a woman's voice marshalling children through their evening régime of food and bed. Yusuf married again after an earlier relationship ran painfully aground. 'That was a very hard experience, and this time round I wanted to do things properly. This time I wanted a marriage that was vocational, honourable, coherent, spiritual, so I went to my maestro and asked for his advice. He put me in touch with a Moroccan family who are excellent people. Simple, humble people. They're actually direct descendants of the prophet. And my wife was *un gran hallazgo* – really quite a find.' One after another the children began to sidle quietly into the room in their pyjamas, fixing me with dark curious eyes. This was how fathers' studies used to be when we were very young: places of power and solemnity, where play suddenly ended as soon as you entered them. And, like an old-fashioned father, Yusuf gently reproved them for disturbing him at his work: 'Off to bed now, son, do as your mother says. And shut the door behind you, I'm busy.'

We talked for three hours, until I felt faint with mental tiredness. Yusuf loved to talk, and mundane considerations like time and hunger tended to pass him by when he roared into exegetical mode.

His conversation was wide-ranging and sometimes hard to grasp, and the more recondite the theme, the more he smiled his little studious smile of pleasure. We talked about the Koran, and he disapproved of my English translation. If I couldn't cope with the Arabic I should read it in Spanish, because the language was spiritually far closer to Arabic than English could ever be. He explained about the *din*, the contract between the Muslim and his Lord whereby the Muslim promises unstintingly to adore and obey, and how the word *Sufi* comes from the Arabic for wool, after the rough-woven clothes of the wandering ascetic, and how the ultimate objective of the woolly ones is to reach, by means of contemplation and prayer, a state of ecstatic union with Allah.

I needed to know whether he'd been helped towards this admirable objective by the medieval Spanish Sufi masters like Ibn Masarra of Cordoba, Abu Madyan Shuaib of Seville and, above all, Abu Bakr Muhammad Ibn al-Arabi al-Hatimi (1165–1240), known to Christians as Ibn-Arabi of Murcia and to Sufis as *ash-shaikh al-akbar* – the Greatest Master.

In answer, Yusuf held up his hand as though silencing an unseen audience, and quoted in a voice trembling with reverence Ibn-Arabi's famous dictum on the precedence of Love over all religions, which scandalised the Islamic establishment of the day and brought the great divine close to being persecuted for heresy.

> My heart is capable of every form:
> A cloister for the monk, a fane for idols,
> A pasture for gazelles, the votary's Ka'aba,
> The tables of the Torah, the Koran.
> Love is the creed I hold: wherever turn
> His camels, Love is still my creed and faith.

Yusuf had read and been inspired by all the great Sufi thinkers, Spanish and foreign, and was particularly devoted to a book called *On the Abandonment of Oneself* by Ibn Ata Allah of Alexandria (d.1309), a follower of Ibn-Arabi, which he encouraged me to buy and read. He loved and admired Ibn-Arabi beyond any of them, but had trouble grasping the slippery complexities of his thought; and I knew what he meant, because I had been dipping into a new Spanish translation of a greatly abridged version of his monster mystical tome *The Illuminations of Mecca* and could hardly get beyond the first page.

Now that it was dark outside, the study window made a frame of the night. And within the frame was a picture, if not to die for, then at least to spend a few weeks of self-mortification for the privilege of possessing. There before me, spread out languidly along the ridge of the Sabika hill, in whose shadow lies the sprawling Albayzín, was the palace of the Nazrid kings, the Red Fort, al-Qal'a al-Hamra, the Alhambra, lavishly floodlit and glowing with loveliness.

'It's beautiful, isn't it?' said Yusuf Idris softly, rhetorically, coming to the window.

'The Alhambra has so much *baraka.*' *Baraka* is Arabic for blessing, magic, spiritual influence. He might have been anti-romanticism, but it was real and undeniable, this miraculous bridge between then and now. 'It's a constant presence in my life. You know, I've always wanted to recite the Koran up there, one night, when all the tourists have gone.' The Nazrid monarchs would invite Sufi brotherhoods up from the Albayzín to their palace on the hill, where they would chant and dance and go into ecstasies among the moonlit courtyards.

'I'd love to do that, if they'd let me. The atmosphere would help so much; if they'd let me.'

And as an afterthought which to the good Muslim is never an afterthought but a going-without-saying, he added: '*insh'allah* – God willing'.

The public face of Islam in Granada is a mini-district of the Albayzín, a triangle of alleys and a tiny square that are collectively known as

Las Caldererías after the makers of cooking-pots – *caldereros* – that must have operated here at one time or another.

I was early for my appointment in the Calle Elvira and walked up the Calle de la Calderería Nueva in search of a breakfast cup of coffee. But there was none to be found, because the drink of choice in the Caldererías is tea. Indian tea, China tea, herb tea, fruit tea, *mint* tea. I counted five, six, seven *teterías* in the same street, most of them fancily decorated with Alhambra-ish arches in moulded plaster and little round tables and signs painted in Arab-ish lettering, and with evocative names: Tetería Al-Andalus, Tetería Tuareg. Some of them had menus in Arabic, and one of them, run by a Catalan Muslim (why does that sound so nearly oxymoronic?), had a sign in the window that kindly reminded customers to stay away on Friday afternoons. Between the teashops were restaurants serving couscous and *brik à l'oeuf*, and pastry-shops selling little sweetmeats made with honey and almonds, and gift-shops full of Moroccan teasets and teapots and delicate painted tea-glasses and packets of Indian tea, China tea, herb tea, fruit tea, mint tea . . . As if this dose of orientalism weren't enough, out of the doorways came tinny blasts of Oum Kalsoum and Algerian rai, just like in a real North African *souk*. In fact the illusion of being in a real North African *souk* was almost too carefully created to be plausible. A touch of scruffiness, a few nasty smells, would have added to the cred of the place.

It was a quiet winter morning in the Calderería Nueva. The only people about were a gaggle of women in headscarves and long leg-hiding dresses who were just heading home with the weekly shopping, and two hurrying men with beards. I had a hunch that I knew where the Beards were going, and followed them at a safe distance down a dark alley that soon opened into a minuscule plaza. They disappeared into a smart new building with Arabic writing above the main doorway, and a heavy oak door boomed shut behind them. Upon this door was a highly-polished brass plaque which read: SPANISH MUSLIM COMMUNITY OF THE FEAR OF ALLAH MOSQUE IN

GRANADA. On the doorjamb to the left of this plaque, as though replying to it through pursed lips and in a tone of barely-repressed indignation, was another plaque which read: 'First Floor. This doorbell belongs to the dwelling of a Christian family.'

The mosque in the Calle Elvira is even more mysterious still, and considerably less impressive. From the street itself, which marks the western limit of the Albayzín and has nothing of the *barrio*'s atmosphere, you'd be unlikely to guess it was there. The only clue might be a dull shop-front with a few sober-looking booklets in racks (it could be a Christian Science Reading Room, until you examine the booklets), and above it a sign in Arabic and Spanish that reveals this as the Granada headquarters of the Islamic Community in Spain – said 'community' being none other than the cultish organisation about which Yusuf Idris had talked so disparagingly.

I waited in the foyer, which was barely furnished and painted institution-green. Just inside the door a man in a long white smock and black beard was mopping the floor. There was a faint smell of Dettol. Expecting to be bored, I flicked through a grey-covered brochure entitled *The Politics of Islam,* only to discover that it was one of the most outrageous documents I had ever come across. Chapter One set out the basic tenets of the Murabitun movement and its recommendations for civilisation as we know it, which included the deconstruction of the state, redefinition of the world map, universal recognition of the authority of the Prophet Muhammad over Moses and Jesus, and the abolition of interest rates. 'Usury is a cancer! Debt is its tumour! Surgery is the cure! Operate now!'

The man I was meant to meet was burly and tweedy and, of course, bearded. So when a burly, tweedy and bearded man walked through the door I assumed it to be him. Beard One had invited me to a Koran-reading class. But Beard Two seemed surprised and irritated by my arrogant assumption that I would be able to attend the reading, especially since he'd never set eyes on me before.

'No, no, I don't think we can allow that. Are you a Muslim?'
'No, but . . .'

'Well, these readings are only for Muslims. You wouldn't under-stand *anything*, you see. *Nada de nada.*' There was hostility in his voice, I felt, and condescension.

'That's not fair! I mean, obviously I would understand *something*,' said I. 'I've read the Koran, I've talked about Islam to people . . . And it was you who invited me. What do you have to do to be a Muslim anyway?'

He looked puzzled and cross. He glanced nervously at his watch. 'I didn't promise you anything. And as for being a Muslim, you wouldn't understand.' If we'd both been in a better mood, he could have reminded me that the Koran says that nobody should say he *is* a Muslim, but that he is *becoming* one. Instead, he turned to the man mopping the floor. 'Tayib, please look after this man, I have things to do.' And he strode off down the corridor.

I tried to leave, but the door to the street was locked. And the man with the mop put his hand on my arm and tried to calm me down. '*Hombre, no es para tanto.* It's no big deal.' He shook his head and gave a wry little laugh. The burly tweedy man, he said, was the emir of the movement, an authority-figure and noted scholar of the Koran, and would not have been used to such insubordination. 'Come with me. I'll talk to you, if you like,' said Tayib.

He took up his bucket and led me away from the foyer, away from the natural light into the badly-lit depths of the building, past the entrance to the mosque where the Beards were congregating in a cross-legged huddle on the coir matting, and into a back room kitted out as a print-shop with a designer's sloping table, a scanner and a big professional colour-printer. I had just registered the state-of-the-art hardware when I noticed a group of contrasting elements: a shelf-ful of Arabic books, a framed photo of some grumpy-looking Ayatollah and a poster on the wall of a Palestinian youth in the act of hurling a large rock.

Tayib was a graphic designer, not a cleaner; but then humility is as considerable a virtue for Muslims as it is for Christians. He had almost finished his current job, the menu-design for the new Café

Fútbol, and a prototype had just finished chuntering out of the printer. (The café menu, I noticed, was mainly sandwiches with fillings of pork loin, *jamón serrano*, York ham, *sobrassada*, and other products of the unclean swine.) But there was something else in the pipeline, and he sat down at his sloping desk and began to scribble with a Rotring pen, talking ruminatively as he worked.

'I became a Muslim practically overnight. I was actually at a college for priests, and then I worked for the Post Office, and *Dios mio*, I had a horrible time. What happened was that I met a Muslim, and thought, "This guy knows what he's talking about." I liked the idea that Islam offered a Society, not a Religion. The structure, the form of living. To me it makes a lot of sense, with everything falling down around our ears. The drugs, the violence, the decadence . . .' He spoke with a quiet, contained intensity, addressing his words not so much to me as to the sheet of paper in front of him, upon which a curlicued baroque bookplate was gradually taking shape. 'I converted *de la noche a la mañana*, practically overnight. But it's taking me a lot longer to be a proper Muslim. Islam is like a woman. You try and get close to her and she says, "No, not that way." And you say, "If not that way, then how?" But she won't tell you. She won't make it that easy for you.'

On his way in to work Tayib had stopped off at a pastry-shop and bought a large cream cake. Now he cut into it with a Stanley knife and gave me half. I ate my half messily and got my fingers sticky. In the bathroom were plastic bottles of water standing around the loo, just like in the Middle East, and two taps and two towels marked FEET and HANDS.

There was a soft knock on the door. In came a businessman with a black briefcase. He muttered '*Salaam alekum*', sat down on a swivel chair and immediately took out a mobile phone and began dialling. His conversation began drifting in and out of our own, forming a peculiar counterpoint to the story of Tayib. 'You don't deal in couscous, do you? No. Well, in that case, I'll just have the usual three kilos of jasmine tea. And cardamom pods, a couple of kilos. And could you let me have four or five kilos of normal tea, you know, the basic Indian stuff – people are always wanting that?' he was saying, as Tayib was expounding his world-view and encouraging me to stay around for morning prayers. The silent complicity between the two men and the atmosphere of the room, its bare walls echoing with religiosity and kilos of herb tea, gave me a shudder of claustrophobia.

Tayib picked up a brochure from the back of his desk and handed it to me with a flourish. It was a publicity handout for the new mosque planned for the heart of the Albayzín, showing an artist's impression of a grand white building with red roofs and a minaret, set in sumptuous gardens studded with fountains and blue-and-white tiled pathways. 'Help us build the mosque of Granada. This will be the mosque of the Islamic capital of Europe,' it said below the picture. Inside was a description of the site, in Arabic and English, and a series of bankers orders you could cut out and send, together with a donation, to the bank account of the Islamic Community in Spain. (1,000 dollars gets your name inscribed on the mosque wall.) Tayib couldn't tell me how much money had been raised so far, but he knew that hardly anything was being donated by Muslim states, as you might have expected. 'Unfortunately it seems the Arab govern-ments have other priorities; wars with each other and peace with Israel,' the brochure noted with a touch of bitterness.

Later, when I left the Calle Elvira, I made my way up the hill to the site of the mosque near the Mirador de San Nicolás, the wide cob-bled courtyard that forms a natural balcony from which photographers get their perfect panoramic picture-postcard shots of the Alhambra. 'During your visit to this Islamic capital do not be the servant of kafir tourism but have the self-respect not only to look at the past but also to visit the future,' said the brochure. But the future was invisible. There was precisely nothing to see.

The site was surrounded by corrugated iron fencing. From what I'd heard, the building had planning permission, and work was about to begin when the town hall suddenly became aware of some Roman remains on the site and decided these had to be fully investigated before the mosque went ahead. Then a rightwing extremist group calling itself Covadonga (after the legendary battle of AD722, in which a few brave Christian soldiers are supposed to have defeated a huge army of bloodthirsty Moors – a sort of Spanish Rourke's Drift) began organising demos and leafletings against the 'foreign' invasion of this ethnically pure Catholic *barrio* . . . An idiotic notion, and Granada's thousand-or-so Muslims in fact had little to fear from a few supremacist loonies. But for one reason or another the project was forced to a halt before it had even begun.

I peered through the fence at the rubble-strewn mess. If there were excavations going on, I could see little sign of them. I thought back to the artist's impression, with its sparkling white walls and hopeful greenery.

The future had either lost its way or was loping ahead out of reach. I was padding down the hill again, dispiritedly pondering the fragility of human ideals, when I remembered that Yusuf had told me about a community of Sufis living out their lives in prayer and devotion to Allah behind the old Arab baths at the foot of the Albayzín. Feeling I had nothing to lose, I stopped at a house with a sign made of blue and white tiles and a name in Arabic, and rang the bell. Above me on a little terrace overhung with tumbling jasmine and clots of pink bignonia, there was someone sitting. The *adagietto* from Mahler's Fifth Symphony was quietly throbbing with F-major promise in the morning air.

A Beard looked over the wall. Yes, there had been a *tariqa* here for a while, it said, but they were gone now, almost all of them. To the *sierra*, to build a community away from the storms and schisms and the politics of Granada. That's where they were now, in the little town of Órgiva, in the mountains a hundred miles south of the city.

So now I really had no alternative but to go to Órgiva.

The Alpujarras is a great place to go on the rebound from disappointment. When Boabdil was kicked out of Granada in 1492 he came this way, though not out of choice. He was given a fiefdom over which he ruled until the autumn of the following year, when he limped south to Fez. But the mountains remained a last stronghold of the old culture and religion for another century or two. The Moors' longest-lived achievement in these parts was a complex system of *acequias*, canals that supplied water to the meanest village, the highest terrace, and certain old families were still charged with its upkeep long after the Reconquest. When Gerald Brenan came to the Alpujarras in 1920, dazed by the horrors of the First World War, he found ice-cream-makers who 'continued to fetch their snow on mule-back from the summits of the sierra just as they had been doing since Arab times', and was once given 2,000-year-old coins as part of his change when buying cigarettes in the village shop.

At the end of the twentieth century little of that legacy is left, and this is now just a slightly undernourished mountain area, magnificently beautiful, where old Spain is still the dominant key of life but has almost been drowned out by modern harmonies and dissonances. The New Age has settled here, as it likes to do in traditional rural societies where rents are cheap. In a paradisical valley outside the village of Cañar, a teepee city has sprung up, populated by gentle people from all over Europe. There are fruit and olive trees, vegetable gardens, and a river of melted snow running among the tents. Before the teepee people arrived, Cañar was slowly dying on its feet. The youngsters had left and the birthrate was plummeting, but in the last two years there have been seventeen babies born in teepee town, and the births have all been registered in Cañar. Swelled by these new citizens, the village is booming now, and the mayor is beaming.

Beliefs and ways of life outside the Western Christian norm have always found fertile ground in the Alpujarras. These days, they have tantric meditation workshops, American-Indian sweatlodge rituals and wild nights of druidic magic. The village of Bubión has its own fully fledged Tibetan monastery, headquarters of the reincarnation of a famous lama in the form of a small Spanish boy. And Órgiva has its Muslims. Or so I'd been led to believe.

In the town's covered market was a noticeboard pinned all over with adverts for drums, guitars, lifts to the airport and flat-roofed Alpujarreño farmhouses – spitting images of houses I'd seen in the Rif mountains of Morocco, where the original Alpujarreños came from – for £10,000 apiece. Among the handwritten notes was one that read: 'Wanted. Mountain bike. Call 34-70-56. Ask for Muhammad Scott.' (A case of bringing the mountain bike to Muhammad?)

The lady at the health-food stall (specialities: goat's cheese, sun-dried tomato bread and hand-made soap) told me where to find the new people, the ones that wear baggy trousers and headscarves in the street. They had made their base in an old boarding-house known to villagers as the Fonda del Pescado: the Fish Hotel. (The Spanish word *fonda* is a hang-on from the arabic *fonduk*, meaning hostel, guest house, *pensión*.)

It was five minutes' walk from the market, in a narrow street behind the village church. A woman in a headscarf and ankle-length patchwork skirt answered the door and peered at me through thick bottle-bottom glasses. She had the pale, squinting face of someone who spends most of her life indoors.

She led me into a courtyard and sat me down at an old multi-coloured splay-legged sixties table, and a chair roughly painted in bright kiddie colours. The little furniture there was in the *fonda* all looked like this; battered, fifth-hand, slapdashly enamel-coloured. It felt like Africa: electrical wires snaked and swooped around the walls, intertwining perilously with a waterpipe that emerged in mid-wall and disappeared back into it a few inches away. There was the same childlike celebration of 'precious' objects, gaudy, tinselly or shiny, in this case a Moroccan lamp with coloured glass facets, a little rug with a floral design, a cheap brass ashtray, that you see in working people's houses everywhere else but in Europe. The metal railing that ran up the staircase to a gallery around the patio had been painted in jumble-sale blue and yellow, and the arched doorways around the ground floor were daubed in brick-red. The walls were whitewashed. Whether by accident or design, out of naïveté or knowingness, the inhabitants of the Fish Hotel had got the Arab style to a T.

The questions started: Where was I from? Was I a Muslim? Was I part of the community (or did she mean Community?) in Ibiza? What did I want, then? 'They keep wanting to study us now, to *interview* us,' said the woman, sounding less annoyed than surprised. 'An American anthropologist came here once but he never came back. He didn't even return the books.'

There are fifteen or sixteen Muslim families in Órgiva, plus five or six single people, and most of them are Spanish Catholic converts. Most of the men had normal jobs in Granada, on the coast at Almuñécar or on farms in the countryside outside Órgiva, and were out at work, but would be coming in tonight for the weekly *dikr*, the litanies and recitations of the sacred names of Allah which all good Sufis celebrate every Thursday night. 'What do the women do? We stay at home and clean and cook and look after the children. *Alhamdulillah* for the children.' Above us on the landing were two more bescarved females with similarly peering, cautious faces. For the moment, then, there was no one here to talk to but her husband, and since he knew everything there was to know, she would put some water on to boil for the mint tea and call him.

Omar Coca was a grizzled, through-the-mill man, looking like an old sailor in his thick blue sailor's jumper. He moved carefully across the patio and sat down gratefully, then launched into a crisis of coughing, first hacking, then phlegmy, through thin leathery lips. Then he lit a cigarette and showed me around his domain.

He and a few Muslim friends were renovating the *fonda* as quickly and well as their precarious economy allowed. It was an old inn, two or three hundred years old in its fabric but with much deeper roots, probably in some kind of *caravanserai* for commercial travellers in the Alpujarras. There would have been a fire in the middle of the patio, where the guests sat around, warming hands and exchanging travellers' tales. Omar showed me the tumbledown stables for mules and horses at the back, with what was left of its beamed roof lined with bamboo canes. This would become the anteroom of the mosque. A chicken shook herself out of a pile of cement and tiptoed off.

There was a presence and charisma about Omar that were partly the result of his years, and partly because you felt that if he chose he might suddenly snap out of his gentleness and turn into a fearsome authoritarian. His wife called him once, twice, from the kitchen door. Seeing that he refused to be interrupted, she retreated patiently to the kitchen to make tea. He was the patriarch, the chief of the tribe, and she was the good Muslim wife.

In a few minutes she came to the table with the tea-things on a yellow plastic tray. The tea was made with a sweet shiny-leaved mint that grew in the Cocas' back yard. It was poured from a silvery teapot with a bird figure on the lid – the classic Arabic type that's so heavy when full of tea and so scalding hot because it's made of such cheap and nasty metal that it's impossible to handle. Omar wrapped a cloth round the awkward handle and poured out two glasses, raising the pot a little higher than usual, arms trembling with the effort, in a nod towards Moroccan tea-pouring practice.

Omar – Christian name Pedro, but he never makes a fuss of the name-change; never had it officially registered – converted to Islam in Seville, under the aegis of the nascent Murabitun movement. He had once been a communist, then followed the common drift from *Das Kapital* to the Koran, which both after all encapsulate similarly regulated, closed intellectual systems. He still admired the social project of Islam and its remorseless, sometimes brutal, practicality. 'There aren't any police in Islam, you know. There's no need for them, because everybody knows the law,' he said. 'There aren't any jails either. At least, there must be some, but there shouldn't be. Think of the cost to society, when a guy's condemned to life imprisonment. If he gets his hand chopped off he isn't going to do it again, *insh'allah*.'

Omar was now retired. Until recently he had been taking regular trips from Spain to North Africa and back, dealing in spices, oils, wild honey and *ajenuz*, which is said to cure every illness apart from death. He has seven children from three marriages, and the most recent of them were now coming back from school with their textbooks under their arms. First in was Abdullah, a little boy of five or six who was already dashing upstairs when his father caught him by the arm, pointed to me, and asked him: 'What do you say? What do you say?'

Lowering his eyes in embarrassment, Abdullah mumbled at me, '*Salaam alekum.*'

'Well said, well said. Now give your father a kiss. Come on, give me a kiss.'

And the boy did so – a reluctant peck – then stamped up the staircase to his room. All Omar's children did the same, the greeting and the kiss, and I found ineffably touching the way he called each of them over to him and the shy, loving obedience of their response. I saw, as I had in Yusuf's house in the Albayzín, that there was something sweetly antiquated in the relationship between these Muslim fathers and their sons, a poise and elegance that you don't see much in families these days. (How many Christian children still kiss their father, and say 'Good afternoon' to guests as they walk in from school? For that matter, how many Christian children still walk home from school, when axe-wielding maniacs lurk behind every tree?)

'Come with me. Let me show you what we're doing.' Omar scraped back his chair and stood stiffly. He directed me first to a cluttered space on the side of the patio nearest the street, which he wants to convert into a halal butchery. Pork is out of bounds, of course, making life difficult for the Muslim in a part of Spain awash with delicious mountain-cured hams. But lamb and goat are fine. 'Anyone can kill, but there are techniques to be learned. What matters is that the meat is killed for God.'

At the back of the patio was a neater whiter place, already fitted

out with low stone benches picked out with coloured tiles and interesting little niches in the wall, just right for depositing Moorish
knick-knacks. This would be the *teteria*, and a much-needed social
focus for the Islamic community in Órgiva. Beyond that, beyond
everything, was the jewel, the heart of the building: the mosque. It
was a dark small room, rustic-beamed and whitewashed, handmade
and human-sized, with arches and a *mihrab* with shelves on either
side upon which Moorish knick-knacks had already found their
place. The floor was of stone, but covered with rugs and rush mats.
We climbed over a half-built wall, voices reverently lowered, and
skirted around the women's section beyond the central arch –
'Don't step on the carpet here. *Don't* step on the carpet' – towards
the back door. Here Omar pulled across an iron bolt, and the sun
streamed in, together with a gust of mountain air, from a courtyard
of a few metres' breadth. This was where Ahmed, the muezzin, stood
to give the call to prayer on Friday afternoons: '*Allahu akbar! Allahu
akbar!* God is great! Come to prayer. Come to your salvation. I testify
that God is the divinity, that there is no other God but God, and that
Muhammad is his messenger. *La ilaha illa-Llah!* There is no God but
God!'

That night the *tariqa* met for its weekly session of prayer and
praise: the *dikr*. Not all Órgiva's Muslims are Sufis, and fewer, perhaps a dozen, belong to the esoteric order of the Naqshbandi. The
Naqshbandi Sufis were all arriving now, in Turkish turban and baggy
trousers, from their flat-roofed houses in the hills. As each man
arrived, he shook hands with everyone else in the patio, said '*Salaam
alekum*' and moved through to the mosque to begin bowing and
scraping and murmuring his praise. The meeting was chaired by
Umar al-Margerit, a learned Sufi originally from Barcelona, with a
perfect command of Arabic and an impressively bushy jet-black
beard that added to his grave and academic air.

In a low voice I asked the imam about the *raison d'être* of the
group. He stroked his beard, half-closed his eyes, and gave me this
learned and eloquent response. 'The objective of this *tariqa*, which

is to say of every spiritual path, is to reach Divine Union, which, following the example of the Seal of the Prophets and Envoys, Muhammad, peace and blessings be with him, is to become the perfect servant of Allah. This means not allowing anything not to be associated with Allah, either externally or internally, which in turn implies freeing ourselves from the tyranny of our ego, the ego which whispers continually in our ear *la ilaha illa-ana* (there is no God but me). This is the adversary that we must fight constantly with the sacred sentence *la ilaha illa-Llah* (there is no God but God).'

Omar's wife had prepared a spicy soup with Spanish *fideo* noodles, and her teenage son Muhammad Ibrahim, in black tracksuit and Nike trainers, handed it around in ill-matched bowls and we sipped it quietly, sitting in a circle on the floor of the mosque. The imam lit a candle in the middle of the circle, telling Muhammad Ibrahim: 'Find another candle, would you, for the women?' The wives and daughters had gathered discreetly at the far end of the mosque, huddling in another tight circle in the half-dark, waiting for illumination.

The ritual began with a long low burbling Arabic recitative from the imam, punctuated with *alhamdullillah*s and *bismillah*s and *la ilaha alla-Llah*s, giving way to a series of repetitions of the names of Allah; we all chimed in with them, half-speaking, half-singing, faster and louder and snatching energetic breaths between each hypnotic repetition, feeling dizzily excited from the overdose of oxygen, until a climax was reached and a new chant began. There are at least a hundred names of Allah. I looked them up later and noted down the ones that appealed to me:

The Knower of Everything
The Provider
The Giver of Openness
He Who Hears All
He Who Sees All
The Designer of Forms

The Absolutely Excellent
The Absolutely Perfect
The Protecting Friend
The Hidden
The Evident
The Last
The First
The Truth.

We launched into a long repetition of *al-haqq*, The Truth, with its guttural Arabic h and q that have to be wrenched from some cavernous unknown region of the throat:

Haqq,
haqq,
haqq,
haqq,
haqq,

we intoned solemnly, slowly; then the pace increased little by little until finally we were barking ecstatically:

HAQQ
HAQQ
HAQQ
HAQQ
HAQQ
HAQQ . . .

Yet at the centre of this sound and fury was a warm, clear, penetrating light; a magical, intimate calm.

'An occasion like this could be seen as a gift,' said the imam in a near-whisper. It was true; there was no doubting the tranquillity and orderliness and sincerity of the Sufis' worship. I have forgotten much of what was said in that Thursday night address; I was still in a hyperventilated daze. I remember something about the corrupting influence of the West on the world, and about the revitalising influence of Islam over Christianity and Judaism, it being the last and greatest of the revealed religions. 'Islam is like opening the window of a stuffy room,' said the Imam; and he spoke at length of the hunger, the nostalgia for spirituality that is sending Spanish Catholics back into the arms of Islam. 'Islam is the only thread that will lead us through the maze. It has the only keys to the past and future,' he said – at which the whole cross-legged circle of Sufis muttered in unison *alhamdullilah* and nodded in recognition, their pointy turbans casting sinister shadows on the whitewashed wall.

At the far end of the room, the women's candle seemed to have gone out.

Short Stories

TWO STAYS IN TWO MONASTERIES

'All strangers that come to the door should be welcomed as
you would welcome Christ, for He will say one day: I was a
stranger and you welcomed me. And let there be given to all
men the honour due – above all to our brothers in faith –
and to pilgrims'

(Rule of Saint Benedict)

1. Abadía de Poblet (Tarragona)

My room is very plain, clean and cold. Only one thin blanket on the bed,
and no bedside light. And of course no minibar, no CNN, no *¡Hola!* I
have two arched windows looking out over the courtyard. Below, a wide
square fishpond, gently dripping, and a group of tall, slender pines.
There are two monks in black and white habits walking in the vineyard
beyond the wall, probably discoursing on theological matters. The
monastery is a maze of butterscotch-coloured medieval buildings, a
community functioning much as it would have done 500 years ago.

Poblet is a Cistercian foundation, one of the 8,012 religious com-
munities in Spain. There are more than 10,000 Spanish monks and nuns
including Jesuits, Dominicans, Carthusians, Marianists, Marists,
Franciscans, Carmelites, Barefoot Carmelites and a myriad other nuances
of belief. According to a book I find in the pillared and vaulted library,

the Cistercian order aims at 'Sanctification through prayer, penitence and manual work. Contemplative life.' Poblet is not 'of the Strict Observance' (Trappist), but the timetable left on the desk in my room looks pretty strict to me. I am horrified to discover that there are no less than three services before breakfast, the first of which begins at the unimaginable time of 5.15 in the morning. There are at least five masses every day, more and longer on feast-days, and in Holy Week it's practically round the clock. Bed is at nine.

Father Matías, the assistant guest-master, is jovial, jokey, tonsured, a cartoon monk without the girth. He fills me in on the monastery routine: as little careless talk as possible with any other monk than himself, absolute silence during meals, no smoking except in cells and in the orchard, punctuality, and payment 'according to your possibilities'. The monastery regularly welcomes guests. 'We get all sorts of religions here – you know, Buddhists, Hindus, Anglicans [sic] . . . Even some people who say they're atheists. But they all go away a little bit changed, a little bit touched.' Father Matías tweaks my baggy linen jacket and suggests I wear a sweater to Matins. It can get down to 3°C in the church at five am. So many forms and observances. Watch what's done, and copy. It's a bit like your first day at school. You are afraid of being late for anything, so arrive early and hang around trying to look nonchalant.

Meals are taken in the astonishing thirteenth-century refectory, a barrel-vaulted hall the same length as an Olympic swimming pool, with an octagonal fountain in the middle. The food is basic and unadorned, though not puritanically so: there might be a simple rice soup made from good stock, a salad of lettuce and tomatoes from the monastery garden; chicken roasted with garlic and oregano; cold cuts of *jamón York* and *chorizo*. (Vegetables can be overcooked, perhaps to spare elderly teeth.) Wine from the co-operative in the next village; good bread; coffee only at breakfast. There is no talking at mealtimes except to mutter *'gràcies'* when they pass you the bread. Instead, a monk ascends to a pulpit set high in the wall and reads from a history of the Cistercian order in Catalonia. Long strings of dates — *mil cinc cent noranta nou, mil sis cent cincuanta cinc* — bounce off the walls in the rubbery tones of Catalan.

There are about thirty monks here. The old ones are bald or balding, bespectacled and squat, the young ones tall, gangly, bowl-haired. They all walk in one of two ways, both monkish. The younger ones glide along as though they had trolley-wheels under their long habits. The oldsters move in a side-to-side, flat-footed, clumping motion (Tom Wolfe might call it the Friar's Roll) that makes them look like clockwork bath toys. All wear a long black tabard tied round the waist and long-sleeved white robe beneath. Over this ensemble, while gliding or rolling from place to place, they might wear a heavy white cloak with a faintly unsettling pointed hood.

The early rise is as painful as I feared. It is pitch dark, horribly cold, and a wind wails round the great cloister. Ghostly hooded figures in the gloom. In the basilica, final resting-place of the Catalan kings, the monks' quiet chanting billows up in the immense darkness. At Matins only the choir is dimly lit. I take my place in an ornate wooden stall, peer at the service book (each monk has his own, marked indelibly with Dymo tape – 'Jesús M', 'Jesús P', 'Matías', 'Josep') – and try following the flat plainsong notes with a fingertip. Before long I can say by heart the oddly beautiful Catalan version of the Gloria: *'Gloria al Pare, i al Fill, i al Esperit Sant. Com era al principi, ara i sempre, i pels segles dels segles, Amen.'*

Today is the feast of Saint Michael and All Angels, so the lesson is apocalyptic and Tolkien-esque: 'And there was war in heaven. Michael and his angels fought against the dragon . . .' The weirdness of it: here I am, in the late twentieth century, sitting in a medieval church in the pre-dawn darkness, listening to tales of dungeons and dragons.

Upping and downing and kneeling and bowing and swivelling east-wards – perhaps to lessen the risk of dropping off to sleep. There are a few yawns at Matins and a lot of rumbling tums. I feel fine, and do also at Lauds (6.45 am). But by the eight o'clock Mass I am fidgety and cross, and want my coffee. This time I sit at the back and watch. I feel as though I am slipping. Then at breakfast I take a third slice of bread and a big spoonful of (monastery-made) apricot jam. Same terracotta bowl I drank my wine from, full to the brim this time with delicious *café con leche*. Can spiritual pleasures ever quite match up to physical ones?

The rest of the morning is taken up with *treball* (work). In the library, I am given my own table with its old-fashioned four-square brass reading-lamp and provided by Father Javier, chief librarian, with a copy of the Common Bible (in English). The catalogue features a surprisingly open-minded selection of religious thinkers, from Aquinas and More to Nietzsche and Shirley Maclaine. On the wall is a notice threatening excommunication for anyone removing books without authorisation (surely a joke?).

After lunch I sit in the vineyard. It is now undeniably autumn. A quality of the light and air, and the way sound behaves in the atmosphere. Everything has the surreal, voluptuous stillness of a painted backdrop. That undefinable autumn smokiness, which in fact has nothing to do with smoke, but the sense of the air thinning and chilling and taking on a sharp new flavour.

I'm unsure about the monks' relationship to the sensuous and sensual. Do they actually enjoy? I think they do. Their food is plain and their meals perfunctory, but aren't the simplicity and shearing-away merely devices to savour more purely the pleasure of eating? Likewise with the music: because it's perceived in a kind of vacuum, free of the buzzing cloud of stimuli that normally surrounds us, it comes to have a greater power.

It is characteristic of the modern world to think first of what is excluded, what is forbidden, and not of what is embraced, intensified.

Father Benito, a charming, literate and good-humoured man in his seventies, invites me to listen to Gregorian chant in the church after Compline. He knows I am leaving, and wants me to take the experience away with me – 'as a souvenir'.

Next morning he finds me in the library and asks me what I thought. He then sings, under his breath, a snatch of Gregorian melody. 'One of my favourites. "*Procul recedant somnia, et noctium phantasmata . . .*".' His voice echoes gently among the vaults and columns.

2. Monasterio de Oseira (Ourense)

I first hear about the glories of Oseira, popularly known as Galicia's answer to El Escorial, from a hairdresser in Vigo who was once a monk there, until for spiritual or worldly reasons (I didn't ask, but I have my suspicions) he decided to leave. In the bar Escudo, in the silent hamlet of Oseira, stuck like a limpet to the grey leviathan body of the monastery, the lady behind the coffee-machine knew who I meant by the hairdressing ex-monk. She smiled mysteriously and set about making me a big *bocadillo de jamón serrano* with Cea bread, a speciality of a nearby village and one of the world's truly great loaves – stone-coloured, rich-tasting, with a thick rust-brown crust.

There were no rooms, despite my protesting that I was in dire need of spiritual retreat, and I was all ready to leave and find a hotel when Father Santiago, a small white-haired old man from Barcelona, feels bad and offers me the spare room, which is clean and has its own bathroom and a view of lofty autumn trees and hills. So far so good. But the good Father is interested in me, touches me repeatedly, and kisses me on both cheeks like a monk, even a Spanish monk, isn't supposed to. I am annoyed with him, and with myself for having built up the image of a studious young nerd steeped in religiosity, even possibly cut out for monkhood.

'*Tienes inclinación de esto?*', 'Do you have an inclination towards this?', he asked me, making a backwards sweep with one hand that I took to mean 'monkdom in general'.

I spent the next few hours chewing disconsolately over the ghastly repressiveness of the monastic life, the way it must deep-freeze sexuality and the capacity for pleasure. From now on I'm pondering my escape. There are four services daily in the great granite Renaissance church, the first being Matins at seven. I've been to two so far and they've not cheered me up. Even the music is depressing, joyless and badly performed. Bald old crabby organist fumbling over the chords, worse than the worst English parish organist, and out-of-tune pseudo-Gregorian singing, made bearable only by the praeternatural acoustic. Whatever happened to doing things for the glory of God? I sat there in the freezing cold, my mood growing blacker and blacker, and tried replaying the Bach B minor Mass in my head, summoning up that splendour and heart-massaging beauty.

Next morning I escape from Oseira, but not before Father Santiago has lavished more attention on me, and the other guests – a creepy collection, like something out of Polanski – have had a chance to quiz me on my spiritual motivation. I am grumpy and rude to them at breakfast, tired from the 6.30 reveille and multiple Mass before coffee and bread-and-hotel-portion-jam at nine. The instant coffee was the last straw.

I leave some money on the table in my room. When I depart, the morning has brightened into a delectable autumn day, twittering and tintinnabulating nature all about. Next time I'll go straight to a hotel.

6

Goose Day

'Any description of the Basques must begin with their language, just as any introduction to their homeland starts with
those arcane road signs, for the Basques more than anyone
depend on their language for their existence as a race'

(James Morris, *Places*)

Travellers in the Basque country have usually been either per-
plexed, fascinated or amused, or all three, by one aspect in
particular of the culture of the country: its utterly weird and apparently impenetrable tongue.

Basque is a survivor, a living fossil, a freak. By all the laws of history and reason it shouldn't exist. It reminds me of the erstwhile
oldest woman in the world, the Frenchwoman Jeanne Calment, all
of whose friends and relatives died half a century before she did,
while she crept on into eccentric solitude. When she was interviewed
on her 121st birthday, Jeanne announced to the world: 'God has forgotten me.'

The roots of Euskera, as the Basques call Basque, lie somewhere
in the linguistic version of a primordial soup, and the precise origins
of people and parlance may never be known. One of the few things
that can be said for sure about Basque is that it is the last surviving
anciently established pre-Indo-European language in Europe. There
are a couple of other pre-Indo-European languages on the fringes of
the continent, Hungarian and Finnish, but their speakers moved

around before settling down in their eventual homelands. The rest all died out in the face of massive migrations from the east – Bronze Age, Celtic, Roman – that gradually swamped the indigenous culture of Europe.

The last non-Indo-European language to leave us was probably Pictish. (Funny to think of the wild and woolly Picts, as they swarmed barbarously north of Hadrian's Wall, having a prior cultural claim on their aggressors the Romans.) God remembered Pictish, and wiped it out somewhere around AD900, but He forgot Basque. It was probably on His list of Things to Do, but it slipped His mind in the rush to get everything done before the shops shut.

So Euskera lived on clandestinely for another millennium, still clinging tenaciously to life, and in all good bookshops you can buy a book called *Colloquial Basque*, which will tell you how to say: 'I want to go by the petrol station to check the tyres' (*gasolindegitik pasa nahi dut gurpilak begiratzeko*) and 'I have been able to learn a little Basque' (*euskara pixka bat ikasi ahal izan dut*).

When my interest in Basque began, this was the book I bought, at Waterstone's in Earls Court. Because it's always more fun to start a language course at the end rather than the beginning, I flicked through the back pages as I sat on the 31 bus to Chelsea, staring through a fog of Zs and Ks and Xs and feeling a little dizzy as this new planet swam into my ken. Because Basque has no relatives, it offers no clues, no room for guesswork. In Spanish, if you're groping blindly for a word, you can always translate directly from a word you already know in French, Italian, Latin or Arabic, and as often as not you'll be right. In Basque you will always be wrong, so there's not much point in trying. There are no easy footholds on its craggy slopes. Luckily for prospective students, the Basques themselves understand what a nightmare it presents for anyone who hasn't absorbed it with their mother's milk, and are thrilled and delighted by even the most half-hearted attempts to master it.

Foreigners who have successfully got to grips with the Language from Hell have been few and far between. One who did was George

Borrow, a bible salesman whose business trips in the Spain of the 1840s form the basis for one of the more irritating travel books of the nineteenth century, *The Bible in Spain*. Borrow was a brilliant linguist, not the least of whose achievements was a translation of most of the New Testament into the gypsy language Calé. He was also pompous, self-opinionated and chauvinistic – not the best of characteristics for the travel writer – and his overbearing attitude to his hosts makes for some cringe-making moments.

This is how he begins his discussion of the history of the Basque language: 'Much that is vague, erroneous, and hypothetical has been said and written concerning this tongue. The Basques assert that it was not only the original language of Spain, but also of the world, and that from it all other languages are derived; but the Basques are a very ignorant people, and know nothing of the philosophy of language. Very little importance, therefore, need be attached to any opinion of theirs on such a subject.' The implication being that a great deal of importance should be attached to *his own* opinion, which is that, 'having closely examined the subject in all its various bearings, and having weighed what is to be said on one side against what is to be advanced on the other', Basque is actually a dialect of Tartar with a healthy sprinkling of Sanskrit words. He gives a column of Basque words alongside their Sanskrit equivalents, and in some cases you can see what he's getting at. The word for 'bird' is *txori* (pronounced chori) in Basque, *chiria* in Sanskrit; 'dog' is *txakurri* in Basque and *cucura* in Sanskrit. Fair enough. But some of his comparisons seem dubious, even taking into account the drip-drip development of languages over thousands of years. It's hard to see how *beguia* (Basque for eye), for instance, can possibly be related to *akshi*, or *hiru* (Basque for the number three) to *treya*.

Another nineteenth-century traveller in the Basque country, Richard Ford, had a more easy-going and wittier take on the subject, as he seems to have done on life in general. 'The Basques have a language of their own, which few but themselves can understand . . . The enunciation is not easy, at least, if the Andalusian's

joke be true, who says that "the Basque writes Solomon and pro-
nounces it Nebuchadnezzar." According to Perochegui, Adam
spoke Basque, as being the language of angels, which seems
strange . . . Angelic or not, it is so difficult that the devil, who is no
fool, is said to have studied seven years in the Bilboes, and to have
learnt only three words.'

There's no doubt that it's difficult. Basque is an 'agglutinating'
language, which means that, instead of prepositions and articles
and other grammatical facts of post- as opposed to pre-Indo-
European life, words alter their meaning by accumulating a series of
extra syllables at the end. Hence Bilboko (of Bilbao), Bilbora (to
Bilbao), Bilbotik (from Bilbao), Bilbon (in Bilbao), and so on.
These suffixes are used according to cases, so the nouns actually
decline, as in Latin. But where Latin nouns have six cases, Basque
nouns have twelve: Absolutive, Ergative, Dative, Possessive Genitive,
Comitative, Benefactive, Instrumental, Inessive, Allative, Ablative,
Local Genitive and Partitive. The only thing that can be said for the
Basque noun is that at least it has no gender, as in English, which
does cut out a fair amount of heartache.

There is only one thing harder than nouns, vocabulary and pro-
nunciation in Euskera, and that is verbs. Looking at the lists of
conjugations you wonder how anyone without an IQ of 150 could
actually retain them all in the memory. The present tense of *etorri*,
'to come', for example, is *nator, zatoz, dator, gatoz, zatozte, datoz*. The
present simple tense of *jakin*, 'to know', is *dakit, dakizu, daki, dakigu,
dakizue, dakite*. The past of *izan*, 'to be', is *nintzen, zinen, zen, ginen,
zineten, ziren;* but when used with indirect objects it becomes
zitzaidan, zitzaizun, zitzaion, zitzaigun, zitzaiuen, zitzaien, and it's at
that point, when your innocent student repetition of verb-forms
begins to sound like a swarm of angry wasps, that you wonder crossly
to yourself: who on earth dreamed this language up, and what was
their problem?

*

By the time I got to World's End, the 31 bus terminus, I realised I was going to need help. Left to myself I would surely perish in the uncharted jungles; I needed a guide, a sherpa, someone who knew the terrain and could show me short cuts and beauty spots and tell me fascinating facts. I phoned the Instituto Cervantes, the Spanish cultural body, and a rude man said No, he knew of no Basque teachers in London. Perhaps it seemed a strange request, like asking at the Shakespeare Institute for teachers of Welsh. Cervantes = Castilian.

Then I remembered the Spanish magazine *Ajoblanco*, an alternative left-wing sort of mag with a 'Contacts' section at the back where druids can leave messages for other druids and ecologically-minded anarchists in Barcelona seek similar, with GSOH. I sent in a plaintive appeal for friendly experts in Euskera, forgot all about it, and a few months later received a single reply. The call was from a girl in Bilbao (*Bilbon*), a professional historian specialising in Basque themes who had been lying in bed with a bad back and was reduced to re-reading back numbers of *Ajoblanco*. She was interested in the fact that I was interested primarily in Basque culture, as opposed to politics and problems and violence, which are the usual focus of foreign approximations to her country, and willing to let me stay in her house and ask as many questions as I liked.

Beneath her prickly intellectual exterior, Begoña had the spontaneous trusting generosity you still find in Spain – correction: in Spain, but also in neighbouring territories annexed by the Spanish state. She turned out to divide her time between a house in the old town of Bilbao and a flat in Lekeitio, a fishing village along the coast with a famously wild *fiesta* in September, the highlight of which, I remembered hearing, involved a goose hung on a rope across the harbour and people in rowing-boats grabbing hold of it as they sailed drunkenly underneath.

Euskera is little spoken in Bilbao and San Sebastián, the main Basque cities, where mass immigration in the nineteenth century watered down what was already a thinnish sense of national identity.

Out in the countryside the roots run deeper and in more nutritious soil. Lekeitio is one of the strongholds of Basqueness in the western province of Bizkaia (the Basque country, or at least the Spanish bit of it, has three provinces: Bizkaia, Gipuzkoa and Alaba) and one of the few places where Euskera is unequivocally the mother tongue. So for someone wanting a crash course in Basque language and culture, Begoña was a splendid contact.

After a summer in London I was short of cash, and decided to save a few pounds by avoiding boats or planes and taking the overnight horror-bus to Bilbao. The coach was full of language students on their way home after the summer, complaining about dreadful English food and dreaming aloud about *tortilla de patatas* when they weren't showing off shiny new coloured DMs and English swear-words. By the time we got to Dover Western Docks I had got to chapter three of *Colloquial Basque*, and could already say: 'I am from London, but I live in Ibiza. Is this the bus to Bilbao?' When the long-haired boy in the seat behind me started muttering to himself in something that sounded pretty much pre-Indo-European, I stuck my head between the headrests and tried it out on him. '*Londreskoa naiz, baina Ibizan bizi naiz. Bilboko autobusa hau da?*' I don't know who was more surprised: he, when this foreigner suddenly started blurting out Basque, or I, when he actually seemed to understand what I said.

Iñaki was born in Ondarroa, a small town a few kilometres east of Leikeitio with a famous humpy medieval bridge over the brackish river Artibai. He told me he had learned 'official' Basque in school, and I made a quick calculation and realised he must be in his twenties, because Franco prohibited the teaching of Euskera – just as he effectively whitewashed the rich tapestry of *euskaldun* culture by banning Basque sports, dances, *fiestas*, ancestral customs – and Franco died in 1975. Iñaki had been away from his homeland for six months in Dublin, and could hardly wait to hang out with his old crowd. The *fiestas* in Lekeitio had started the day before, and he would be there just as soon as he could, dressed in blue and swilling

Coke and red wine, as tradition demands. 'The gang'll all be there tomorrow night,' he said with a homecoming smile.

Begoña and I met at midday outside the Arriaga Theatre, a toad-like nineteenth-century monument to Bilbao's glory days, and we walked through dark, smelly canyons of old-town streets lined with expensive shops that were just clattering down their security gates and shutting for lunch. She was nervy, intensely intelligent, kind; a tiny woman who moved with quick birdlike steps. As soon as we arrived at her home she dashed out again to visit her mother, while I lay on the sofa and tried to get my psychological bearings.

I turned on the telly. It was a local soap, a spin-off of the language industry that has come into being along with limited Basque autonomy. In a laundrette, as the sudsy water circled in its portholes all around them, two girls were whingeing about their parents. I knew this because the boy on the bus had just told me that *ama* means mother and *aita* father. Within the universe of soap, there are more similarities than differences. Even in Europe's oldest language, when people aren't having illegitimate children or lying in hospital beds beside bleeping machines, they are sitting in laundrettes complaining about their parents.

The city of Bilbao lies in the deep brown hollow of an ancient river bed, crammed with dead or dying industry and grime. Up above it, the countryside is green, gentle, Swiss in its richness and sparkle. Up and down the hillsides, like Swiss chalets, you see the pitched wooden roofs of farmhouses. Every Basque countryman (*baserritár*, or dweller in a *baserri*) has his own vegetable plot, which at the very least will probably include several ranks of green beanstalks, a patch of high-grown tomato plants that in midsummer give an amazingly fat, sweet fruit that tastes of the south, a row or two of flowers for cutting, and an apple tree or two. In the mornings the farmers' wives take their produce to market, once upon a time on donkeys, now in Ford vanettes, and this is what anyone with any sense fills their fridge with, and not with the common-or-garden stuff from the commercial stalls.

We drove along the coast towards Lekeitio, stopping at a big deserted summerhouse with a view of the sea. We walked around in the thick grass. My senses were confused: the warm air and blue backdrop of sea conjured up the Mediterranean, but an Atlantic freshness blew in from the north. The house had an orchard of old uncared-for trees, and we gorged on fragrant pears and bitter apples of a vibrant purple red. I felt suddenly euphoric and full of life, swept out of my tiredness by the view and the air and the apples' acidity.

Apple in Basque is *sagar*, wine is *ardoa*, cider is *sagardoa*, and if you're going to be in the Basque country round about September or October, *sagardo bat* (one cider) may be the most important thing you need to know. In a bar in the sunlit main square in Lekeitio I tried out my first bit of functional Euskera. *Sagardo bat eta zurito bat*, (a cider and a beer), I said. But requests are easy. Questions are trickier, because they bring with them the additional problem of answers. Buoyed up by my first success, I daringly asked the girl, *Zenbat da?* (How much is it?), only to have my self-satisfaction cruelly dashed when she replied, *Berrehun hirorogei hamabost pezeta*, and I was humiliatingly forced to retreat into Spanish in order to find out that I owed her 275 pesetas.

The *fiestas* of San Antolin were well under way, and a humdrum fishing village of 7,000 souls had swollen to five times its normal size with busloads of *bilbotarrak* and *donostiarrak*, summer visitors from Bilbao and San Sebastián, and *baserritarrak* in clean check shirts and black berets. (The plural in Basque is formed by adding, not s, but k.) Every five minutes Begoña met someone she knew, and there'd be stereo-kissing and smiling introductions to this *Londresko kazetari* and more rounds of *sagardo* and *zurito* and louder and faster conversations. The clicking, purring sounds of Basque were all around me, and I felt myself drifting off into a linguistic ocean – or perhaps, in view of the fact that a mere 20 per cent of the population of Euskadi actually speaks the language, it would be better described as a linguistic *lake*. From the big speakers set up on the stage in front of the church came the Basque pop hit of the summer with its chorus of *bai, bai, bai* – 'yeah, yeah, yeah'. Through the mists of my ignorance I could see the word *bai*, pronounced 'bye', being formed on hundreds of pairs of lips, giving me the surreal impression that people were constantly taking their leave of each other, when all they were actually doing was agreeing.

Someone had told me I could learn a lot from the slogans. We took a turn around the village and they assailed us at every step – on banners slung along the harbour wall and the balconies of the town hall, scrawled on handwritten placards in bars and as graffiti in the streets. The most popular ones seemed to be EUSKAL PRESOAK EUSKAL HERRIRA and PRESOAK ETXERA. '*Presoak*' sounded like something to do with laundry. What was this: a protest against the outmoded labour-intensive practices perpetrated by the reactionary forces of the garment industry? No, it was a deadly serious appeal for Basque (*euskal*) prisoners (*presoak*, plural of *presoa*) to be brought back home (*etxe* = house, *etxera* = to the house) to the Basque country (*euskal herri*, plus the allative ending *-ra*). The Spanish government slings ETA convicts into jails all over the country but never within Euskadi itself, in an attempt to strangle at birth any possible solidarity between prisoners, and forbids the use of Euskera in letters home.

The slogan on the harbour wall required less interpretation. *HEMEN EZ DA ESPAINIA, EZTA FRANTZIA ERE*: This is not Spain, nor France. This is a belief that hardcore Basques truly cling to – that not only is it wrong for their land to be a corner of some foreign field, but that culturally, historically and in every other way it's unique and indivisible. I'd already got myself into trouble over this, and it was bound to happen again. Slips of the tongue, usually, as when someone cooked me a meal of pork chops and chips and fried green peppers and I said how much I liked Spanish food, and I felt a chill run round the table. It's not even a matter of not saying 'Spanish' when you don't mean it. I could have said how much I liked the food of the lands under Spanish state control, but it still wouldn't have sounded right. Better to say 'Basque' whether you mean Basque *or* Spanish, and let them have the best of both worlds.

The main square, church, town hall and harbour of Lekeitio are a beautiful collection of buildings and spaces, beautiful not in some twee Heritage way but in a robust knocked-about way that results from the fact that the village isn't some post-modern tourist ghost town but is lived in by real people still doing the things they've always done, more or less. From the harbour, the fishing fleet goes out in pursuit of tuna and anchovy, though there are eleven boats now, not the sixty of a decade ago. Along the harbour are piles of nets to be mended and cleaned, and behind them is a row of tall houses with wooden balconies glass-framed to catch the sun and protect, in winter, against the bitter north wind. On the ground floor of some of these houses are cavernous shops selling all manner of nautical equipment: ropes and brass lamps and floats and baskets for fish. In one of these shops was a sweet-faced woman whose father and grandfather ran it before her. 'Is there a market for the stuff you sell?' I wondered.

'There is now. But if the fleet keeps getting smaller, I shall have to think of other things.'

In the square in front of the town hall a demonstration of *Herri Kirolak*, otherwise known as Basque rural sports, was coming to an end. Basque culture boasts a wide range of ludic activities of which only one, *pilota*, a fast and furious ball-game a little like a cross between rackets and fives, has crossed the dividing line between primitive ethnic proto-sport and the elegance of the real modern thing.

This is not to say that the others aren't fun to watch. Some of them are funny, others movingly resonant with collective cultural memory. There is *segolari*, cutting corn with a scythe, and *lastoaltxari*, hoisting straw bales on a pulley, which has its roots in the time when hay and straw would have to be removed to the hayrick by hand. There are *hartxaintxa*, sheepdog trials, and a variety of weight-lifting that, instead of weights, employs a 225-kilo wooden cart – historians say it derives from when carts got stuck in the mud and had to be pulled out by brute force. And there's my personal favourite, *korikolari*, running in a circle, which has a Beckettian absurdity to it that to me brilliantly symbolises the futility of sport and the pointlessness of life in general.

Lumps and chips of wood were strewn about the square, and a few *aizkolaris* (axemen) were still working away at a series of by now rather tired-and-emotional-looking logs. Wood-chopping is an ancestral sport that chimes in nicely with Basque tree-loving tendencies. Euskadi is a nation of, I suppose it would be 'dendrophiliacs', though in this case the love expressed is of a sadistic kind. The *aizkolari* stands on the log at one end and savagely hacks it with a sharpened hoe or axe, the object of the exercise being to slice it in half before his fellow choppers, who are all chopping away at their own logs. The wood in question was traditionally hard, green beechwood, until deforestation made beech a rare commodity, only for special occasions, and pine became the norm. As the demonstration ended, I saw a little boy run up and grab a handful of wood-chips as a souvenir, showing them off proudly to his father, who assumed an expression as if to say 'That's my boy!', or rather *Hori nere mutila da!*

We walked up above the harbour into the maze of cobbled streets, stopping at the birthplace of Lekeitio's most famous son, the historian and linguist Resurrección Maria de Azkue (1864–1951), whose great *Basque–Spanish–French Dictionary* of 1925 is a classic tome, still used today. In his study of Basque ethnology, *Euskalerriaren Yakintza*, Azkue relates the history of certain customs peculiar to his home town, like the bizarre *katxarranka*, which is still performed every year on the feast day of Saint Peter (29 June). A wooden chest is carried around the town by eight fishermen. On top of the chest a *dantzari* in black tailcoat, white shirt and trousers and a red sash around his neck, clutching a flag with the insignia of Saint Peter, dances three dances in three different places in the town. Azkue traces the *katxarranka* back to the fifteenth century, when the accounts of the local Fishermen's Guild were kept in the chest and solemnly transferred to the counting-house every year at the end of June. During the reign of Philip III the *fiesta* was taken extremely seriously, so much so that the Church began to fret about what it saw as the *katxarranka*'s indecent mix of sacred and profane. 'Seeing the chest pass through the streets, and upon it the dressed-up Saint Peter, the simple people would go down on their knees and beat their chests,' wrote Azkue. Two centuries later, in 1861, the saintly disguise was banned, for it 'scandalised Christians from outside the town and was a motive for laughter among the enemies of the Church.'

There were other even odder customs in Lekeitio, all adding up to a ritual repertoire of amazing richness for such a small town – such as the dance at dawn in which a man with a firebrand held between his mouth had to set fire to the (fake) beards of the other dancers. (Azkue comments that 'those who were watching the dance received much contentment and a great desire to laugh.') I also like the sound of the *txukun-arrapatzea*, a pig smeared in grease which was let loose in the street and had to be caught. These, plus the barefoot procession of children to the Hermitage of Saint John to pray for the fleet on stormy days, the wine-shop exclusively for the sick and ailing (a medical prescription was necessary) and the cow-fights on the beach, have all gone to that great *fiesta* in the sky.

Others, though, have lived on. Under the watchful eye of Saint Peter, in the same little courtyard a few steps up from the harbour, I stood in disbelief as a series of children and adults stepped up to a microphone, opened their mouths and produced a sound unlike anything I had ever heard before. I had stumbled on the annual *irrintxi* contest, held in September as part of the *fiestas* of San Antolín. The *irrintxi*, a Basque battle-cry transformed in recent times into a cry of general exuberance and glad-to-be-Basqueness, is a high-pitched warbling scream held for as long as the lungs will allow, and finished off with a three-note cockadoodle, an arabesque of joy.

As practised in Euskadi, the genre varies in pitch and shape according to the performer. But in musical notation a typical one might look like this:

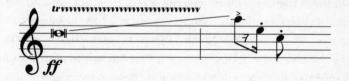

Highlights of the contest were a teenage boy whose voice was in perfectly quavery mid-break, a little girl with Down's syndrome who gave it all she'd got and shook her fist at us when she'd finished, and an experienced chap with a beard and the all-white costume of the *pilota*-player, who impressed us all with his bravura and lung power and was eventually awarded First Prize. I'll also remember Sara, whose performance was a crescendo of sound like a jet plane reaching the sound barrier, and Tesa, who stood with her arms held back, as if preparing herself for take-off. But my heart went out to Edurne, a large lady with a big blonde beehive of hair and typically Spanish (oops, Basque) middle-class uniform of shoulder pads and polka dots. She smiled a confident smile, planted her sturdy thighs on the flagstones, positioned her mouth near the microphone – but not too close, for maximum sound quality – and blasted us with a mighty wail that could have scaled fish at 50 metres. It seemed to go on for ever, and by the time she got to the final triple whoop her face was as red as a red pepper. I pictured her children, cowed into dutiful submission by the threat of a noise like that.

'She wins most years,' said someone in the crowd. By rights she ought to have won this year, too. For a real battle-cry, after all, you need a battle-axe.

That evening I took Begoña's little dog out for a walk, practising my few words of canine Basque – *kalera* = to the street, *etxan* = sit, *etorri* = come – and delighted that I was able to make myself understood.

The next day was Goose Day, highlight of the Lekeitio party calendar, and the temperature was rising in the town. I ran into Tesa from the *irrintxis*, a brassy friendly woman in a blue headscarf, and her son. 'We're from the North,' she said, which puzzled me. We were already on the Atlantic coast – how much further north could one go? But Tesa's accent had a familiar flavour about it, and soon the penny dropped. They were in fact, though I would never have dared let the dread word pass my lips, *French*. 'We have some customs in common; some dances and music,' she said in Spanish. 'There are some differences in the language, but we understand each other pretty well.'

In a square at the centre of the town I stopped to get money out of the cashpoint. A number of Lekeitio's banks bore the marks of vandalism – graffiti, shattered glass, crude posters – but this being a branch of the Bilbo Bizkaia Kutxa, a Basque bank, was one that didn't. On the wall next door were posters and slogans galore, and one particular image caught my eye. It showed a villageful of shiny, happy people dancing round an oak tree. The dancers in the picture, in traditional Basque *bleu de travail*, were holding hands and smiling. On a bench sat an old man reading a newspaper with the headline PRESOAK ETXEAN: literally 'prisoners at home' (*exte* = house and the suffix *an* gives the sense of 'at' or 'in'). Birds twittered in the trees; the sky was almost as blue as the *bleu de travail*. The style was naïf, sugary, idealised.

I led the dog across the square and it was as though I'd walked into the 'before' of the poster's squeaky-clean 'after'. A row of solemn-looking people held cellophane-wrapped baskets tied up with pink and purple ribbon. In the open space before them, a group of young people danced a slow, sad dance of homage. They were girls with thick black long hair and boys with earnest faces, wearing blue shirts and thick blue trousers and blue espadrilles, and they hopped and turned in elegant unison to a sober music of flute and drum. Beside them was a *txalaparta*, the Basques' very own aboriginal musical instrument, consisting of planks of wood arranged on top of large resonating baskets and hit with wooden beaters. And above them on home-made banners were three giant photos of the three *presoak*, overpainted to look as though they were staring out from behind thick black bars. The families of Lekeitio's ETA prisoners were holding an impromptu demo.

The dance ended; there were tearful embraces between Blue People and ETA relatives. A group of traveller types with ratted hair and babies milled among both groups, clattering syllables of Euskera. And I felt a sudden chill run down my spine: the cold disagreeable shiver of Ideology.

The *presoak* in question, for the record, are Atxurra Egurrola Julen, José Luis Gallestegui Lagar and Juan Karlos Lezertua Urrutibeaskoa, currently in prison in Fresnes (France), Córdoba and Cádiz respectively. Their black-and-white pictures are stuck up in most of the bars in Lekeitio and some of the shops, together with the addresses of their prisons so that concerned fellow Lekeitiarras can help to keep their spirits up with a card or letter. Later on, at the aperitif hour, I went to a makeshift taverna set up in someone's garage or store-room especially for the *fiestas*, its walls whitewashed and pinned with hand-written menus. There they were again, the grim-faced trio, leering down from behind the bar. But the atmosphere in the place was light-hearted and friendly, and I got talking to a lady from Bilbao who had relatives in the village and had spent her summers here ever since she was a child. Her name was Itziar: Basque for 'star'. I ordered *bi sagardo* – the ciders arrived with free tapas: morsels of fried *chorizo* on pieces of bread stained blood-red with the peppery oil – and confessed to her my slight confusion. First, I wanted to know, what exactly were the crimes of the three *presoak* and why did no one ever want to talk about them?

'Well, they're all *delitos de sangre*, crimes of blood,' said Itziar, casting a furtive glance about her. 'They might have been involved in terrorist outrages, or been found in possession of explosives, or simply harboured other terrorists.' There was a note of surprise in her voice at hearing herself say the words. They were seldom uttered by anyone, it seemed, either because the facts were already all too well known or because around them hovered the force-field of a taboo.

'But I'm completely against violence. Completely against it, however noble the ideal,' I protested.

'Me too, me too,' she said energetically, 'and this is a situation that can't go on. But, you know, there's violence on both sides here. There's the violence of the State, the police violence, and that doesn't come out in the newspapers. There are doors kicked down in the night, apartments burned out, torture . . .' Noticing the camera that hung by my side, Itziar grabbed my arm and said earnestly, 'I hope you got a picture of the dance this morning? You ought to have done, so that this kind of thing gets out. What did you think of the ceremony? I found it very simple, very moving. Would you like me to get you an interview with one of the family members? Here – let's ask this lady.'

Before I could say No, she had turned to a group standing next to us at the bar. The woman held one of the gift-wrapped baskets from the ritual dance that morning, containing a couple of apples, a couple of pears and a rose. 'Products of the region,' she told Itziar firmly in Basque, gripping the gift tightly in her hand so that the cellophane crackled.

'The young people at the dance – are they related to the prisoners too?' I asked her in Spanish, and she said something in Basque to her mates at the bar, and when she answered my question it wasn't to my face and in Spanish, but to Itziar and in Basque.

'She says they are just young people from the village,' said Itziar.

'Were all those people at the dance supporters of ETA?' I said, once more to the face of the woman with the basket, who was refusing to look me in the eye. She bristled, said something crossly and turned away. It was clear she had overheard our previous conversation about violence and crimes of blood, and had taken an immediate dislike to us both: Itziar, because she'd stepped out of line by speaking, politically incorrectly, of the prisoners' 'crimes', which were crimes only in the eyes of the evil Spanish state; and me, because I was blundering about like an ignorant bull in the china-shop of Basque politics. For the traveller in Euskadi, I decided, discretion – or was it repression? – was the better part of valour.

No one knows when Lekeitio's *antzar joku*, the game of the goose, was first dreamed up, but it'd probably be safe to say a few hundred years ago. Certainly, the kind of sport where the object of the exercise is to cling on to the neck of a goose while being thrown thirty feet into the air doesn't seem like one that could realistically have been invented during the twentieth century. The earliest reference to it is in 1818, when a municipal source records that '460 *reales* and 10 *maravedis* were spent on the amusements of the geese, which took place in the town square'. At some point between then and now the venue for the game must have been moved from the square to the harbour. Until the Society for the Protection of Animals heard about it in 1975, the goose used for the *antxar joku* was actually *alive*, and the Society threatened to have the whole thing banned unless a dead one was substituted. Hardline traditionalists still complain about that decision even today, but few would deny that it's improved the *fiesta*.

How to define Goose Day? It's a sport, a spectacle, an affirmation of *euskaldunatasuna*, a powerful bonding ritual among families and groups of friends, an orgy of drinking, a collective catharsis of incredible intensity. It's also a gruesome charade that implies the slaughter and maltreatment of several dozen geese, even if they are dead by the time the maltreatment occurs. It begins in the early afternoon and goes on for hours. In some ways it's extremely boring. More than having to be seen, it has to be lived. This means wearing the gear, drinking the drinks, and trying to feel some of the things that people typically feel on Goose Day. In the morning there is a fussing and nervous rush to get things done, as mothers cook up pots of food that will serve to revive faint hearts in the early evening between the geese and the greasy pole and the Bull of Fire and the other bits of the endless *fiesta*, when everyone is drunk and ravenous. Meanwhile, everyone else assembles their costumes and mixes the drinks. Convention dictates a uniform of blue shirt and trousers in a thick blue cotton fabric called *mahón*, and a blue-and-white handkerchief round your neck. (Blue espadrilles are optional.) In the little clothes-shop, which had wisely stayed open to catch the badly organised, the lady advised me against the trousers. Cut-off jeans would do – just. But the shirt and scarf were essential. 'You must have them, or you won't enjoy the *fiesta*,' she said in a tone that brooked no argument, wrapping up my purchases in paper.

The streets were already a sea of the same deep purplish blue, intermingled with occasional waves of faded denim and white T-shirts with blue Basque slogans in the pseudo-Gothic 'Asterix' script that Basque typographers love. There were babies in mini-suits of *mahón* and dogs with blue bandannas round their necks. On street corners great plastic bottles were being filled with a dark slippery liquid – the day's supply of *kalimotxo*, an unpleasant combination of red wine and Coke that for some unknown reason (perhaps because of its associations with anarcho-rebellion and punky squalor) has recently become Basque youth's tipple of choice.

A girl and a boy came by, she with a tambourine, he with a little accordion (the *triki-trixa*; it has no keyboard, only buttons), playing a chirrupy dance music punctuated with indecipherable yelps and shrieks. Behind this human couple, as if it were the most natural thing in the world, came a couple of giants: twice-lifesize figures with heads of *papier mâché* that tottered as they sauntered. Around them ran a pack of scary smaller figures with wolves' heads; these carried inflated pigs' bladders on strings and whopped people over the head with them as they passed. And around the wolf-pack scuttled an even scarier pack of wild-eyed cackling children, terrorising old ladies with the bangers they tossed carelessly underfoot.

Down to the square, to meet the *koadrila*. The culture of

koadrilask, loosely-formed gangs of friends that have known each other for years and will continue to go out partying *en masse* until the day they die, is one of the building-blocks of Basque society, sometimes compared by sociologists to the institution of marriage in terms of the seriousness with which *koadrila* members commit emotionally to the group. This lot were friends of friends of Begoña, and happened to be mostly gay men and glamorous straight girls with an appetite for *martxa* (good times, nights on the town) such as I've never seen.

Koadrila culture is a complex thing whose functioning is not easily understood by *Kanpotarrak*. At the start of the night money is donated to a central kitty looked after by a treasurer whose job it is to get the drinks in at every bar the *koadrila* visits. The drinks are usually *zuritos*: tiny beers in flat-bottomed glasses, meant for sipping, not swilling. It's an uniquely civilised and convenient arrangement that ensures you are kept refreshed but radically slows down the onset of drunkenness. The time you spend in a given bar is the time it takes to consume a single round, after which you're off to another bar, and the fresh air and exercise only increases your enthusiasm for the next *zurito*.

The *koadrila* forms an amoeba-like blob governed by a collective brain that mysteriously decides in which direction the amoeba should move. As the blob negotiates the narrow streets, some of its constituents are inevitably lost, but others are gained, so that the amoeba's size remains stable. You are never quite sure where you are going and why, but at the end of the night you think back and realise with a shock that in the last few hours you have probably drunk in eight, ten, a dozen bars, or more. And the miracle is that you are still standing – more or less.

With so many people to order for, I needed to get my Basque numbers right, so I sat down with Begoña and got one to ten off pat. Naturally enough there were no short-cuts, and apart from *bi* (two) and *sei* (six), which sound like numbers in other languages, I was on unfamiliar ground. I wrote the first five on the fingertips of one hand – *bat, bi, hiru, lau, bost* – and the next five on the other – *sei, zazpi, zortzi, bederatzi, hamar* – and fought through the blue-clad crowd at the bar opposite the church and shouted out '*Bederatzi zurito eta sagardo bat*!' The girl set to pouring the drinks, and as I waited I caught sight of the three *presoak* again, glaring down accusingly from above the till. The one on the right had a big black hippy beard that merged imperceptibly into his big black hippy Afro hairdo. He looked like a cross between Cat Stevens and the hairier of the two males on the cover of Fleetwood Mac's 'Rumours'.

The Basques love their music, and it was everywhere on this *fiesta* day. Loud Basque rock music in the bars, and loud Basque folk music over the PA, and wandering minstrels tootling away on Basque musical instruments. What was the angry blaring I was hearing as I ferried the drinks from bar to street? The song was called '*Askatasun Egarriz*' – 'Thirst for Freedom'. Begoña took me through the first few lines until I got the gist, which didn't take long.

> *Herria jarrai hadi zutik*
> (the people are still standing)
> *Etsaia dabil etahaik*
> (the enemy is still out there)
> *Arrotza daukagu gainetik*
> (aggression is on top of us),
> etc etc etc.

We sat on the balustrade and watched the crowds. The atmosphere was one of an intense, untrammelled happiness that flowed among the crowds like honey. There were no rules any more. Shaving foam and Christmas-tree snow sprays were now being liberally applied by small children to the hair and clothes of their elders. One man had come prepared for this eventuality by rigging up a loo-paper dispenser on his back, with two rolls. *Koadrila* members wielding white chalk scribbled slogans on the backs of their colleagues: one said *Nació pá' matá'*: 'born to kill'.

A man with seventies sideburns and a long, grave face came by playing a little drum and a *txistu*, the black-and-silver vertical flute whose tootlings make the hearts of all good *euskaldunak* swell with pride. Basque literature is full of references to the *txistu*'s bitter-sweet sound, its nostalgic soulfulness born of the tree that was nurtured by the soil of the ancient Basque homeland, and so on and so forth. In pre-modern times the *txistulari* fulfilled an important social function. His presence was obligatory at baptisms, weddings, funerals; he was the messenger of war and peace. Every *koadrila* also had its pet *txistulari*, and Gorka, currently resident in Barcelona where he must feel like a tuna out of water, was one of the last upholders of the great tradition. Later in the day he'd be playing on one of the *txalupas*, the big rowing-boats in the harbour as they made their chaotic assault on the suspended goose. He gave us a burst of tootling, a lilting dance in five-eight time, and it really did sound bitter-sweet, nostalgic, soulful.

The harbourside was seething now with blue-clad people, and the water with hundreds of little boats themselves crammed with so many drunken laughing people it looked like a single lurch to the side would tumble them all in. Kids were hurling themselves off the quay in waves and the water heaved with squirming brown bodies.

Begoña and I climbed into a green-and-red rowing-boat and manoeuvred our way among the harbour jostle towards a position under the overarching rope of a fishing-boat, the *John F. Kennedy*. The little fleet was due to leave for the Straits of Gibraltar in search of tuna, but was waiting for the *fiestas* to finish before it weighed anchor. The boats were built in Lekeitio's boatyards at the mouth of the estuary. From up close you could see how exquisitely made and maintained they were, their squat thick-lipped forms newly painted the same dark *mahón* blue as my shirt, a heavy-duty turquoise, or a bright industrial green. Their colours shone proudly in the September sun.

There were sixty-seven *txalupas* in all, sixty-eight including a Russian miniature submarine that had been sliced in half and now fulfilled the function of a rowing-boat. The *koadrilas* had been busy customising their boats, and some of the more eccentric ones were decorated with New-York-subway-style graffiti or Tolkien swirls and symbols or coloured checks or nationalistic battle-cries and decked out with flags and banners. The boats made their way tipsily along the port and the *apresoroa*, the goose-grabber, stood at the end of each boat and grabbed the bird under his arm. He plunged into the water, and then the really bizarre thing happened. The goose is attached to a rope which runs along the quayside, where it's held securely by a team of hefty guys lined up like a tug-of-war team. They tug on the rope and the *apresoroa* hurtles meteorically into the air, crashes down into the water again, and the process is repeated until he has to let go, and the next *txalupa* comes sailing by. Sometimes the goose came loose from its rope: other times the neck broke in mid-ascent, and the goose-grabber ended up in the water, triumphantly clutching a purple tube of flailing veins and nerves.

It was five in the afternoon and there was madness in the air. The little boats came by one by one, each with its *koadrila* crew high on adrenalin and alcohol. Goose Day is a sort of drunken Dunkerque. At water level there was already a pungent smell of beer and salt and pee, and the spaces between the boats were filling up rapidly with a flotsam of plastic cups, empty 2-litre Coke bottles and sodden, swelling *bocadillos*. The attempts on the goose fell into three types. Either the *apresoroa* failed to grab the bird altogether and was good-naturedly booed by his *koadrila* as he floundered in the water, or he succeeded in grabbing it but failed to go more than one 'dunk', or he went more than one 'dunk'. A voice on the PA shouted '*Aurrera ya!*' – 'And they're off!' – as the boats left the start-ing line and *bat! bi! hiru! lau!* as the grabber rose and fell. But he almost never got beyond *bat*. Occasionally there was a pause as the goose-boat chugged in to replace the bird, which had fallen off or become excessively bedraggled, and this tended to prolong the proceedings. Luckily there were plenty of things to do to fill the time, like taking dips in the grimy water, cracking open cans of beer and singing along to the perky Basque pop song with the chorus that goes *Bai, bai, bai* . . .

Memory turns most Spanish *fiestas* into an Impressionist blur, but there are always highlights. One was a guy who peed pissedly from half-way down the harbour steps, slipped on the algae in mid-pee and tumbled flailing into the water. Another was the goose-grabber whose trousers fell down as he kicked wildly in mid-air. Kicking is a technique used by most modern-day *apresoroak*, who claim it gives extra 'lift', like the mid-air running movements of long-jumpers. The trousers started to fall on the first ascent, and were down at his ankles by the second. But he went on in his underpants, rising and falling *bat! bi! hiru! lau! bost! sei! zazpi! zortzi! bederatzi!* times to produce by far the best result of the afternoon.

He turned out to be Jon Elordi, a lifeguard on a nearby beach. Jon later told the TV interviewer: 'I'm the fucking boss!', which everyone was happy to agree that he was.

The night after Goose Day there were wild warlike *irrintxis* and mingled shouting in the street, and a car was firebombed a few steps away from where I slept. It left a black stinking mess of rubber and metal on the cobbles and stained nearby houses black with the smoke. The retired couple in the flat above, with its covered balcony, had to be evacuated. The car had French number-plates, but the owners weren't representatives of the evil French state, but tourists here for the *fiestas*. This was violence of the stupidest sort. It was the work of Jarrai, the ETA-sponsored gang of juvenile delinquents that is mainly responsible for the recent massive increases in street crime in Spain. Hardly a day goes by in Euskadi without some bus being burned out, a car bombed or bank window smashed. Not long ago half the parking meters in Bilbao were immobilised by somebody pouring acid into them; an innovative expression of parking rage, but hardly likely to bring about Basque independence any more quickly, one would have thought.

As a topic of conversation the day after Goose Day, the firebomb in our street was even more popular than the man whose trousers fell down. Lekeitio's mayor, Xabier Txartegi, came on the TV news to denounce the crime. Families came especially to stare at the wreckage and recite to each other a litany of disapproval. 'Apparently they cut off the electricity in the whole street before they did it. There's a box they know how to tamper with, on the wall. They were all in masks; a bunch of thugs. The whole neighbourhood's built of wood, they might have killed us all. And the couple upstairs . . . Just as well someone got them out, or they might have choked to death. Just a bunch of young thugs . . .'

On our way to the beach we dropped in at the photo-shop in town, where the photographer was hard at work sorting through his pictures of yesterday's events. Thousands upon thousands of smiling faces; but his own face wore an angry frown. 'We're going back to prehistory, I tell you seriously,' he said, putting down another shot of the trouserless lifeguard to jab at the air with an emphatic hand. 'Burn a car if you want to, but make it your own, eh?, not a couple of foreigners having a nice time at the *fiesta*. Better still, let them set fire to themselves. They could climb in the oven and I'd be glad to shut the door.'

Begoña and I spread out our towels on the sand opposite the wooded little island of Saint Nicolas, where someone had managed to get across at low tide and hang a banner among the trees. *GORA ETA*, it said. I swam slowly in the grey-blue sea, letting the warm water nurse my hangover. We lay in the afternoon sun and talked, and the conversation turned to tradition. Goose Day was a popular *fiesta* with plenty of life left in it. Could the same be said of much more of Basque culture and society?

In my bag I carried a sheaf of photocopies from Richard Ford's nineteenth-century *Handbook for Travellers*. I found the pages that describe Ford's tour of the northern Spanish provinces, read out relevant chunks and waited for the comments of my friend. It turned into a quiz-show, a game of 'True or False?'

'Commerce and fishing form the occupations of those who dwell on the seaboard, and agricultural and pastoral pursuits of those who live inland; the ores of the iron-pregnant hills are worked by both native and foreign capitalists.' *True.* It's a broad-brush view that's still lifelike after a century and a half. Pastoral pursuits are on the decline everywhere; less so in the forests and mountains of north-eastern Navarre where the rural traditions of Euskadi are deepest-rooted. As for the foreign capitalists, if you take 'foreign' to mean 'from outside Euskadi', they are still here, not only in charge of the mines in the iron-pregnant hills, but at the helm of banks, paper mills, chemical works, breweries . . . The Spanish government, conscious of the economic backwardness of Euskadi after a century of decline, gives tax-breaks to companies willing to make the move.

'The towns are Swiss-like, surrounded with green hills and enlivened by clear trout-streams . . . the *alamedas* [avenues] are always pretty; a *juego de pelota* or fives-court, a *circo gallístico* [cock-pit] and a public *plaza*, are seldom wanting.' *True*, apart from the cock-fighting, which died out in the early years of the twentieth century. (Ram-fighting, on the other hand, lives on in certain village fiestas of the interior.)

'The towers of the ancient factions between the Gamboino and the Onecino are fast disappearing.' *False*: these relics of the historic local feud that escalated practically into warfare are fast being bought up and turned into chic dwellings for beautiful people. Begoña turned over in the sand and pointed to a hilltop high above the *ria*, where a four-square medieval fort now stands amid manicured lawns.

'The elevated slopes are covered with oak and chestnut trees.' *False*: most of the ancient forests have been cut down, and the trees of the future are pine and eucalyptus.

'The Basque farms are small, many not exceeding five acres, or so much land as a man, his wife and family can labour' (*true*); 'cultivation with a sort of prong-fork or mattock called *laya* is much in vogue' (not now, but within the memory of grannies). 'Corn ripens only in favoured localities; maize is the favoured "bread-stuff".' Wheat is the favoured bread-stuff now, but corn-bread is chic 'peasant' food and therefore twice as expensive. How the whirligig of time brings in his revenges! 'Fine apples are plentiful.' *True.* No one could argue with that, least of all me, who had gorged on a glut of them in an orchard overlooking the sea.

'The Basque women wear their hair in long plaited tresses, *trenzas*, and cover their heads with a hood or *capuz*, which is more convenient than picturesque: when young they are fresh and fair, although somewhat muscular; and their beauty, from overwork, poor fare, and exposure, is short-lived, for they pass into haghood after thirty.'

After some amused discussion, Begoña and I came to the conclusion that these days haghood is more a state of mind than a physical condition, but that 'overwork, poor fare and exposure' were less likely to hasten its onset than strange no-holds-barred *fiestas*, political meetings and excessive alcohol intake. The Atlantic sun was losing its warmth, and, feeling suddenly haglike, we rolled up our towels and walked back up the beach for a coffee.

Short Stories

WORLD OF INTERIORS

Spain harbours a wide variety of housing possibilities, from mansions to holes in the ground. Few, though, can be more archaic or uncomfortable than this: a roughly circular, squat dark stone structure with a roof of straw, heather and rye grass that comes down low, and no chimney.

These are the *pallozas* of the Sierra de Ancares, on the border of Galicia and Castilla y León, a wild landscape that has finally shrugged off human efforts to scratch a living from it and reverted to wilderness. Deer, boar, pine marten, foxes, squirrels, birds of prey, have the run of the place. The *urogallo*, forest cockerel and ancestor of all farmyard fowls, is now so rare that the few wild examples of it are known by their Christian names.

The books say that in 2000 there will be less than half the *pallozas* there were in 1900, and that the last time anyone lived in one was 1992.

I met a man who used to live in one a few years before that. The house is now a stable, but he still spends much of his life in it, stacking fodder and wood and squatting in its smoky shade when it rains. He showed me round. It was certainly smoky. The fire simply had no outlet; it was thought preferable to smoke the house out rather than lose heat through a chimney. (The smoke must also have helped to preserve the all-important products of the *matanza*, hanging up near the roof on a spindled wooden frame.) It felt chillingly damp, even though the roof had recently been repaired with sheaves of fresh straw.

We stood outside for a few minutes in contemplation of an extra-ordinary house that was very much a living, breathing building even now, in the final years of the twentieth century.

'Old? Yes, it is. Yes, I did live in it for a while, because when there's nothing else, you have to live however you can.' Now there is something else, and he has made his choice. He lives in the light-and-water, smoke-free house next door.

7

Catch 'Em While You Can: Six Spanish Customs on the Verge of Extinction

1. La siesta

The *siesta*, like so many other Spanish cultural phenomena, is a product of the rural environment. Country people wake up at dawn, when the animals wake up and want feeding, and spend most of the afternoon resting. In summer the early mornings are cool and pleasant, but the afternoons are unbearably hot, so the *siesta* is really just a clever way of getting the most out of your day.

In Spanish cities the *siesta* tends to be a clever way of getting the most out of your *night*. People who were staggering out of discos and going straight to work at eight in the morning would get home at two in the afternoon, eat something and collapse for the rest of the day. By midnight they'd be ready to hit the town again.

A newspaper survey informs us that a mere 10 per cent of the population still sleep in the *siesta*. This seems like an exaggeration, but there's no doubt it's less common than it used to be. In the old days you couldn't do business over the phone after two o'clock – everyone was either devouring a three-course *comida* or sleeping it off. But as Spain becomes ever more guilt-ridden about its reputation for laziness, it is gradually giving in to peer pressure from more anally retentive societies like Germany and Britain, where nine-to-five-with-an-hour-for-lunch is the norm. And as more and more offices install air-conditioning, there is less and less excuse for the afternoon flop. It's a pity, really, because the *siesta* seems to me an exquisitely evolved and healthful habit, perfectly in tune with the realities of nature and climate.

2. *Free* tapas

The *tapa* is almost by definition, or *used* to be almost by definition, a freebie. It was a morsel of something, a mussel, an anchovy in vinegar, a chunk of *tortilla*, meant to keep the wolf from the door while you sipped your glass of wine/beer/sherry/vermouth. It was usually served on a little saucer, and the saucer placed on top of the glass – hence the name *tapa*, which means 'lid', and it came with the drink, with the compliments of the house.

Then something happened, or rather a number of things happened. *Tapas* became an institution, people realised they were getting something for nothing and could eat a free meal if they ordered enough drinks, and barmen realised it was a great way to get people out of the restaurants and into the bars. In Madrid, Seville and Bilbao in particular, the *tapa* became rather elaborate, sophisticated and expensive, a culinary art-form in itself. In other places there was no elaboration; people just started charging a few pesetas for something that had always been free.

The *tapa* on the house is hard to find these days. I had one not long ago in Ribadavia, the medieval wine town in southern Galicia. The *tapa*, a bite or two of octopus-tentacle-tips in spicy sauce, was the perfect foil to a glass of yeasty-cloudy-acid new *Ribeiro* wine – a snip at 50 pesetas the pair. And I had one in Madrid: mussels in half-shells, dressed up with a perky *pipirrana* of peppers and onion, washed down with a cold Mahou. (Mahou is the best beer in Spain, in my opinion, and one of Madrid's great contributions to human happiness. The others are the Prado, the Rastro street market and the bar near the Puerta de Toledo which serves snail *tapas* from a miniature cauldron bubbling away on the counter.) It was in Madrid, too, now I think about it, that I had a freebie recently at a Galician octopus bar round the corner from the new opera house. So perhaps this admirable practice isn't entirely dead, but it's certainly on its last legs.

3. Black tobacco

Ducados, Celtas Cortos, Ideales . . . Rough, tough, powerfully aromatic cigarettes, dripping with tar, known generically as *tabaco negro*, to set it apart from the effete and flavourless *tabaco rubio* ('blond tobacco', artificially dried where the black sort is not) of Fortuna, Camel, Marlboro and the rest.

In old Spain, everyone smoked black fags. The Ducados packet, squat and squashy with a big blue stripe round the front, was the one you saw in the top pocket of farmer and functionary, and that heady reek, like the smoke from a bonfire, was the one you smelt when they lit up, and that terrible retching sound was the one you heard as they coughed their guts out immediately thereafter. *Rubio* was for women and sissies and wallies with wads of cash (Fortuna *et al.* were and are a few pesetas more expensive).

As so often, it was the influence of American fashion that changed the *status quo*. Spanish people in cities heard that smoking was actually a rather nasty and dangerous habit, and they began to give up in their droves, and those who couldn't give up changed to less aggressively tar-laden brands. Fortuna became Spain's most popular cigarette. But this was in the late 1970s, when feminism was just beginning to chip away timidly at the edifice of machismo. Women who thought of themselves as strong, independent-spirited, more than a match for the *machos*, turned on to black tobacco – single grrrrls in their mid-thirties like my friend Marisa, who keeps a packet of Ducados by the bed and has one in her mouth before she's even opened her eyes.

The result is that most men in Spain now smoke *rubio*, and Fortuna has become a male brand, whereas very few younger men smoke Ducados, which is rapidly turning into a women's cigarette, as Fortuna was before. *Tempora mutantur et nos mutamur in illis* – and not even ciggies are safe from the nicotine-stained hand of Time.

4. Not saying please and thank-you in bars

Por favor and *gracias* are two of the first things the package tourist learns as s/he ventures cautiously out of the womblike security of the tour group. S/he uses the words as s/he would at home: freely and often. Much too freely, and much too often. I once counted the number of times 'thank-you' was used during a simple transaction in a south London newsagents'. Five times: with the passing of the newspaper and chewing-gum across the counter; with the offering of the £5 note; with the returning of the change; and two last times upon leaving the shop.

Compare that with, say, the procedure for ordering a drink in an old-fashioned Spanish bar. Having approached the bar and decided what you want, you merely announce your choice – not loudly or aggressively, unless there is a lot of noise – and the barperson brings it to you a.s.a.p. When you have drunk it, you ask how much it is, the barperson tells you, you pay for the drink and leave. No *por favor*, no *gracias*, although *buenos días* or *buenas tardes* might not go amiss at some stage of the proceedings.

When I first came to Spain I was shocked by the apparent rudeness of this, but now I see in it an elegant emotional economy: there is no point in pleading or thanking people for something as basic as a small *cerveza*, and then finding these words cheapened and thinning, like secondhand carpets, when they need to be used for weightier matters; when you really need a favour done (*por favor...*) or you're genuinely grateful to someone who's gone out of their way to help. (That's why the British have to say: 'D'you think you could possibly...?' and, 'It was so incredibly nice of you to...', because please and thank-you aren't enough any more.) This would all be fine, except that in Spanish cities there is more and more phatic, meaningless Anglo-Saxon-style communication and less and less of the old brisk emotional honesty that meant you never said a thing unless you thought it was worth saying. Before we know it, they'll be coming out with: 'Have a nice day! Missing you already!'

5. *Traditional names*

Adoración, Encarnación, Asunción, Inmaculada Concepción, Purificación, Visitación, Presentación – there is a girl's name in Spanish for almost every phase and facet of the Virgin Mary's life. There are women out there who owe it to their devout parents that they are addressed as Pains (Dolores), Anguish (Angustias), Remedies (Remedios), Kings (Reyes), Snows (Nieves), Shelter (Amparo), Sweet Name (Dulce Nombre) and any number of traditional names associated with Our Lady and Her surpassing qualities. In some cases, local legends of the Virgin's apparition on the road, on a plain, on top of a pillar, at sea and so on produced names of their own, hence Camino, Llanos, Pilar, Mar; not to mention others that are basically place-names of sacred Catholic sites: Covadonga, Montserrat, Fátima, Leyre, Begoña, Guadalupe, Lourdes and Almudena. (Almudena is one of the famous Virgins of Madrid, the other being Atocha. But since Atocha is also a main line railway station, even devout Madrileño parents seemed to have steered clear of the name. It would be like calling your daughter Waterloo.)

Traditional boys' names were never so interesting, despite the clutch of superbly sonorous Latinate or Visigothic ones – Fulgencio, Virgilio, Hilario, Cayetano, Bonifacio, Saturnino, Valeriano, Hermenegildo, Gumersindo, Norberto – which were never very popular and now appear to have disappeared.

It is a fact that before 1977 in Spain the only names that could be given to children were Spanish ones. As late as 1989, Spanish *Gastarbeiter* returning home with babies they had joyfully christened

Gerhard or Elisabeth found them re-baptised Gerardo and Isabel by bureaucrats on official papers. In 1990 the law was repealed, and suddenly there was an explosion of imaginative new names. Hippies could now call their offspring Amor, Paz or Armon'ia with impunity. Film-fans were free to go ahead with Kevin, Harrison and Melanie (after la Griffith, popular wife of la Banderas). Anything went, apart from Cain, 'derogatory' names like Tadpole and Shit, numbers, and boys'-names-for-girls or *vice versa*.

Fashions have come and gone, and now the most popular Spanish names are safe, simple, anodine, international things like María, Laura and Cristina; and for boys, Daniel, David and Alejandro. (In Catalunya the Virgin of Montserrat, powerful patroness of Catalan identity and wealth-creation, still holds some attraction for parents, as does Jordi, her saintly male equivalent. Otherwise the story is the same; the names to conjure with now are straight-down-the-line Joan, Jaume, Josep, Anna, Rosa and María.) Like so much in Spain, something rich and strange has suffered a sea-change, into something plain and ordinary. The old names had resonance, poetry, a sense of history and conviction. It seems a shame. But perhaps a kid called Inmaculada Concepción gets a hard time in the playground.

6. The squat loo

Whatever happened to this historic sanitary device, upon which you squatted with both feet on ceramic bases that always reminded me of a rocket-launcher? The most likely answer is that it is going, gently but irretrievably, down the pan. Time was when you expected to find 'holes in the floor' in every bar, café and railway station, apart from the very grandest examples of each. In the summer of 1983, when I was Interrailing around Spain, I don't think I saw a toilet seat in a month and a half of travelling. Now it might be the other way round: the 'pedestal' is all the rage, and the 'launch-pad' is on the way out, apparently regarded by modern-minded Spaniards as a disgraceful archaism.

Many people might see this as an example of positive progress: the launch-pads often either failed to flush at all or flushed over-enthusiastically, creating a horrid tide that washed around your feet and crept towards the cubicle door. The new kind sometimes do that too, and they can get just as stomach-churningly filthy as the old. But the good thing about the old kind was that you never actually had to make physical contact with any part of it. With the new kind, of course, you are touching where thousands have touched before.

Anyway, I miss the launch-pad. It was amusing, unsettling and deeply foreign. It was an Experience.

Short Stories

COME BACK TO THE VILLAGE, JUANITO IGLESIAS

It was the night of the *fiesta* when the boy ran away. In the village of San Juan de los Chopos (pop: 235), among the peaks of the Sierra Cualquiera, the annual celebration of the Night of Saint John is a moderately wild affair, given the size of the place, with only a modest complement of bonfires and drunkenness and firecrackers tossed in the road. A few of the older villagers can remember when spells were cast to keep the demons of the night at bay. More than one old woman still hobbles around the edges of the fields collecting flowering thyme, in the vague belief, in the face of modern reason and ridicule, that the thyme flower picked at Saint John has a special efficacy against colds and flu.

Juan Iglesias was last seen walking unsteadily out of the village towards the *barranco*, the dried-up bed of the stream with its grove of mangy poplars, swigging Spanish whisky from a bottle. According to a couple of old ladies who sat on a bench in the square, pulling their cardigans about them as they clucked at each other about grandchildren and husbands, it seemed that Juanito had simply wandered off to relieve himself. But he was never seen again in San Juan de los Chopos.

Ten years later, after a thorough search of the surrounding villages of the Sierra Cualquiera had come to nothing, Juanito's mother Dolores decided to get in touch with *¿Quién Sabe Dónde?* (Who Knows Where?), a TV programme that specialises in reuniting lost loved ones with their families. Probably the most-watched of all Spanish television programmes, *¿Quién Sabe Dónde?* is presented by the genially diplomatic and honey-voiced Paco Lobatón ('. . . and I mean that from the bottom of my heart'). For three hours every Monday night the programme serves up a lipsmacking menu of tragedy (decades of wondering and loneliness) and joy (when those decades finally come to an end). Incidentally, as it were as a backcloth to all the human drama, it also reveals a secret society with its own intimate history, parallel but incommensurate with the history of cities, States and continents.

So now we see this heavy-faced, thick-fingered country woman, Dolores García, sitting uncomfortably in the studio, and hear her talking quaveringly in her dense country accent.

'Juanito, if you're watching this, it's your mamá,' she sobs. 'Come back to the village, please come home, or at least give us a call and tell us where you are. It's been ten years now and we've heard nothing from you. Your auntie has cancer. Your grandmother is very sad, she wants to see you before she dies. Your little sister Lolita is married in Barcelona. If you've got into trouble or something, we won't bother you, we won't say a thing. But we miss you. We want you back. Why did you go, Juanito? Why haven't you been in touch with your mamá, who loves you so much?'

A film is shown of the village, to forlorn-sounding chamber music. It is a small, off-white place of flat buildings that seem to be digging themselves gradually into the ground, perhaps as a refuge from the summer heat. We see the village on one of the 364 days of the year when there's no *fiesta*. The two or three streets are empty apart from an old woman in an apron sitting on a low chair in a doorway, glaring at the world.

The Juanito item finishes and Paco moves on to another story, about a woman who was separated from her twin sister during the chaos of the Civil War, and is going on air to launch a final appeal for clues. The programme is nearly over when the telephone rings in the studio.

'What is your name, and in relation to which case are you calling?' asks Paco.

'My name is Juan Iglesias García, and I wish to speak to my mother,' replies a dark voice. Whereupon Dolores, who is sitting in the studio in her Sunday best, crumbles on to the shoulder of her sister beside her.

Falteringly she grabs the microphone: 'Juanito, I can't believe it, after all these years! Where are you, my son? What happiness to hear your voice!'

But Juanito's response is not what she expected. 'Mother, all I want to say is that I'm never coming back, so don't make me try. I left San Juan because I was fed up — with the village, with the family, with everything. There's no future for me there. I'll never come back. You ask me why I never called you. Because I knew you'd try to find me, and I knew I'd feel bad. Because I never wanted to have anything to do with that place again. I'm sorry, mamá, but that's the way it is. Here in the city I'm fine, I've got a job, I've got a girlfriend. We may be married next year.'

Thinking back to the film, the village, you could understand why he left. The shuttered tedium of weekends, the feeble amenities (one bar, a single bus a week to town), the rule of the elderly. As he talks, his mother crosses herself and gasps into her hands. There's something in the air, seeping like ectoplasm from the TV. A feeling in the air you can almost taste, a darkness and bitterness, like the taste of an olive from a poor harvest.

8

2010: A Fleece Odyssey

'*El pastor hizo grande a Castilla*
Castilla hizo grande a España
Y España hizo grande al mundo.'

'The shepherd made Castile great,
Castile made Spain great,
And Spain made the world great'

(*Spanish proverb*)

Modern life doesn't have much time for things that take much time. It likes things that are instant, disposable and require no effort. Most aspects of traditional life, however, are rather time consuming, arduous and long lasting. So it hardly comes as a surprise to find them being killed off with incredible speed. If there were a term, something like 'genocide', to describe the wholesale destruction of rural culture, this could be the moment to apply it.

When summer comes to the south of Spain, the grass dries up and sheep-farmers and their flocks move north in search of pastures new. In winter it gets too cold up north and there is pasture in the south, so they make the return journey. There are two ways of doing this. The contemporary solution is to hire a train or a fleet of lorries and ferry your sheep to their destination in a day or two.

The old way of doing it, known as the *trashumancia*, took, and takes, twenty-five times as long and hundreds of times as much effort. You and the livestock set off on foot, remembering to take food, water and anti-wolf protection gear, and you tramped over moor and mountain until you reached your goal. It is, to put it mildly, a considerably more troublesome procedure. But the one thing modern life loathes more than anything is trouble. And that may be the main reason why the *trashumancia*, one of Europe's longest-lived and loveliest traditions, is dying on its cloven feet.

The past is getting harder to find: the present is crowding it out. In mid-June I flew to Madrid carrying a backpack and an old cotton umbrella, once black, now purplish-black after half a century of Mediterranean sun. I sat in a café in the FNAC bookshop in the Plaza de Callao and skimmed through a book about the Mesta, the sheep-farming brotherhood that dominated Spanish country life for five centuries. For most of those centuries wool was the country's most important industry, thanks to the merino sheep whose delicate fleece made a fabric that was the envy of Europe. In the first half of the sixteenth century, at the height of the Mesta's power, there were three million sheep making the *trashumancia* every year on special livestock roads called *cañadas reales* – '*cañada*' from the cane bushes that often grew in the gulleys they followed, and '*real*' because these routes enjoyed the protection of the Crown.

'Sheep no longer follow the ancient *cañadas*, which have mostly disappeared', wrote the historian Julius Klein in 1910. 'In their place there exist special small railway carriages, with a capacity of 100 head of livestock each. These carriages ply the railway lines during the traditional bi-annual epoch of the *trashumancia*, and in many cases follow the same routes as the *cañadas*.' He was trying to make it sound all up-to-date and efficient, but to me it was a worrying thought – all those sheep crammed wearily on to trains, packed in shoulder to shoulder like British Rail commuters.

I remembered reading in the papers about an organisation that was trying to revive the custom of the *trashumancia* and had actually taken an enormous flock of sheep down the Calle Alcalá in central Madrid, which turned out to be a *cañada real* unused for centuries. Extraordinary photos had appeared in the press, showing the little *arc de triomphe* of the Puerta de Alcalá marooned in the great woolly sea that swept and billowed around it. In the background stood office workers on their way to work, little old ladies who had just popped out to buy a loaf of bread and kids who had probably never seen a sheep before, all of them in a visible state of amazement.

The Fondo Patrimonio Natural Europeo are the organisers of this and other escapades with livestock across the length and breadth of the peninsula. The Fondo has good reasons for thinking the *trashumancia* a tradition that ought to be revived. One is the welfare of the animals. Another is the disappearance of a perfectly ecologically correct and benign form of extensive agriculture. And a third is the state of the *cañadas*, which, if you add them altogether, make up 420,000 hectares of virgin land. But of course they're now being built on, cultivated, turned into rubbish dumps and generally maltreated. So the Fondo is busily spending European Union money to make sure the *trashumancia* lives on.

I finished my coffee and went to see them at their headquarters, a poky top-floor flat full of earnest green people thinking green thoughts. A jolly girl called Maribela plied me with leaflets and told me there was a *trashumancia* in progress, an authentic one lasting six weeks. It had set off from a farm outside Cáceres a week earlier and would end up in due course in another farm outside León, more then 600 miles further north.

While she munched on a large salad I sat in her office and wondered about sheep, farming as big business, and whether Conservation wasn't just a matter of city people forcing country people to comply with their own fantasies of rural life. But Maribela at least, like a lot of urban Spaniards, had her country roots pretty near the surface. 'I know I'm trapped here in Madrid, but I used to spend the winter here and the summer in a tiny village north of Palencia, a place that has no roads. My father's from there. I've got

my own bees in the village, you know, making heather honey for
me,' she said proudly. 'So, you see, I'm not such a town mouse as
you think.'

Maribela knew all about the rigours of walking the *cañadas*. If I
wanted to join the *trashumancia*, she said, I'd have to take a sleeping
bag, a tent, a torch, a water-bottle, sun cream, and plenty of *chorizo,
salchichón*, dried fruit and nuts and other dry food that wouldn't go
off. The nights in the *sierras* of Castile could be cold, even in June;
there could be rain; that umbrella might come in very useful. On
the other hand the days could be scorching hot. That umbrella
might come in useful as a parasol.

If I set off the next day I could meet up with the flock in
Montemayor del Río, a hamlet in the far south of Castile outside the
old wool town of Béjar. The only disadvantage was that on that very
day the Spanish Minister of the Environment, a big-haired right-
wing woman who had trained as a nuclear engineer (true), was due
to descend on the *trashumancia* along with her accompanying media
circus. 'She obviously has no fucking idea what she's talking about,'
said Maribela. 'She'll probably turn up in a new suit with her hair
permed, or something.'

It would doubtless be a fantastic photo-op for Señora Tocino
(which translates roughly as Mrs Bacon) and her newly-created and
somewhat improbable ministry. What could be more calculated to
dispel any doubts we might have about her sensitivity towards
Nature, towards Tradition, towards the social and financial crises of
agricultural Spain than a cute shot of Minister with Sheep in a
Landscape?

The sad thing, we agreed, was that the issue of the dying *trashumancia* and the decay of its historic pathways might have to take
second place to Mrs Bacon's political posturing. There are 125,000
kilometres of *cañada real* in Spanish territory – more than the whole
railway network put together – but for most of that distance the
cañada is hardly recognisable as anything but scrubland, forest,
marsh, dusty backroad. Until not long ago the *cañadas* were smooth

green runways, walled in on either side and gently curved so that sheep could surge down them at high speed. The Mesta, which controlled its own sophisticated bureaucracy, employed a special rank of officer to make sure that nothing and nobody interfered with this perfect pasture – on pain of death. Since the demise of the Mesta in 1834 there's been a lot of interfering. Farmers with arable land on either side of the path have gradually nibbled away at the *cañada* until their crops practically meet in the middle. Houses, sheds and factories have edged their way on to it. Where it passes through a town, it's often been found the handiest place for the municipal rubbish-tip.

Next morning I hitched a lift with two Green men from Maribela's office, and we arrived in Montemayor just as the minister's limo was pulling into the village square. A folk group played a raucous *jota*, the curious one-step-forward two-steps-back dance of Castile, and a crowd of local well-wishers pushed forward to greet the big-haired one with bunches of flowers. 'I keep *telling* him to get a video-camera. This is the sort of thing we need it for,' said a woman in a flowery apron to her friend.

I found the *trashumancia* on a hillside above the town, against the backdrop of a mountain range that glistened with the year's last snow. I couldn't see the flock yet, but I knew it was there from the policemen roaring around on bikes and TV crews setting up their cameras and processions of villagers in straw hats twittering excitedly. 'I used to be a *trashumante*. A lot of us around here did, you know. But it's been forty years since I left the shepherding profession,' said a small stubby gentleman from the nearby village of La Aldea. 'Of course there used to be *trashumancias* coming through here all the time, down the Real Cañada de la Plata, that's the one that comes down all the way from León to Cáceres and goes through Montemayor. They came in from Avila too. That was something really beautiful; world without end, amen.' The man shook his head in the way that can only mean 'the world is not what it was'.

The sheep were making their way across the plain, accompanied by two dozen goats, four shepherds, eight dogs and the Minister of the Environment. You could hear the tinkling bells in the distance, a gently persistent tide of sound that lapped ever closer, mingling with the mobile phones of the hacks from Madrid. A policeman barked into his walkie-talkie, 'Don't let the journalists through, they'll break up the flock!', but the hacks were already sprinting across the plain. The sheep approached slowly, heads down, quietly chomping, a stone-coloured mass, while the media danced around them on their photo-op, an unruly herd compared to the much-better-mannered sheep.

The dancers from the village had made it up here too, in their party outfits of lace and leather. Among them was a tall guy with a bandanna round his head and skin-tight black trousers, clanking with medallions, buckles and bells. He was playing a skin drum painted with an image of the Virgin garlanded with ivy leaves, and a bamboo flute; twittering and banging away like the star of the show, which he assuredly was. He strutted through the knee-high under-growth at the edge of the wood, brushing past clumps of lavender that filled the air with sweetness. 'Look at the countryside,' I heard him say. 'It's for making babies in. Tell all the couples to get up here and get to work!'

Meanwhile, the minister sat on the grass and spouted platitudes. 'We need to preserve this land, this culture and these traditions, and in whatever we have to invest we will invest,' she said. Then she danced a few steps with the folk group, picked with carefully concealed but none the less evident disgust at a greasy lamb stew specially prepared for the occasion, climbed back into the ministerial limo and left in a cloud of dust.

The shepherds had made a little encampment next to an oak wood and were chortling into their coffee over the absurdity of it all. It was a broiling afternoon, and I sat in the shade with a family from Béjar, who offered me marzipan pastries, coffee, and a glass of cold, sweet water from a spring at the base of the still snow-capped Sierra de Candelario that loomed in front of us. Antonio, the elderly father, seemed well versed in ovine ways. 'See how they're on their feet, squashed together so tightly in the heat? That's to make a cool breeze pass under their bellies. Funny thing about sheep, they're not quite as silly as they look.'

The early rise, the journey from Madrid and the temperature were taking their toll, so I lay down under an oak tree within sight of the shepherds. Now that the sheep were at rest, their bells made a minimal tinkling. It was highly relaxing on the ear after the squawking journalists, and in a few minutes I was asleep. When I woke up, my family had gone, the forest was empty and the tinkling had mysteriously increased in volume and urgency. The shepherds were nowhere to be seen. I jumped to my feet, grabbing my black umbrella, stricken suddenly with nerves. The flock was on the move. On the little plain outside the wood the sheep were spilling all over the place. I ran to the edge of the flock and set to rounding up the stragglers in cowboy style, grabbing a stick from the hedgerow and waving it behind them while simultaneously making what I imagined were appropriate whooping noises. But where was the *cañada*? Amid the baaing and clanking, at the other side of the bobbing ocean of sheep someone in a hat was doing a frantic sem-aphore in my direction. His arm moved up and down, from vertical to horizontal. Clearly he meant 'straight ahead'. I moved off at a cracking pace and a breakaway group of sheep scampered ahead of me.

But I had got it all wrong. When eventually I met up with the head shepherd Victor Muñoz, a dark-skinned angry-looking man wearing a panama hat and mirror shades, he gave me the biggest telling-off I'd had since schooldays, punctuated by some highly educational Spanish.

'What the cunt d'you think you're doing?' (I translate literally.) 'When I tell you to come here, you come here, I shit on God.' (Again, I translate literally.) 'D'you understand me? You don't just wander off wherever you please, d'you understand? I shit in the sea.' (From now on, please assume my translations are literal unless otherwise informed.) 'If you want to follow this thing you stay at the back, you don't go round the side frightening the sheep. I shit on the mother who gave birth to you.'

'I'm sorry, I didn't know . . . But I thought the *cañada* was that way.'

'Well, it's not that way, I shit in the sea. It's the other way, round this wall here.'

He suddenly seemed to see me for the first time through his shades, and said, 'Who the devil are you anyway?' The sheep were not to be hassled or scared, I shit in the milk, but gently pressurised. 'And what the cunt are you doing with this shit of a stick? You need a decent stick. Take this.'

Victor Muñoz shoved into my hand a slender rod of hazel wood, strong and light and perfectly straight and balanced, for beating through undergrowth and coaxing the animals and for support when the going got tough. 'Now let's get these sheep of shit out of here, shall we? We've got a job to do. Just watch what I do and see if you can learn something.'

Until I recovered from the sting of Victor's tongue, I followed meekly in his footsteps. I became sheep number 2011. I began to see that he was right, that the path to ovine expertise was a *via negativa*, a kind of pastoral Zen in which all you had to do was watch, and wait, for enlightenment to appear.

You'd expect 2010 sheep to give off the sharp stink of wet wool, sheep-grease and sheep-shit. Even up close, this lot had almost no smell at all, unless you counted a sweet unpindownable aroma that was somewhere between fresh grass cuttings and the fur of a sleeping cat. ('Don't they smell sweet?' I said cautiously to Victor, who managed a grim little smile, and grunted: 'If they smell good, they'll taste even better.')

The animals were clean and neat and healthy-looking. They had long necks, compact bodies and tails that formed a neat little flap. They had been sheared at their winter quarters in Talaván, outside Cáceres, but the wool had grown a little since then, so that they now wore a thin little downy wrapping, like Mayfair ladies in their twinsets. You could tell by their markings and the discrepancy in their tail lengths that they belonged to two separate flocks, one belonging to the Fondo Patrimonio Natural Europeo in Madrid and the other to a rich Castilian businessman with his fingers in various agricultural pies. The businessman's sheep were a cross between Entrefina and Lancha, with long tails and a number, 1, 2 or 3, branded on their backs. The others were Merinas, the classic breed of the Mesta, brought from Algeria to Spain by the Beni-Merin tribe in the twelfth century. These bore the mark of an eight-pronged star: once the sign of the sinister and powerful Mesta, and now of the good-hearted FPNE.

Looking at these timid beasts with their big eyes and delicate faces, it was hard to believe that for centuries they, or their distant ancestors, were the cornerstone of Spain's economic greatness. Merino wool was so light and fine, such an improvement on the lank, dark, heavy wool of the Romans and Visigoths, that within a century or two after its introduction it was a sought-after commodity all over Europe. Spain was 'famous . . . for its fine cloth long before the English knew what it was to be properly dressed,' wrote Adam Smith. In 1313 the Spanish Parliament made it illegal to export live sheep beyond the Spanish border, thus safeguarding the lucrative monopoly on merino wool. The monasteries of El Escorial and Guadalupe each had its own flock. Velázquez even chose a merino lamb, trussed up on a table, to symbolise Christ in his still-life 'Agnus Dei'. In those days, the sheep commonly went unshorn, because that way the wool got dirty and sweaty and heavy and was therefore worth more when it was removed from them at special shearing-houses in the north called *esquileos*. This is now regarded as barbaric, since the fully-clothed sheep suffered terribly in the heat and effort of the journey, and then, being sensitive creatures, caught chills and fevers when they were suddenly left to go naked in the cold mountain air. This flock, my flock, had been shorn some time before leaving their winter pastures. By now they

had grown a comfortable travelling coat, suitable for almost anything the Spanish climate might throw at them.

The *trashumancia*, as much an economic necessity, an age-old
custom, a visual spectacle and all the other things it is, is a universe
of sound. Perhaps half the sheep wore bells, and each had a slightly
different tone and pitch. From a distance the noise was like cool
running water, a complicated rippling. (The French composer
Olivier Messiaen used to go on treks in tropical rainforests, noting
down streams and waterfalls in musical form.) Close up, when the
sheep were jostling all around you, the noise was less unified; certain
bells were louder than others, because they were closer to the ear,
and these produced weird jazzy melodies that stood out against the
background of multitudinous clanking and tinkling. At night, or in
the depths of the afternoon *siesta*, the music became avant-garde,
minimalist, Japanese. Once or twice I fell asleep at night thinking of
an enormous windchime. But the bells, the bells; they could never
be completely silent. They were with me day and night, filling my
head with echoes.

Whenever the flock set off again after a rest, the routine was the
same. Among the 2010 sheep were a dozen *mansos*, castrated merino
rams with curling horns, deep booming bells around their necks
and the star-shaped mark of the Mesta on their foreheads. In the
trashumancia these males lead the flock, tempted by goodies fed
them by the shepherds, and the ewes follow them, well, sheepishly.
Victor would start off down the *cañada* with a leather bag full of biscuits, whistling a sonorous, swooping whistle of encouragement.
The rams followed him greedily, like a bunch of old queens after the
Milk Tray. And, quietly and without fuss, though after a moment or
two's dithering, the rest of the flock gradually fell into line.

From now on, the dogs came into their own. Picking themselves
up from the cool holes in the earth where they'd lain quaking in the
heat, they yawned, stretched and got to work. There were two breeds,

four or five of each. There was a scruffy whiskery energetic type, the *carea*, used by Spanish shepherds to control the flock. (The world I heard was *definir*, which to me perfectly describes the way the shepherd gives shape and motion to what would otherwise be a formless, directionless mass.) And there were huge burly heavy-furred mastiffs, sluggish, slavering brutes that contributed little to the team, or so I thought until I noticed their enormous iron collars bristling with spikes that looked like something out of some medieval torture chamber.

The mastiffs grow up with the flock and come to think of the sheep as their own property. While the *trashumancia* is still in the lowlands they slope along amiably enough, but as soon as it reaches the mountains they undergo a complete personality-change. In the forests of the north there is a real danger of attacks by wolves. The mastiffs smell them on the mountain air. Armed with their medieval collars, they turn into ferocious and fearless defenders of the flock. They have even been known to make pre-emptive strikes on the wolves in their forest lairs. Their presence is vital: on the one occasion a *trashumancia* made the journey without these splendid dogs, in 1995, more than thirty sheep were lost to wolf-attacks.

And so the party moved majestically down its royal road. The pace was slower than I'd expected, and the shepherds spent much of their time sitting under trees chatting while the flock trickled by along the *cañada*. The better the pasture, the slower the progress, said Victor. Last winter it had rained in Spain, not only on the plain but in the *sierras* as well, and in a quantity that no one could quite believe. Everywhere you looked there was lush grass, deep green foliage speckled with the lighter green of new growth, and water running down the hillsides in streams, bubbling out of the rock and seeping up in marshy pools.

The dynamics of the flock were endlessly fascinating. I began to see how, under the hands of Victor and his colleagues José Manuel, Antonio and Indarecio, it behaved more like a pool of thick sticky liquid than a series of solids; pouring through narrow gulleys, leaving great gobs stuck to walls which would then be peeled off by the sheep-dogs and stirred back into the mix; surrounding immovable objects in a relentless tide of wool. The shepherds had a special way of sending the dogs among the sheep, sometimes in pursuit of a stick or a stone, and splitting off a clump of sheep from the flock as if by force. It looked entirely counterproductive – wouldn't the clump be left behind for good? – until you realised that what was involved was a kind of kneading motion, giving energy to the mass as you would to a lump of dough. The sheep folded back in, oxygenated and gathering speed. Sometimes we would cross a road, and motorists, marooned in the flock and gradually realising this could be a long wait, would turn off their engines, wind down their windows and abandon all hope of arriving on time.

With us on the *trashumancia* were twenty-five goats: bearded billies with fierce faces like the devil in 1970s horror films, and smaller cuter females with soft brown coats and mischievous eyes. For the first time in my life I fully understood the meaning of the phrase 'to separate the sheep from the goats'. While the sheep meekly toed the line, never straying from the conventional greenery of the *cañada*, the goats had more guts and took more risks, leaping up on the teetering stone walls on either side to chomp the tender shoots of vines and fruit trees. There was a political analogy in there somewhere. The sheep were like old-fashioned Communists, happy to suppress all individual action in the name of the group; the goats were anarchists, rampantly individualistic, independent and unpredictable.

The first day's journey was an easy stroll along the ridge of a hill that stared straight up into the face of the Sierra de Candelario. The *cañada* was in reasonable shape, except where it had been slashed nearly in half by an ugly fence of orange-painted iron uprights and barbed wire.

'What's this fence doing here?' I asked Victor.

He gave one of the iron poles a whack with his stick. 'Because some son of a prostitute wants this land for himself, that's why, I shit on God!'

In fact the land might have been annexed by the son-of-a-prostitute's father, or his grandfather, at a time when it seemed a shame to waste this perfect, unused fallow land. But that doesn't mean it wasn't illegal. Further on, the path was closed off by a set of double gates. Also illegal. Both the fence and the gate would be noted down and the Fondo would be notified. It now boasts a legal service aimed at stamping out appropriation, contamination and other abuses of this land, which is public land and in theory belongs to everyone, whatever their connection with livestock. Later on, there were several sets of double gates across the *cañada*. Illegal, too. Victor Muñoz cursed and swore in Technicolor.

A man from the local government environment department turned up in a Renault van and, hands on hips, fired the usual questions at the shepherds as he stared in wonder at the immense flock. How many, how long, how goes it? He was a trim, tall elderly chap in a safari shirt with the crisp, no-nonsense air of the retired soldier. On the subject of these illegalities he had strong opinions: 'You've got to sort them out. You've got to be like Hitler. You know someone's been building a *chalet* a couple of kilometres further up?' A *chalet* is a modern Spanish detached house, and the definition of bourgeois self-improvement. 'You've got to say to these people, I don't care if it was your father or your grandfather or the twelve tribes of Israel that took this land, we're taking it back. Let there be absolutely no doubt about that.'

So you restore the lost chunks of land, I put it to the government man, and the *cañada* looks as pretty and pristine as it did in the seventeenth century, but what do you do with the space if there's no more *trashumancia*?

'You open it up for public use. The *cañada* could be a public space where anyone could bring their sheep or cows and not be in anyone's way. Or, maybe' – a felicitous image had just flashed across his mind – 'people could come with their wife and kids on a Sunday afternoon, set up the barbecue, have some lunch, a glass or two of wine . . . It could be like a public park, a nature reserve and a picnic site all in one. But first we've got to get rid of these fences and these *chalets*. We've got to find these bastards, and when we catch them, I tell you, we'll be like Hitler!'

We stopped for the night on a wide grassy esplanade where the sheep could be parked and there were flat spaces for pitching tents. The support vehicle, a glittering Japanese four-wheel-drive bought by the Fondo Patrimonio with German money – in the old days it would have been a mule or two – had got there before us and twenty-year-old Antonio Mendoza was already busy peeling potatoes.

I was dreading the meals, the social stuff. The daily routine of tramping and working the sheep was one thing, but the business of bonding with the shepherds was quite another. They were tough-as-nails country people, uncomfortable with clever talk and city nonsense. At first they were suspicious, chilly, or openly aggressive. They took the piss out of my black umbrella: 'What a fairy! Get yourself a proper hat, fairy!' This succeeded in offending me, mainly because the umbrella was a genuine old countryman's umbrella, not some frivolous urban fashion-statement, as they seemed to think.

The first of the four to thaw out was Antonio, the *trashumancia*'s driver, map-reader and cook. As I helped to unfold folding chairs that first evening, he told me a little about himself: born, bred and still living in the tongue-twisting village of Navacepadilla de Corneja, near Avila, Antonio is the nephew of one of Spain's most distinguished shepherds, Don Cesareo Rey, who led the Fondo's first *trashumancia* in 1993 and brought young Antonio along for the ride. 'But I don't really know anything about sheep. At home I keep cows, *soy vaquero*,' he said. *Vaquero* means 'cow farmer', but also 'cowboy'. I made a brief mental video of this thin, somewhat shy young man from a Castilian village on horseback, thundering over the dusty plains of Texas.

He had made a juicy *tortilla* and a packet soup with extra hard-boiled egg and chunks of *chorizo*. 'Where did you learn to cook like this, Antonio? In your military service?' said Victor as he washed the sheep-snot off his hands with the aid of a plastic water-bottle held between his knees.

The shepherds snapped open their pocket knives and began hacking off hunks of raw bacon and *chorizo* which they ate with oily-fingered relish, washing down the food with squirts of wine from a leather bottle. The talk was *Blazing Saddles* campfire talk, punctuated with swearing, burping, farting and other sounds which, though prohibited in the company of women, are apparently essential in the company of men.

Machismo is a peculiar creature. By night and at certain times of day it might be livid and swollen, but shine a bright light at it, and it cowers and shrivels into nothing. Earlier that afternoon we'd seen three women bathing by a stream. One was dressed in bra and panties, and was stretching cat-like into the sun, looking like some 1950s cover-girl. As the flock passed them, the shepherds went into a frenzy of wolf-whistles, growls and baroque sexism: 'Gor, get a look at that! I'd fuck her right now, I feel that horny. I shit on God, what a great-looking bit of skirt, look at the tits on her, she looks like she'd be a horny bitch in the sack . . .' But now we were talking as we scoffed *tortilla* and drank wine from a leather bottle, and I felt a bit drunk and so I asked them straight out: 'So come on, then, what about women? You don't mean to tell me you go six weeks without a single . . . you know . . . ? Where are the women on the *trashumancia*?'

There was an awkward silence. I wondered whether I'd overstepped the mark. Then there was some nervous tittering and somebody said, 'But we've got 2010 women with us all the time. That's 500 each, and ten left over for you!' Everybody laughed, and the embarrassment was over.

I wasn't surprised to discover that, of the four shepherds, all except Victor were unmarried and unattached. Part of the social crisis afflicting country life in Spain is that there aren't enough women to go round. Young men are logically drawn into farming, as the only real career-option. But rural society isn't ready to accept female shepherds and female tractor-drivers, and a farmer's wife is seen as a glorified housewife. So the daughters leave home and become secretaries or find a place at university in the nearest town; then they marry some city-slicker who promises to whisk them away from the boredom and misery of village life. And their brothers are left to ogle girls in bikinis and make jokes about their Casanova-like prowess with sheep.

Each of them had arrived at the *trashumancia* by a different route. Victor Muñoz, Mr Mirror Shades, was a professional carpenter who'd been laid off and on the dole. But he'd known about livestock ever since he was a child, and the time was ripe for a change of career. At the time the Fondo Patrimonio Natural Europeo was just building up its flock of Merinas in the next village, and it needed an experienced shepherd. Victor was recommended by the mayor of his own village, a person who was used to having his recommendations taken seriously. He was hired there and then.

Indarecio Riba was the full-time hired hand of the rich man from Salamanca whose long-tailed Entrelancha sheep were under our charge. Inda was OK: he was a big, sturdy guy who might not know very much about some things, but he was unbeatable when it came to livestock. He'd grown up with cows, goats and sheep in his village north of Salamanca, though for him the three were hardly on an equal footing. 'I've never liked cows,' he said decidedly, mouth full of bread and raw bacon. 'My favourite are goats. They're more *bad*. They climb walls and trees. Sheep are more innocent, more quiet, they don't get about so much.'

Then there was Antonio, from Navacepadilla de Corneja. And shepherd number four was a small ferociously energetic person called José Manuel Galán. José Manuel came from Robleda, a few kilometres from the Portuguese border. He had been working part-time in the Sierra de la Peña de Francia, clearing tracts of woodland against forest fires, when he saw an ad in the local paper for a temporary shepherd. 'I'd still be up in that forest if I wasn't down here, I shit in the milk.'

At the end of the road the four of them would receive 150,000 pesetas each, around £750, for their six weeks' hard labour on the *trashumancia*. Expenses like food and drink were all paid for. It seemed to me an incredibly bad deal, bearing in mind the discomfort, the responsibility and the huge amount of physical effort involved. It was a far cry from the days of the Mesta, when to be a shepherd was a fine career and shepherds in general were one of the most favoured classes of Castilian society. As a shepherd under the aegis of the Mesta, your privileges were many and various. You couldn't be thrown into jail for debt. You were automatically given a licence to bear arms, as protection against 'wolves, gypsies and marauders'. Occasionally villages would organise wild parties called *momarraches* or *mojaraches*, in which drunken people dressed in masks and bird costumes would spill out down the *cañadas* and torment the shepherds and their charges. It sounds unlikely, but the Mesta took the threat sufficiently seriously to provide the shepherds with special bodyguards when *momarraches* were in the air.

The perks didn't stop there. In the sixteenth century, Mesta shepherds had extraordinary rights over the pasture on either side of the *cañada*; they could take their sheep into the field of their choice and spend as long there as they wished, in return for a nominal rent. Where the *cañada* passed through woodland, they were encouraged to cut down the youngest, tenderest shoots of trees for animal feed and burn the rest to create new pastures. They did this so efficiently that within a few years Castile was suffering the terrible ecological after-effects of deforestation: erosion, desertification. There was also no more wood. It was a bad business because, at that time, the Spanish desperately needed timber for their shipyards; they needed boats to seek out new worlds, exploit the natives and rip off their silver. They had an empire to build, and they were in a hurry.

Victor, Antonio, Inda and José Manuel slept in tents, or on the back seat of the four-wheel-drive. I chose a patch of long grass beside a lavender bush, vaguely remembering something about lavender's soporific powers, laid down my sleeping-bag and tried not to think

about the cold and the damp and the fact that 2010 sheep were sharing my bedroom with me. Throughout the night they made their
rather beautiful avant-garde Japanese bell-music, comically inter-
spersed with the occasional ripe fart.

The morning was, like the night, cold, damp and dark. I rolled up
the sleeping-bag in which so little sleeping had taken place, and
pulled on the same jeans, T-shirt and Doc Martens I'd pulled off a
few hours earlier, and it felt like a continuation of the day before. I
could have felt downhearted and miserable. Instead I was buzzing
with exhilaration, the nervous fizz that tiredness gives you and a
kind of blind determination not to fall by the wayside.

The morning routine: freshly-squeezed goat's milk, courtesy of
Inda and the goats, with cocoa or instant coffee and the little sweet
Spanish buns called *magdalenas*. Followed by the daily inspection of
the flock and cure of sick animals, undertaken by Inda and José
Manuel, spray and syringe in one hand, hooked shepherd's crook in
the other. The sheep were in good condition, despite a few out-
breaks of maggots and a few sore feet, and fat with grass. A sheep
can put on 10 or 15 kilos during the *trashumancia*.

Inda lit his first fag of the morning and gave me a short lesson in
pasture quality. 'Last year there was drought and they had a bad
time. This time the pasture is good – d'you see it's a little bit short?
That's the best, you don't want it too long. Look at the sheep now,
they're *de maravilla*,' he said, leaning down to grab one of his little
beauties by the hind leg and spray her dainty feet, much against her
will, with purple antiseptic.

The morning's entertainment: a dog-fight. Two of the great hulk-
ing mastiffs began a slow dance of power. They struck heroic poses,
like two old lions, tails poised, and they pulled back their lips and
roared at each other, saliva glistening on their teeth, before clamp-
ing their jaws into each other's necks. Since they were both wearing
their Chamber of Horrors collars the fight wouldn't last long, but
there was blood on fur as the two of them loped off quietly into the
undergrowth. The shepherds laughed like drains.

We were off again, the rams leading the way with their sonorous bells. Little by little the sun began to burn off the cold mist of the early dawn. By eight o'clock it was a hot day. The Spanish timetable, so incomprehensible to foreigners, evolved in rural societies in extreme climates like this and still makes most sense in them. Deep Spain starts at dawn, often with a black coffee, a shot of cheap brandy and a high-tar ciggie, and gets in six good hours, has lunch at midday and sleeps a monstrous *siesta* for most of the afternoon. Then, when the heat goes out of the sun until nightfall, there are still a few more hours of work. It is a highly evolved way of living, and it works.

We climbed a steep escarpment covered with granite rocks, flowering broom and lavender whose resinous fragrance was so strong it made your nose hurt. On the other side of the hill, the *cañada* had been eaten away almost to nothing by walled vineyards, and we funnelled the sheep through, five or six abreast.

By mid-morning we'd arrived at Valdehijaderas, a tiny, dirty, smelly little *pueblo* where a few old people came out of their houses and stood open-mouthed as the flock went past.

'*¡Hola!* How many've you got there?' called one.

'Two thousand.'

'*¡Caramba!*'

'I'll give you 2,000 pesetas for the dog – what do you say?' called another.

'You, stay at the back now,' Victor commanded me as we threaded the baaing, clanging sheep through the village, 'and make sure none of them gets left behind. Or stolen. You can't trust these people, I shit in the sea.' In that sentiment was an echo of the ancient social conflict between *trashumantes* and the towns they passed through, between a nomadic form of life and a settled one; as Julius Klein puts it, 'between pastoral and agrarian interests, between *crianza* [rearing animals] and *labranza* [cultivating land]'.

Outside the village was a narrow Roman bridge over a stream of mountain water. The first sheep to arrive at the bridge swarmed on to it, forcing their companions to cross the stream. Nervous swimmers, they teetered on the bank, jostled from behind, until one slipped and fell, sploshing across to the other bank, and the others began to jump one by one, leaping high into the air with legs tucked neatly underneath them. Further upstream the mastiffs wallowed luxuriously in the muddy shallows, like water-buffalo.

A podgy little lady in a straw hat had waddled out from Valdehijaderas to watch us cross. She was quietly curious.

'Where are they from? Cáceres?' she murmured. 'I'm from Cáceres too.' She smiled at the coincidence: 2010 Extremaduran ladies and her, 200 miles from home. 'What happened is that I married a Castilian, and here I stayed.' As if to emphasise her point, she promptly turned and marched back towards the village.

Our path now took us across a wide dusty plain. The *cañada* was clear of rock and scrub and properly walled on each side, and it was lush with clover and wild wheat, and buzzing with crickets. I measured out its width in forty-seven long strides. Now I understood why people called the *cañadas* 'motorways for sheep'. This was a perfect highway, an airstrip, a green ribbon of prairie stretched over the plain. There were no houses to be seen, no human traces of any kind except the stone walls on either side, and here I was, walking along a track that had been walked on for thousands of years. I began to have an odd feeling of *déjà senti*. The scene was so completely pure and primitive – me and my hazel stick, the sheep and their bells, and the untouched landscape all around – that I forgot my jeans and T-shirt and fantasised that I had travelled back in time. I was a neolithic farmer dressed in animal skins, leading my flock along the ancient roads just as my Roman, medieval and twenty-first century descendants would do in the distant future.

North-east of Béjar the Cañada Real de la Plata crosses the Cañada Soriana Occidental, which runs east for a while before meandering north through Ávila, Segovia and Soria. (The map of the *cañadas* is a strange filigree of quavery lines, covering the face of Spain like broken veins.) There was an important decision to be made. Continuing north would take us down a stretch of *cañada* in bad condition, according to Antonio's researches in the four-wheel-drive; much of it sown with wheat. It would also take us to Salamanca, where the Cañada Real de la Plata arrives at the city in spectacular fashion across a Roman bridge. Everybody loves it when the *trashumancia* goes through a big city: the journalists, the photographers, the children, the office-workers on their way to the metro who find the street packed with farm animals. Everyone, in fact, but the shepherds, who worry and bite their nails. The *cañada* gives them right of way, of course, but they still have to ask permission from the town hall, and shepherds, being earthy no-frills sort of people, have no truck with officialdom and powers-that-be. The sheep also suffer from stress and sore feet from all that hot tarmac, and there isn't much pasture in city centres these days. So we'd take the right-hand fork: the Soriana.

At the last village before the turn-off, beside a stretch of *cañada* that an errant stream had turned into an almost impassable bog, Victor found a patch of ground surrounded by a sturdy metal fence and gate. 'A perfect stable, I shit on God! We can lock them in here for the night and go out to the bar!' As a place to stay it was none too salubrious, being also the village rubbish-tip. Empty bleach bottles and broken glass were dotted about. But the boss felt it was worth a try, so we went to ask the mayor.

Valdefuentes de Sangusín: big name, small grotty old village of 400 souls. The streets were paved with animal shit. In this late afternoon there was no life in the place but a woman in a straw hat and a boy, perhaps her son, driving a cow and calf down the main street, whacking the cow with a stick. A gothic church, of the Assumption of Our Lady, was in a dismal state of repair and had fig trees sprouting from its walls. On a stone bench by a wall, a fat man was sleeping the *siesta*.

We found the mayor in the bar. One mayor, one bar. We knew he was the mayor because of his Yves St Laurent shirt and his stick and his indefinable air of authority. The shepherds surreptitiously

brushed off their hands on their trousers and doffed their hats at
Santiago Moreno, who put on his town-hall voice, took a sip of his
café solo, heard their shy request, and announced that the dump was
not on municipal land but belonged to the village carpenter. If we
would allow him to finish his coffee, he would accompany us to see
the gentleman in question.

The carpenter and his family were sawing and scraping away at a
pair of doors, in a workshop with a view of the snowy *sierra*. He was
an irascible man with a deep mistrust of the Environment. We knew
this because when we told him we had recently been with the
Minister of the Environment, he said: 'Environment? I shit on God!'
(His oaths were, curiously, of the same hue and vocabulary as
Victor's, who had, curiously, also once been a carpenter. I imagined
some Masonic brotherhood in which foul swearwords were passed
from mouth to mouth, in whispers over the workbench.) 'What the
fuck does that mean, *environment* . . . ? Hasn't the Minister got better
things to do than come around here dressed as a shepherdess, I shit
in the sea?' His family had all seen the event on the news, and
brightened visibly when they realised we were the very people they'd
seen the other night, as if something of television's peculiar magic
was rubbing off on them.

The dump was Faustino's, but when we asked to borrow it for the
night he kept a long silence, a long pondering manly Spanish pause.
His wife, dumpy and sparkle-eyed, in a frilly apron, answered for him:
'But that place is full of dirt and filthiness! It's a bad place, that place.
What if a sheep steps on a bottle of some chemical, or rusty nail, or
something? Faustino, what about the other field down the bottom?
We haven't got that planted, have we? Why can't they go there?'

The other field was walled in, of a good size, and possessed a
solid metal gate, and it was gradually agreed, by an agonising process
of weighing up pros and cons between Victor, Faustino and the
mayor, that the sheep could lodge there for the night. The sheep
were funnelled into the carpenter's field, and they were counted for
the first time since leaving home. There were 2010 exactly, and the

shepherds were very satisfied. But the matter did not quite end there.

That night Victor and the lads went out to the bar as planned, but I was exhausted and needed a night in, or rather, out. I unrolled my sleeping-bag on a bank of grass, stared at the stars and tried to let the gentle chiming lull me to sleep, but my mind was haunted by worrying visions. Suppose the flock escaped from their *corral* and all 2010 were let loose to terrorise the countryside, destroying everything in their path? I was their baby-sitter for the night, and should anything happen, the full responsibility would fall on me. I thought I heard an increase in the volume of tinkling bells, and got up to check; but it was only a few of them like me unable to sleep and nervously pacing around in the dark.

The shepherds rolled back long after midnight. I was dimly aware of giggling and slamming doors. Then, later, I was aware of another series of sounds, followed by a deep, uncanny silence. Now even the gentle night-time chiming had stopped. I sat up with a start and ran across to the field. It was empty. The sheep had gone. The metal gate was wide open, and the entire flock had disappeared into the night.

Gripped by panic, I found Victor sleeping fully-clothed in the car and shook him till he woke with a stream of 'fucks' and 'what the cunts'.

'They've gone! They've gone! The sheep have escaped!'

'What the cunt . . . What d'you mean, "they've escaped"?'

'Somebody must have left the door open and they ran straight out.'

'*Mierda!* Which way did they go?' He was sleepy, drunk, and raging.

'They went thaddaway – towards the village.'

'I shit in the milk. What the cunt . . . Where are my fucking shoes, I shit on the mother who gave birth to them. Where the cunt did I leave them? I shit on the great prostitute.' (This last was a new one on me.)

What followed was a military manoeuvre: shepherds and dogs on full alert, car headlights like searchlights, and a mission to capture 2010 deserters and return them to base. I was ordered to guard the entrance to a country lane which the sheep, being vague and useless, might wander into by mistake on their return to the fold.

Being vague and useless, of course, they had not got very far; not even to the village. All they had wanted was a refreshing stroll in the cool night air. 'Sheep like to walk with the wind in their faces,' said Inda. Since the wind was blowing down the hill, they'd begun to walk up it. But they were rounded up with a commotion of whistling and calling and baaing and clanging; Victor got out his bag of goodies for the rams, and eventually the flock was persuaded to turn full circle and get back to bed. It was four o'clock. In a couple of hours it would be goat's milk time again, and Victor would open the gate again and light up a cigarette and shout, 'Good morning, *señoritas*! Did you sleep well, I shit in the sea?'

I spent five days with the *trashumancia*; five richly comical, terrible days. By day three I was footsore and filthy, and there was still no water for washing. But forgetting to be clean was part of the experience. 'Until your trousers stand up on their own you can't say you've really done the *trashumancia*,' said Victor. By day four, mine did; and so I had. The going began to get tough. We left Guijo de Avila over football pitches and building sites littered with rubble, along great barbed-wire fences, and under towering pylons. And at Guijuelo, an ugly industrial town, our path led us right through a gravel factory with chimneys belching smoke and a mini-mountain range of slag-heaps over which the sheep picked awkwardly, no doubt feeling as out of place as they looked in this barren environment. We filed through a subway under the main N603 road to Salamanca and across a local railway line. This prompted Inda to expatiate on the nightmare of transporting sheep by train: 'You have to wait for the wagons, load them on, wait for hours in the heat, you get to Salamanca at midnight, with the sheep half dead, no food or water . . .' The world took on a melancholy greyness suddenly, and I was half dead too, and almost without realising it I had decided to follow a *cañada* of my own making: to Salamanca, Madrid and home.

That afternoon we came upon a stretch of water and stopped by its banks to have lunch. The reservoir of Saint Teresa, fed by the river Tormes, had obliterated a chunk of *cañada*, which meant the sheep would have to wind their way around the lake and cross a stream before rejoining the track on the other side. There were obstacles everywhere you looked. It was a Saturday. Dozens of cars were parked along the shore, and fishermen were sitting by the water while their children screamed and romped in the stream. The shepherds took all this in with anxious eyes. The noise and the arriving cars, they said, would be sure to frighten the flock.

More people were arriving to join the *trashumancia*. A German girl and her American friend came on a day-trip from Madrid. A couple of Japanese students, dressed to the nines in new designer hiking gear and loaded down with cameras, had read about it in the paper, taken a taxi from Salamanca and wanted to spend a few days with the flock. They were sweet, polite and, as it seemed to me then, extremely brave. When the shepherds saw them they burst out laughing, and the racist remarks came thick and fast. I felt sorry for them, and hoped that rejection would turn, during the course of things, into grudging respect, which seemed to be what had happened to me. Remember the umbrella? Now the shepherds all envied it and wanted one for themselves.

I packed up my rucksack and left after lunch. With these new people, the rapid-fire questions they asked, and the way they ate their own little picnics instead of sharing them around, the magic of these days had softly and suddenly vanished. To my surprise, Victor seemed sorry to see me go. He slapped me on the back and swore affectionately. When I asked him whether he thought I had the makings of a shepherd, expecting the answer: 'Not in a million years! Get back to the word-processor,' he said something supremely flattering. What he said was: 'You haven't got the makings of a shepherd. You were *born* to be one.'

Well, I thought about that compliment as I hitched a lift to Salamanca, and took off my smelly clothes in a room in a cheap *pensión* and had the longest hottest shower of all time. And I thought about it as I sat in the Plaza Mayor and looked at the evening light on the renaissance stonework and the crowds in their Saturday best, and sniffed the air fragrant with eau-de-cologne. In the centre of the Plaza Mayor a man in Castilian costume was playing a pipe and drum. It was the man from the minister's visit in Montemayor del Río, nearing the end of a thirty-six-hour marathon of non-stop playing that would shortly qualify him for the Spanish edition of the *Guinness Book of Records.*

I thought about it all as I ordered a beer and some almonds, feeling a great tidal wave of tiredness wash over me. And I decided that Victor was probably wrong.

Short Stories

THE WITCHES OF O MATO

In a village in Galicia lived two sisters, Nieves and Aurora. Nobody knew how old they were, and even they had all but forgotten; neither would ever see eighty again. Perhaps because of the strange crosses painted in white on the front wall of their house, or the collection of dolls they had rescued from the rubbish and hung around the entrance, locals called them the Witches of O Mato, and parents forbade their children to go near the house. But they weren't really witches, just a couple of elderly women whose lives had turned sour a long time ago and preferred their own company to that of the outside world.

When their mother died, nearly thirty years before, the family property had been split up and part of it sold. Aurora and Nieves – their names mean 'dawn' and 'snows' – never trusted humankind after that. They gave up answering the good-days of their neighbours, and painted those strange white crosses to scare away potential visitors. For a quarter of a century they spoke to no one but each other. Like all good country women in Galicia they kept chickens, and had vines, and grew cabbage on head-high stalks in the garden. Their diet consisted mainly of vegetable soup. They collected car bonnets and Private Hunting Ground signs from the rubbish-dump with which to fence in their property. Their income came mainly from begging in the streets of the nearby town of O Carballiño.

The house had no electricity, running water, or furniture, and the sisters cooked what little food they had over an open fire. Perhaps that was how their house burned down one cold November night. The neigh-

bours rushed to their help, and for once Nieves and Aurora seemed grateful for the attention. But, after the fire, they relapsed into their double
solitude. They moved into the only room left untouched by the flames, a
tumbledown stable with an earth floor and a leaky roof, and made this
their final fortress. Only one of their neighbours, a shopkeeper called
Rosita Bertolo, was allowed over the threshold. They told her God had
warned them about the fire and wished the burnt-out house to remain
untouched. Rosita brought them milk and biscuits. They told her: 'God
has sent you. You are the Virgin of the Remedies.'

Attempts were made to move them into more suitable accommoda-
tion. Aurora was now blind and suffered from a bad limp, no one knew
whether as a result of the fire or some other accident. One day the
Guardia Civil arrived on their doorstep, but were scared away by Nieves'
medieval threats. 'Get away from here, or I'll throw boiling oil on you!' the
old lady shrieked. They came back later, of course, with a judge, a coro-
ner and the parish priest. A pot of vegetable soup was bubbling on the
open fire. This time the officials managed to talk the sisters round. Their
house would be repaired by the local town hall, if they would only see
reason. They were taken away to a hospital, where the doctors said they
were 'quiet and well'.

Where are Nieves and Aurora now, I wonder? Maybe in their house
again, squinting at the electric light and puzzling over the stove. Or
maybe in some twilight home, dosed up with drugs, staring at the telly
and missing their vegetable soup.

9

Our Lady of the Sewers

'Contrary to some common notions, a pilgrimage is not necessarily penitential, it need not be performed under
conditions of physical discomfort or with great solemnity,
nor are ordinary means of travel, e.g. by train or motorcar,
necessarily out of harmony with it'

(*The Catholic Encyclopaedic Dictionary*)

Romería: pronounced ro-me-*ree*-a. A word thought to originate
from the days when pilgrims arrived from all over Christendom
to worship in the shrines of Rome. These pilgrims were known to
the Spanish as *romeros*, and the act of pilgrimage – the outward journey, the stay and the return journey – as *romería*. The business of
going to Rome.

Theoretically this is a religious rite but, like all Christian celebrations worth their salt, the *romería* is at least 50 per cent pagan,
ludic, Dionysiac and disorderly. One Spanish writer defines *romería*
rather well, if pompously, as 'a term used to refer to certain trips
made on foot to visit a holy place, or, to the *fiesta* of a popular character in which people move to the surroundings of a hermitage or
sanctuary, in order to show their devotion to the sacred image that
may be found there; but also intending to have fun with their
friends: dancing, singing, drinking and eating.'

The most famous *romería* in Spain certainly fulfils that definition,
though some people might quibble with the bit about walking.

Contemporary followers of Our Lady of the Dew, better known as El Rocío, are more likely to make their way to Her shrine by car, or at least on horseback, than to bother to make the pesky journey through the mosquito-plagued marshes of the Coto Doñana on foot.

15 April

I boast to a friend about my planned trip to the Rocío. Expecting her to be impressed and envious and ask to come with me, I'm stunned by her reaction. She puts down her cup of coffee emphatically and launches into a vivid description of her nightmare. 'The Rocío was one of the worst experiences of my life. The whole thing's just got completely out of control. The people, the noise, the madness of it, the heat, it's "Bring more sherry!" and "More *sevillanas*!", and more sherry, and there are piles of rubbish everywhere, and I felt like screaming "Get me out of here!". To dramatise this she pulls a face like a hysterical person, her long black hair flailing around her. 'But there's no way of getting out – you're in the middle of nowhere pissed out of your head and it's six o'clock in the morning. It's changed completely from the way it used to be. It's a *fiesta* for the toffs, for the *señoritos*. It's commercialised, everything costs a fortune, even a *bocadillo* costs a fortune, and as for seeing the Virgin, forget it. You can't get near the chapel. Never would I go again, never. *Ay, ay!* It was terrible!'

I am surprised by her attitude, and wonder for a moment whether it has anything to do with tribal loyalties. My friend is from Extremadura and the Rocío is pure 100 per cent Andalucía. But I tentatively ask a few more people about the Rocío and they tell me similar things. Someone says if you want to go on horseback, as was always the preferred mode of transport when the *romería* was a down-home, gypsy thing, a day's hire of a horse will set you back a million pesetas (£5,000). Elsewhere, I read that a million people regularly pitch up at the hamlet of Almonte, where the Virgin has Her usual residence, from Seville and Cadiz and Huelva and Madrid and Frankfurt and Paris and Rotterdam.

Then I read an article in *El Pais* with the superbly cynical headline '*La Felicidad Obligatoria*' ('Obligatory Happiness'). When the week-long charade comes to an end, when the last frilly skirt has been flounced and the last sherry swigged, the writer claims that 200 tons of rubbish are left scattered among the reeds and rushes of the Coto Doñana – in theory one of Spain's last unspoilt wildernesses.

Under such a barrage of negativity, gradually I forget about the Rocío. It is only when I am talking to another friend about some other matter (coincidentally the girl is called Rocío; perhaps that's what triggers the thought in my mind) that I begin to ponder the subject of pilgrimages again. She tells me about a village near her father's home town of Córdoba where there is a particularly lovely *romería*. Unlike the Rocío, Rocío says it's small-scale, genuine, hasn't lost touch with its roots. The pilgrims spend the night carousing by a hermitage on top of a hill, and the next day they carry the Virgin down to the village of Belalcázar through lovely countryside, fording a river on the way. '*Es una cosa enloquecedora*,' says Rocío. It's a thing that sends you crazy? Or a crazed thing? Probably both. Oh, and the Virgin's name is rather amusing too. She's called Nuestra Señora de Gracia de Alcantarilla, which can be taken, somewhat sacrilegiously, to mean Our Lady of Grace of the Sewers.

I put down the phone from talking to her and ring the town hall in Belalcázar, which puts me on to the majordomo of the Brotherhood of the Virgin, who runs the village supermarket. José Medina, the main brother, is all grave politeness. Yes, it would be a pleasure to welcome me as a pilgrim (tinkle-crunch of a cash-till in the background); he'll just pop down now to the hostel and make me a booking. If I'm coming for the weekend, I'll need two nights, Friday and Sunday, because the Saturday is spent 'up there', carous-ing. You mean people actually sleep up there? Well, nobody actually sleeps much, but you might want to snatch an hour or two's rest. Bring warm clothes, he says – 'that'll be 1,545 pesetas, I've charged you for the washing-powder. Lola, would you get this lady some Ariel from round the back? – Sorry, yes, warm clothes and a blanket or two. It might be spring already, but the nights up there can be cold enough to peel you'.

The *romería* de la Virgen de Alcantarilla de Belalcázar is not one of the better-known ones in Andalucía; few books mention it. Looking at the map, the reasons for this are obvious. Belalcázar is off every beaten track. It is one of those places you would never set eyes on unless you made a conscious decision to go there, which would be highly unlikely in itself. No one ever 'just passes through'. Belalcázar is not quite on the way to nowhere, but it's not on the way to anywhere, either. Within a few hours on either side are three major tourist hot-spots: Toledo, Guadalupe and Córdoba. But tourists make no effort to negotiate the terrifying gulf between the three, where there are no minibars or buffet breakfasts; they simply retreat to their bunkers in Seville and Madrid. The result (there are also other reasons, like political neglect and poor communications) is that this northern corner of Andalucía, bordering on Extremadura to the east and Castilla-La Mancha to the north, is one of the least visited, least appreciated, deepest bits of deep Spain.

23 April
Nacho has borrowed a four-wheel-drive from his sister. It's a Korean-made monster with space to sleep at the back and certain peculiar characteristics, like an aerial with a life of its own and an infuriating little carillon that tinkles incessantly if all doors are not shut and seatbelts fastened.

We drive south through the mountains of Madrid, stopping in Ciudad Real and not being surprised that Pedro Almodóvar fled its provincial slumber as soon as he came of age. The car has a number-plate NA, for Navarra, stronghold of ETA terrorists. So, suspicious stares as we drive slowly along dusty back streets. Things begin to look up as we reach Almadén, where I have heard that mercury is stored in great underground swimming pools, and enter the valley of Alcudia on a bad single-track road. The countryside is pure

dehesa – an untranslatable term that implies extensive plantations of
holm oaks, whose acorns are used to fatten pigs for cured *serrano*
ham, and pasture for sheep among the trees. The valley is perhaps
100km long, and there are no houses, no power-lines, no litter.
Immense pools of colour are formed by the wild flowers, pushed
into overdrive by a winter of Big Rain. Around every corner is a new
outrage: a whole hillside coloured in pastel pink between the oaks;
a bloodbath of poppies; surreal mixtures of purple lavender and
yellow dandelions. Colonies of sugar-pink *campanillas* spread out
daringly into the road. The air reeks of pollen, stinks of flower perfume. We decide it is all a bit much.

La Bienvenida is a minuscule hamlet with a church and a farm
that sells its own cheese. The name means 'The Welcome'. We turn
off the road, intending to buy cheese, and see two ladies legging it
across the fields towards the house. They have seen the car. At last,
a customer! At the last minute I realise we have no money, and
therefore, tragically, cannot in fact be customers. The four-wheel-
drive swings back on to the road, crunching on the dry track.

The first thing you notice in Belalcázar is the castle – quite rightly
so, because *al-qasr* means 'castle' in Arabic and *bel* means nice to
look at in Romance. It is a four-sided Gothic structure, romantically
tumbledown, with a soaring tower on one corner from which hang
two banners reading:

B	N
E	O
L	
A	N
L	U
C	C
Á	L
Z	E
A	A
R	R

Driving further into town we see other banners, similarly home-made if not quite so dramatically sited, hanging from first-floor balconies and in the windows of shops. The message varies, but often seems to include the words CEMENTERIO NUCLEAR. They are wherever you look. I even see them spray-painted like urban graffiti (CEMENTERIO NUCLEAR NO! and the universal peace sign) on the half-walls of a ruined farmhouse.

The streets are cobbled, the houses white-fronted, low, with grey granite lintels over the front doors and simple black grilles over the windows. Some of these doors are open, allowing you to see that there is no central patio, as in Andalusian town houses, but a long corridor leading from front to back. For a place about to explode into its major good time weekend of the year within twenty-four hours, Belalcázar seems strangely quiet. I creep along the main street in the evening light, and all I see are caricatures of old-fashioned provincial life: a dog asleep in the road, two boys kicking a football against the wall. But as I turn up the Calle Federico García Lorca a woman is making her way home with a dozen Catholic-family-sized bottles of fizz in two bulging bags, and one or two front steps are building up an impressive stack of white plastic folding chairs. Subtle, but unmistakable signs of a *romería* in preparation.

Someone at least is busy: in the dark little supermarket they tell me José, the Virgin's majordomo and the big boss of the *romería*, is talking on the local radio and has left a message telling me to meet him at the radio station. Rafa, quick, take this *señor* to see José, says the girl at the cash-till, and Rafael (black-haired, gangly, face indelibly *andaluz*) runs me round the corner to a one-room studio next to the veterinary surgery.

While I'm waiting for the majordomo I flick through a copy of a Municipal Information Bulletin which contains a thousand fascinating facts about the town, such as that it has 4,200 inhabitants, 3,500 cows, 20,000 sheep, a swimming pool and two railway stations – 'although these are closed, both of them, to passenger traffic'. The Bulletin bursts with pride in Belalcázar's history and achievements, something that tends to look ugly in cities and nations but is sweet and splendid in little towns. The, notably short, list of Illustrious Personalities produced by the town includes Sebastián de Belalcázar, *conquistador* and founder of Quito, Ecuador; Tomás Morillo, 'eminent botanist'; and Muhammad Ibn Qassan Ibn Aslan 'el Gafequi', oculist and ophthalmologist whose nickname, I conjecture idly, must surely be the origin of *gafas*, the Spanish word for 'glasses'.

To judge by the Bulletin, this is a town with everything: history and culture by the lorryload, and a range of amenities to satisfy the most demanding citizen. A series of crepuscular photos shows the fine town hall, the parish church of Santiago, the castle and various hermitages, and then trails off into images of half-built municipal parks and light industrial warehouses. There is even a picture of the very modern and sparklingly clean bathroom (basin, loo and bidet forming a graceful trio) of one of the brand new bungalows in a clearing outside the town in which the town hall hopes to accommodate visitors.

All country towns in Spain dream of tourists; the money and glamour they bring, the flux and reflux they create in stagnant rural societies. But Belalcázar's dream is a long way off and, for the moment, ridiculous though it may seem, I am the only glamour around. There is a knock on the studio window: it is José, bluff, gruff, more farmer than shopkeeper, beckoning me to come in and sit down. There is much shaking of hands and reciting of names and titles – town councillor this, ex-mayor that, a struggling local journalist who asks me eagerly about Rupert Murdoch – all of which I immediately forget, caught up as I am in the amazing new realisation that I am *about to be interviewed!* It crosses my mind that I am probably also the first foreigner to set foot in the town for many a month.

My interviewer is also a town councillor for the right-wing Partido Popular, a solidly handsome man in his forties with a fine set of teeth which he flashes at me between questions. Knowing almost nothing about Belalcázar other than what the Municipal Information Bulletin has just told me, I hold forth on the natural beauties of the valley of Alcudia, the architectural excellence of the town and my eager anticipation of the coming celebrations. The faces around the table are straining with pleasure.

Then there is a change of tack, a sudden seriousness. Have I noticed the banners, have I read about the controversy in the Spanish press, do I perhaps have any opinion about the government's plan to install a nuclear dumping-ground within a stone's throw of Belalcázar? Hastily I formulate an opinion, and my opinion is that it is a scandal, a typical piece of political perfidy, an outrage which the people of Belalcázar will surely never permit. The table practically erupts into applause. I have said the right thing. The engineer fades in the music, there is more hand-shaking, and the ex-mayor, the councillor and I retire to one of the bars on the town's diminutive main square, where we shall drink camomile tea and light will be shed on the cunning passages of Belalcázar's recent history.

The place is not what it was, that's the truth of the matter. Under the Arabs the population reached 20,000, and Gafiq, as it was then, became quite a centre of learning. It was conquered by Ferdinand III in 1236, and never quite recovered its glory after that. By the late 1950s the head-count was around 10,000, but then came the tourist boom on the Mediterranean coast and half the town emigrated, mainly to Catalonia, Alicante and the Balearic Islands, but also to Madrid, Germany, the UK and wherever else there was work for Spaniards willing to wash dishes and mix cement. Today there is a community of 700 Belalcazareños, for example, in Menorca, and 2,000 in Madrid. In the summer and the last weekend of April, when the emigrants return, the town swells again to the size it might have been. You can see it happening now, on the night before the great *romería*. Local boys made good, or not so good, are trickling back, and the streets are filling up with smart cars with 'foreign' number-plates – A for Alicante, B for Barcelona, PM for

Palma de Mallorca. As the *fiesta* feeling gathers momentum there is a reunion scene on every corner, and people are stereo-kissing through automatic windows.

Bernardo Delgado Rodríguez, the right-wing councillor, tells me he too was an émigré for many years. The 1970s saw him manning the barricades of the class struggle in Madrid, though, oddly enough, from the side of the Communists, not the Right. As leader of a powerful trade union he once succeeded in getting all the workers in VIPS, a cheap and nasty convenience store analogous to 7–11, out on strike and effectively closed the entire chain. He says this with an oblique kind of pride, such as you might feel for an achievement you no longer value quite so highly. Bernardo has since changed his spots in spectacular fashion, and now runs a factory in the town making, 'How do you say it in English? *Bragas para mujeres.* Knickers for women. Business is good. There's certainly plenty of demand! It's funny; when I started studying management I began to see Marx from the other side. Now I think, the *workers' revolution . . .*' He says it with a kind of playful scorn; a childish thing he has put away. 'There is no point in having a workers' revolution if there are no good managers. That's the revolution we're waiting for now – the *management* revolution.'

The eager young journalist in the studio, the one who asked me about Rupert Murdoch, has what used to be known as a hang-dog look. He tells me he went to Córdoba to look for work as a hack, spent three years there and failed to find any, then came home again. We engage in hack-talk. Javier agrees with me that in journalistic terms the *romería* de Nuestra Señora de Gracia de Alcantarilla de Belalcázar is a better bet than El Rocío, because it approximates much more closely to an expression of genuine feeling. It's the commercialism of the big *fiestas* that kills them off. 'As soon as you put money into these things, you ruin them. The folklore thing in Seville has become an industry. As soon as Christmas is over, they're already planning the campaign for Holy Week and the April Fair.' Up the road in Andújar, this same weekend, there are half a million pilgrims at the *romería* of the Virgin of the Head. We agree that it's wonderful not to be among them.

José Medina pushes back his chair. 'Well, must be getting back up the Hermitage, there's a lot of hassle to deal with,' he says.

Nacho and I check into the only *pensión* in town. We take room 15. Room 16, across the hall, has a door and a number just like ours. The window blows the door open a crack, and I can see that the room is a half-finished, windowless shell of breeze-blocks. From the ceiling hang countless hams, twisting slowly in the draught. It's a Hitchcockian scenario: the remote little town where no foreigner has been seen for years, the only hotel, the room at the end of the corridor, the slices of sweet *jamón serrano* served downstairs in the bar . . . 'Nobody checks out of Room 16.'

We drive to Hinojosa del Duque, a few kilometres south, for dinner and end up dancing to techno in a scruffy little provincial disco where the atmosphere is as crazed and intense as you'd expect it to be tired and timid. The scudding, remorseless beat of techno is the soundtrack of the villages of deep Spain, where raving as an antidote to chronic boredom and social claustrophobia never outlived its function.

On the wall of the disco is a poster of the Virgen de Alcantarilla. She is in 'Divine Shepherdess' mode, wearing a bright red voluminous dress and little ermine cape over her shoulders, a simple straw hat, and clutching a crooked staff. The baby Jesus squatting on Her left arm looks almost like an afterthought. Our Lady's neighbour on the wall, a blonde on a beach with her skirts up, looks at Her with a combination of pity and amusement: 'Come on, woman, free your mind, this is 1997, not AD97!'

24 April
There is a certain amount of vagueness as to where exactly the *romería* starts from, where it ends, and when it occurs. People wave their arms energetically in two ways, one suggesting 'here' and the second 'elsewhere'. The time-check for today's events is *por la*

mañana, 'in the morning', which of course is an outrage to northern notions of exactitude. What if we set off too early or too late, from the wrong place, and miss the *romería* altogether?

I pounce on the boy in the hotel and ask him, 'Where are you going today?', hoping he'll tell me or, even better, show me the way, and he replies airily: '*Voy p'al campo*', 'I'm off to the country.' Finally, with the air of one explaining the obvious to a simpleton or granny, he gives us directions: out of the village on to the main road, second left, follow the crowds. The Hermitage is up on a hill, 13 or 14 kilometres out of town. You can't miss it, there'll be hundreds of cars and horses and people and noise and music.

The pilgrims are strung out along the road, cars and carts go by, but the *romería* is a more or less peaceful tramp in the spring sunshine. It feels like a nature ramble; to left and right, gentle slopes of cornfields are hazed with colour, and the roadside spattered with it. Falcons wheel in to investigate us. We overtake a group of guys getting nicely pissed as they walk. One of them swings a half-chewed ham in one hand, another a leather *bota* of wine. They offer us a swig.

Then we spy a hill crowned with a low white building with a stubby tower. This is our destination – it's obvious from the peculiar blare of noise and energy emanating from it. We cross the river Zújar on a modern bridge. The river is higher than it's been for years, and now looks khaki-green and contentedly sluggish. We wind up the hill on a dusty track towards the Hermitage, mouthing wordlessly at each other in amazement at the sight that unfolds before us. Here, in some of the remotest countryside in Spain, it's as though an army has marched out of nowhere and pitched camp. Similes crowd the mind: there is something medieval about this joyous disorder, half-way between Christianity and paganism – and something biblical. It's a settlement in the desert, a ziggurat, a pause in the wanderings of the Israelites.

On either side of the approach road are stalls selling sun-hats, cheap and nasty sun-glasses, cassettes of tacky Andalusian folk singers, fell-off-the-back-of-a-lorry trainers with brand names like Pierre Carton and Adinas, green and pink plastic toys with plastic mould-lines you could cut yourself on, lurid pink candy-floss and *churros*, those deep-fried strings of dough that are delicious but so unhealthy. Apart from the Andalusian singers and the *churros*, everything else in the fair appears to be made in China.

Everywhere you look, people are producing tents, tables, blow-up beds, fold-up beds, hammocks, chairs and cooking equipment from the backs of hatchbacks, estates, four-wheel-drives, horse-drawn carts and fruit lorries covered with blue tarpaulin decorated, *romería*-style, with leafy branches. Some families have harnessed trunks of olive and oak to their roof-racks and are now unloading them, the better to construct monstrous bonfires around which to gather when the chill humidity of this spring night falls like a lead curtain at four or five in the morning. A soundscape of roaring generators, banging tent-pegs, arguments about who is sleeping where, thudding techno and swirling *sevillanas* from the P.A. is borne around the little hill in fluctuating waves with each gust of the fresh spring wind. Above it all, the shrill single bell of the Hermitage tolls somewhat hysterically in an attempt to get the pilgrims into church for the afternoon mass.

Down below in the sprawling countryside, the main task in hand is the search for a vacant oak tree suitable for conversion into a campsite. It's hardly a difficult task – there are thousands of trees, stretching away from here to *eternidad* – but as Saturday goes on most of the trees near the hill will have been occupied, their branches festooned with hams and wine-boxes that spin gently in the breeze.

The Hermitage is a simple white church, built in the thirteenth century on the site of a Roman fortress which before that had been a settlement of some neolithic Ibero tribe. On top of the bell-tower a pair of grimy storks in a fat bowl of a nest survey the chaos below them with a bemused air. 'The only thing they really don't like is the fireworks,' says José Medina. 'They usually fly away when the rockets go off and come back later. The rest they don't mind.' It's hard to believe. As I watch, the male leaves the nest and flaps off into the sky, visibly irritated by these goings-on.

The majordomo is wearing a silver medal around his neck – the insignia of the Brotherhood – and carries the silvery staff of the Order, with the same image of the Virgin cast into the top. Today is his big day, and it's all going according to plan. How different he looks up here in the Hermitage from down in the supermarket. He looks somehow radiant, transfigured by responsibility. He ushers us into the church for our first sight of Our Lady. 'She spends six months a year up here and six months down in the village,' whispers José. 'Tomorrow we take Her down, and in October She comes back up again. *¿A que es bonita?* Isn't She pretty?'

We agree that She does look rather fetching in Her shepherdess garb, even if the red velvet dress and ermine cape do suggest a Marie Antoinette level of acquaintance with the reality of livestock management. In Her left hand She carries a staff with its top curled over like a question mark. She is diminutive, not much taller than a toddler, and She peers out from within a flower-strewn canopy. Her face has a curiously shiny, plasticky, doll-like look. The thing to do is apparently to touch the sweep of Her dress and say a little prayer, and a queue has formed for this purpose. Clearly the prayers have been answered on occasion, to judge by the miniature waxen limbs hanging from the back of the virgin's canopy (a leg for a cured leg, an arm for an arm).

The church is abuzz with the very southern European piety that says you should express your faith publicly and unembarrassedly, but not feel it any the less sincerely. In Protestant countries the former is thought to cancel out the latter; showiness equals falsity. As we stand in line, there is a slight commotion at the back of the church, and a well-to-do *señora* in a twinset and pearls is seen to sink to her knees and begin shuffling ostentatiously down the aisle. She wears an unforgettable expression of smug delight, like a hen that's just laid an egg. Meanwhile the queue looks on admiringly. They are longing to do the same thing, but they're afraid their knees might never recover.

The woman in front of me clutches a small child, which she shoves forward when her moment comes, whispering, 'Go on, kiss Her!' The little boy leans forward shyly in her arms and touches his lips, not to the Virgin's cheek (this would be too much of a liberty) but to Her hand. Then it's my turn, and I touch the cape. I can't think of anything to ask Our Lady for, except to get me through the next twenty-four hours, which are certain to be some of the most punishing I and my liver have ever known.

It is one o'clock. Time for a drink and a *tapa*. Gastronomically speaking, northern Andalucia is not up to much, but it does possess two of the major ingredients of the good life: good ham and good cheese. So we go to one of the scruffy tents set up around the dusty dance-floor, and I order a plate of *jamón serrano* and another of sheep's cheese, and the ham is sweet – the pigs live under the oak trees and spend their days munching acorns – and the cheese is rich and fresh, densely-flavoured, nutty, just completely delicious. These morsels are washed down with *fino* Montilla. It comes ice-cold, in a plastic cup. Altogether the little meal is a glimpse of heaven.

The *fino* is irresistible, and the cup is deliberately small. So I order another, and another, and another. Truly this wine is *un regalo de Dios*, a gift from God. The effect of it is like champagne, euphoric and upful, *whoooosh*. At the next-door tent the barman has slapped on a tape of the hit *sevillanas* at this year's April Fair in Seville, and a few couples have already embarked on the deliriously formal stepping and waving and gyrating dance. It looks and sounds out of place up here in the wilderness, so far from the frills and furbelows and fripperies of Seville, but I do a few steps anyway. The *fiesta* spirit is coming on strong now, carried along by the smells of generator-oil and frying *churros*.

Time to make friends. I order a shot of whisky and push through the crowd rapidly forming at the bar towards a man who looks as though he's got a few stories to tell. He has more white hair in his beard than on his head and a filigree of broken capillaries across his cheeks. He's as wiry as a Giacometti, and in one hand he carries the staff of the Brotherhood.

'Are you the guy who was on the radio this morning?' he asks when I introduce myself, and he laughs behind his hands, and the young girl he's with, Lola, laughs too, and for a few minutes I'm having the piss taken out of me in a raw, slangy Andalusian accent I barely understand. For a few minutes I feel I'm blushing, confused, the dumb foreigner. They are glancing at my shot of whisky, joking about how only a dumb foreigner would drink white wine with ice.

Suddenly they snap out of it, Lola wanders off and the whole atmosphere changes. It was a trial by fire, a ritual dressing-down. 'They call me The Monster,' he says. I naturally want to know why. He takes me by the shoulder, says, 'Come', and leads me round the back of the drinks tent, to where the generators roar and the night's supply of beer and *fino* is stored. We are on the edge of a precipice looking out over hundreds of miles of *dehesa*. As far as the eye can see, it's all shared out between two or three immense farms whose grand farmhouses, dazzling in their recent coats of whitewash, look like cruise liners in a turbulent ocean of oaks.

'They call me The Monster because I like to take big jumps,' he says. 'One year I jumped off this cliff and rolled down the hill to the bottom. Last year I jumped off the bridge down there into the river. Trouble was, the river was almost dry. So I didn't fall in the water, I fell on a patch of concrete – see there, by the base of that column?' (Is this guy for real? He is telling the story with a smile on his face.) 'This year I've decided not to do any more jumps. I mean, look at me! I'm a wreck! But they still call me The Monster.'

It turns out that Serafín Vigara – his real name – is actually the brother of the mayor of Belalcázar. This is not as much of a surprise as you'd think, and I'm at a loss to explain why. Something to do with small towns, perhaps, and the greater visibility of black sheep in them. He is an exceptional man in several ways. He spent many years abroad and in other parts of Spain, earning his living however he could. Most of his peers left the town for good, but he came back to stay. He has found regular employment on a building-site. He's a pillar of the Brotherhood of Our Lady of the Sewers. In short, he's now quite a medium-sized fish in Belalcázar's diminutive pool.

On the subject of the nuclear dump, he points to a distant spot on the *dehesa* where some men came a few months back to make the first soundings. Nuclear people love granite, and it's kilometres deep around here. Also the area is practically uninhabited, so if anyone starts growing extra limbs, the P.R. repercussions will be minimal. But Serafín says they'll put that thing near his town over his dead body. 'Just let them try – I'll bomb the bastards first, I'll become a terrorist!' Coming from a man who happily flings himself off bridges at the drop of a *sombrero*, this is not a threat to be taken lightly.

We totter off, the Monster and me, to meet the mayor. The Vigara family are camped under a tarpaulin, in a prime position by the church. I am sat in a deck-chair and introduced to them all, a seemingly endless string of brothers, cousins, sisters-in-law, offspring. Talk about the extended family . . . Plates piled high with slices of ham and cheese are immediately thrust towards me, accompanied by injunctions to eat, eat, eat.

I am already comfortably full from the *tapas* and don't wish to eat more just now. But I'm secretly thrilled that this cruel old-fashioned Latin generosity still exists. On other occasions I've found it terrifying. In Athens once, as a teenager, my friend's big fat Greek mum made me eat so many cheese pies and *tzatziki* that I had to creep into the garden and puke under a rose bush. Why don't those situations occur any more? Partly because one is older and more confident, and able to say No when one really means No. But also because the traditional Spanish generosity towards strangers, once big-hearted and intense, has cooled and dwindled under the influence of northern manners.

I used to find dealing with that kind of total hospitality a torture. Now I tend to see it as a game, even though one that the invitee is destined to lose. It usually goes something like this:

'Our ham and cheese are the best in Spain. Eat.'

'Mmmm. It looks delicious, but I couldn't possibly, I've just had lunch and I couldn't eat another thing. Honestly.'

(*offended*) 'What, you don't like ham and cheese?'

(*ingratiating*) 'Oh yes, they're my favourite foodstuffs in all the world, but I can't eat any more just now.'

'You must be sick, or something. Go on, have a little bit of ham, just a little bit.' (*Plate waved threateningly in front of guest.*)

'No, no, I really . . . Oh, all right, if you insist, just a tiny bit. For the taste.' (*Takes smallest available slice, chews and swallows with difficulty. Hosts look on expectantly as face assumes expression of ecstasy.*) 'Fantastic, absolutely fantastic. You were right: this ham and this cheese are each the best of their kind in all Spain.'

(Repeat *ad infinitum*, or until guest explodes.)

The announcement having been made that I am foreign, it is time for each of the family to try out his few words of Foreign. Of the group, two or three have spent time in Germany, one or two in Britain. Several of them have their base in Madrid, like the self-satisfied man smoking a big cigar who has just tried out his German on me. I bond with his wife Maruja, a smiley woman in a turquoise shell-suit who tells me about their apartment next to Madrid's Barajas airport.

'When I look out of my window, I can see the planes coming in, as near as that stork up there'. The poor stork is still wheeling about confusedly. I say dumbly: 'Great.' There is a small pause. She takes a swig of *fino* from her plastic cup, and then it's as though she's read my mind, because she says: 'You probably wonder why I don't live in Belalcázar. Well, I couldn't live here. A week or two for the *romería*, a month in the summer, that's fun. But all year round, *Dios mío*, I'd go out of my mind.' She leans towards me and almost whispers, 'You know, there's nothing to do here. Absolutely nothing.'

Maruja's brother-in-law Antonio, the mayor, left Belalcázar at ten. 'Well, I didn't so much leave as they took me away, to a seminary in Cadiz. I was there till seventeen, then I went to study in Córdoba, and ended up working in the construction industry in Catalonia – a question of tubing, electrical installations. There were quite a few people from Belalcázar in the same business. Are you hungry? Won't you have a *tapita* of ham, a beer?'

He's not the type of guy you'd expect to be mayor of anywhere. He's a gruff, rough-hewn guy with nothing of the pomp and circumstance of the town hall. Like a lot of Andalusians he was a Communist in the 1980s and, despite a dramatic Right turn in the 1990s, all that comradeship and classlessness obviously made their mark. In any case, his farming roots are a good deal deeper than his political ones. Even his voice has dirt under its fingernails.

He talks about his town, its modest resources, its cautious dreams. No one starves in Belalcázar. Not with all that cheese and ham. Most families have their own kitchen garden, earn their living from live-stock and are propped up financially by the local government. But the town hall wants to get ahead. The word 'agrotourism' is one that it's heard recently and is very fond of, and it sounds fantastic, even if nobody seems to know exactly what it means. If there are agro-tourists about, it reasons, they will surely be lured off the beaten track by the four new little cabins up on the municipal camping-site, each with its own sparkling bidet and floral counterpanes.

Then of course there are the cultural marvels of Belalcázar: the castle of the Sotomayor family, crumbling Gormenghast on its hill-top; the Roman bridge and baths; the church of Santiago, stripped of its decoration during the Civil War; and the Convent of Saint Clare, apparently described by some civil servant in some official list-ing as the second most important historical monument in the province of Córdoba – the most important of course being the Great Mosque. It may not add up to a whole hill of beans, but it might be enough to make assiduous culture-vultures make a day or two's detour from the historic schlep around Extremadura. Then if

tourists could be persuaded north from Seville and Córdoba, forming a kind of pincer movement with the ones coming in from the
west, the picture would be complete. Hotels and restaurants would
spring up, the émigrés would return like nesting storks, the birthrate would soar . . . No longer would the mayor's sister-in-law have
cause for complaint. There would be things to do in the evening. It
would be like the *romería* de Nuestra Señora de Alcantarilla all the
year round.

What does the *romería* mean to the town? The mayor tells me
what I can already see. For Belalcázar this is a Big Deal. '*Es algo muy
grande.* It's something very great,' he says, smiling through his moustache, opening his arms very wide to show just how big. 'It's religious
and pagan at the same time. The church is full all night, but the
band plays all night as well. People really live the thing to the full –
you'll see tonight at the Rosary, and tomorrow at the Crossing of the
River, how people are moved to tears, how they shout at the
Virgin . . .' For a moment he seems on the verge of tears himself. But
then he stops short, gulps back his emotion, and says: 'It's something that can't be expressed in words.'

We drive the Ssongyang into the *dehesa*, feeling like yuppie weekenders as we crank up the four-wheel-drive and join the hunt for a
vacant oak tree. Within a mile of the Hermitage every tree has its car
and tent and circle of deck-chairs. Here more than anywhere you
can see the social variety. From oak to oak, there are émigrés in big
Mercedes with Alicante number-plates, groups of grunge kids in
scruffy vans, country people in tractors wearing flat caps and old-
fashioned check shirts, *romería* obsessives in mule-drawn carts with
green tarpaulin covers stuck with branches.

I kip down for a *siesta* on the grass. When I wake up, furry-
mouthed with *fino*, it's dark and the holy hill is ablaze with lights, its
generators roaring. The storks have had enough and left for the
night, like neighbours fed up with a rowdy party. More and more

cars are still arriving, their headlights snaking in a weird procession over the blacked-out landscape.

There is a Mass going on, and the church is rammed. José of the Brotherhood tells me this year it's a musical service inspired by the Rocío, with guitars and a choir. We reckon this sounds dowdy, and decide to worship at the bar instead. More *fino*. It's so fresh and cold and crisp; we discover if you knock back a cupful in one go, it's like snorting a line of coke. Gabriel, next to me at the bar, lives in Villaverde, an unpleasant suburb of Madrid. Short black curly hair, young guy from Belalcázar, trying to get ahead in the big city, back here for the *romería*, this year as every year. He shakes my hand, invites me to another *fino*. The interfering, hectoring warmth of the Spanish, it's balm to the wounded, cramped British psyche. 'I'm involved in the construction industry. Well, actually I'm a builder.'

He calls over his friend Manolo, a student of English. 'Say something in English for us,' he demands. I think for a moment and say, in a deliberately phoney beginner's accent, 'I yam from Eengland.' This sends all of us into a convulsion of hilarity, Manolo mock-punching me in the stomach and me mock-falling over, doubled up, into the dust.

A blonde beautiful girl in a bright red puffer-jacket is walking past the techno tent, sees the commotion and barges in. Marieta. She is loud, proud, has big tits and is also from Belalcázar, also based in Madrid. When she finds out I'm English she invites me to a *fino* and drags me off bodily to her tent. I am now adrift on the waves of the *romería*'s social ocean, tossed in a pleasurable confusion from one whirlpool-like encounter to another. By this stage of the evening everyone is drunk as a skunk, but there's not a whiff of aggression or Attitude about. It's an in-your-face sort of charm these people have, but it's charm none the less.

In Marieta's tent, a throng of friends and relations. I am merci-lessly quizzed. Ham and cheese are pressed on me. I refuse both. Marieta's brother has a bottle on a string, hanging round his waist, which contains a foul mixture of hyper-sweetened black coffee and some kind of cheap supermarket vodka. He says it's a local speciality – this should be warning enough – and thrusts the bottle in my direction. I take a swig, and my mouth is instantly coated with the sugary muck. I gag theatrically, clutching my throat.

Seeing my tape-recorder, they all try to grab it and record themselves, and listening to it now I have got their dumb jokes and 'Is it recording? Which button do you press?' and silly songs jostling with sensible things like the interview with the mayor. Eventually the machine gets passed to Inma, a nervous girl who is brutally forced by the others to sing something. 'Go on, give us one of your *coplas*, let's hear it. The machine's on! *Venga*, get on with it!' The poor girl is suffering, but dithers for a moment and then breaks into song. It's an old Spanish number, all about a girl called Trinidad – '*Trini, Trini, Trini, ay!*' – and she sings it beautifully in a clear but quavery voice that gives me a momentary pang of boozy sentimentality. When she finishes, everyone screams their appreciation and pleads for more, but Inma's had enough and we stagger off in search of more fun.

Leaning on my right shoulder as we stagger, I find a girl who answers to the name of Virtudes. Virtues. A fabulous name and a tough one to live up to, though she shows no signs of trying very hard. She is a brassily charming Belalcazareña and a mustard-keen pilgrim who intends to get through the whole of the programme – the Procession of the Rosary, the Crossing of the River and the triumphant return of the Virgin to the village tomorrow night – on nothing more than adrenalin, alcohol and sleeplessness. 'And I wanna see you there at the finishing line, or there'll be trouble,' she says, fixing me unsteadily with a pair of dark green eyes. I say I'll do my best, and feel suddenly feeble and northern. No staying power. Insufficient devotion to Our Lady of the Sewers.

We have stumbled into a neighbouring tent-and-caravan construction in which is seated Belalcázar's leading intellectual, Luis Delgado, amateur historian and owner of the town's emblematic castle. '*Es el que más sabe, es el que más sabe.* It's he that knows the most!' chorus the girls, and push him forward to meet me.

Luis, a mischievous-eyed elderly man, launches excitedly into a bookish disquisition as to the reasons why the roots of Belalcázar are actually in Castille and not Andalucia, and how the neighbouring village of Hinojosa del Duque is socially inferior for historical reasons and its people speak a rougher sort of Andalusian Spanish and its houses were always poorer than those of Belalcázar but more pretentious, with all sorts of fancy decorations on its doorways, whereas the people of Belalcázar had no need for such airs and graces because they, lucky souls, had the court of the Dukes of Sotomayor on their doorstep. And, without noticing it I've been furnished with another *fino* and am really quite enjoying the lecture.

The dukes' ownership of the castle, says Luis, ended when one of their line was posted to Russia as a diplomat at the court of the tsar. In those days it was *de rigueur* in Moscow to throw lavish parties, and the duke found himself spending such a fortune on champagne and caviar that he was humiliatingly forced to sell the castle in Spain to his own administrator – who was of course Señor Delgado's ancestor.

The man is a mine, no, a brimming fountain of stories, and I have them all on tape. One day I may transcribe them all and publish them in a slim volume, proceeds of which will go towards the upkeep of the castle, which is in a scandalous state of disrepair, with rooks squawking among the naked architraves. But night is already falling, and the girls are eager to haul me away to church, where Our Lady of the Sewers will shortly be emerging for Her jaunt around the hillside.

We make our way back to the dusty dance-floor, lose the girls and hitch up with a gang of girls and boys from the dusty mining town of Peñarroya down the road. We talk about the Virgin of the Sewers, sorry, of Alcantarilla, and they virtually spit on the floor in disgust. 'She is very small and very ugly,' they say, making no effort to keep their voices down, and Ana whips out of her pocket-book a postcard of the gang's particular fave Virgin, Our Lady of Bélmez. I recognise the name Bélmez from the Spanish legend of the Faces of Belméz, whereby a series of mysterious faces are supposed to have appeared on the wall of a house in this otherwise completely uninteresting town.

'Look at that. Now there's a real Virgin for you!' says Ana proudly. I'm forced to agree that Her Lady is elegant and refined, with an aquiline nose that actually looks a little like the nose on Ana's brother Federico. The dance-floor is emptying, but the scratchy techno pounds on regardless, so that when Our Lady finally appears at the door of the church and wobbles out shakily on the shoulders of Serafín and three other Brothers, She does so to a techno beat. The waxen limbs swing from Her little canopy as she moves. She has bunches of flowers stuck around Her feet and festoons of twinkling Christmas-tree lights. (Actually it's just the one festoon.) Federico points out Her battery-pack, hidden not very effectively under the Virgin's copious skirts.

People are thronging at the church door, clutching lighted candles like garden flares, eyes raised in wonder to the Virgin's face. Some of them break into song, the song being a traditional hymn in praise of Our Lady of the Alcantarilla. It is a slow rather beautiful tune, with rambling lyrics that implore Her to water our fields with copious rain and rescue us from the wolf. Two old ladies bustle forward to touch the palanquin as it passes, then retreat to cross themselves in unison, and finally to nurse and admire the fingers through which had passed such a charge of holy energy. I find the whole scene inexplicably moving, and in a moment or two my vision is a blur from the tears in my eyes. But I'm also surprised to find I'm laughing too. For a second I wonder if I'm going mad. Rocío was right in her use of the word *enloquecedora* – there is a kind of Dionysiac lunacy at the heart of the *romería*. It's springtime, and spring does funny things to the brains of animals and people. Mad March hares. Stirring dull roots with spring rain.

Now Our Lady wobbles off down the hill and we all fall into line chaotically behind Her, struggling to light our candles (hastily acquired in the sanctuary shop, along with T-shirts and badly-made figurines of Our Lady) with cigarette-lighters that the wind keeps blowing out. The Peñarroya gang say they have hash, so we fall out of line at a point where the chain of flickering candles can be seen as it winds down the hill, and loll on the bonnet of a car to roll joints and admire the procession.

I am just sober enough at this point, as my back muscles adjust to the cold metal of the car, to take in Federico's shouted story of how the image of Our Lady was found. 'Some guy from Hinojosa, out hunting with his dogs in the fourteenth century, saw Her under a pile of stones. Spent the whole night there on his knees in front of Her, silly bastard.' And, even odder, how the child She holds in Her arms was found. 'Some old guy from Monterrubio, swimming in the river, right at the start of the Civil War . . .'

(The image of the Virgin had been burned in the early years of the war when Republican wrath against the Church ran high, but the child must have survived, because one torrid August day in 1936 Ramón Prado Romero, aged twenty, was taking a dip in the river Zújar with some friends not far from the holy hill when his feet touched something that felt like a doll. The tiny figure had a rope round its neck and a stone to stop it floating. Ramón, who had seen the figure often enough in the church on the hilltop, said nothing to his friends but went straight home and told his father, and the two of them came back in the *siesta* hour, when the rest of the world was asleep, fished up the image and hid it until the end of the war, when a new Virgin was carved and the original child deposited somewhat awkwardly in Her arms.)

I am practically comatose on the roof of the car, and when the rest of the gang move back to the dance-floor I stay put. I lie there for what could be hours, the lights and noise of the *fiesta* flowing around me, and eventually peel myself off the roof and slope off back towards the Ssongyang on its oak tree island in the *dehesa*, past clumps of people huddled around great glowing tree-trunks, swigging on the *fino* like there's no tomorrow. Which in a way there isn't.

I slouch past an old man who tells me off for deserting. '*Hombre*, if I'm staying up, so can you. This is a *fiesta* – you ought to make the most of it.'

25 April

Two or three hours of something it would be inaccurate to call sleep, under the oak tree while a cold spring dew fell on me like a concrete blanket. It's still dark as I make my way back up the hill, stopping at a stall to buy a bag of *churros* and a cup of thick sticky hot chocolate. The *churros* are freshly made, crunchy in their dusting of sugar and commendably low on the grease. But I pass on the chocolate, which reminds me too much of primary school puddings.

As daylight comes, the devastation of last night is increasingly clear. A *romería* would hardly be a *romería* without its corresponding grotesque mess of strewn plastic cups and Coke cans. But now would hardly be a good moment to clear up either, because Our Lady is about to emerge once again from the church, to be carried through the countryside for Her six-month summer stay in the parish church. In the dawn light I can make out a wild-eyed Serafín, looking like the Ancient Mariner, leading the cheers of the *fino*-fatigued, bedraggled, euphoric crowd: '*Viva la Chiquinina! Viva la Virgen de Alcantarilla!*' (La Chiquinina is this virgin's special affectionate nickname. The Virgin of El Rocío's is 'white dove'. Impossible to translate, '*chiquinina*' means something like 'cute little thing'.) Among the loudest cheerers is Virtudes. She congratulates me on getting this far. I don't tell her I flaked out for a while half-way through. 'See, what did I tell you? All you need is *fino* – and a little bit of faith.'

So the Virgin starts out on Her journey, winding down the hill and across the *dehesa*, sheltered in Her golden canopy with the cross on the top and the scallop shell of Saint James at the base, and followed by a straggly crowd of devoted followers. We watch from the brow of the hill; the procession wanders away among the oak trees. The sun comes up, bringing out the poppies and the purple-blue lavender and the *campanillas* the colour of granny's pink sugared almonds, the kind she could never eat because they messed up her teeth, and the yellow cornfields. And before our eyes the scene crystallises into a first class, unselfconsciously gorgeous, absolutely fabulous idyll.

We seem to float for an hour or two, through a smiling landscape wildly daubed with ridiculous colour, like a 1960s acid trip. As we walk, we sing songs about the Virgin's miraculous ability to bring rain to parched crops – though to judge by the countryside around us there isn't much need for Her miracles at present – and good-natured satires aimed at the people of the next-door towns of Hinojosa del Duque (to the south) and Monterrubio de la Serena (to the west). Inter-village rivalry is another *topos* of deep Spain, fast disappearing as our human rivalries grow in size and scope. What happened was that the Virgin of Alcantarilla was originally shared more or less amicably by all three towns, who could borrow Her whenever drought or famine or disease threatened. One town must have benefited more than the others from Her miracles and made the others jealous, because in 1600 Hinojosa and Belalcázar took the matter to court, each having to prove why the Virgin belonged exclusively to them. (Monterrubio opted out.) Fourteen years later it was decided: She was the patroness of Belalcázar, and of nowhere else. The rivalries lived on, though oddly they seemed to be more with Monterrubio than with Hinojosa, perhaps because Hinojosa eventually acquired a lovely and miraculous Virgin of its own, the Virgen de la Guía, and thereafter had no need of Our Lady of the Sewers and all Her works.

The stories are still told. They say that if for any reason (river too high, Brotherhood can't get it together) on the last Sunday in April the Virgin isn't taken from the Hermitage back to Her home in Belalcázar, She'll fall immediately into the greedy hands of Monterrubio. Now, as we carry our patroness through the flower fields, we sing a silly little song of triumph:

'*La Virgen es nuestra*
Y nos la llevamos
Y los de Monterrubio
Quedan llorando.'

'The Virgin is ours
And we're taking Her away
And the ones from Monterrubio
Are left crying.'

By the time we arrive at the river, it is a gentle spring morning, the dew has finally burned off the grass and the one word on everybody's mind is 'coffee'. But we are in one of the loneliest spots imaginable, many a weary kilometre from the nearest Gaggia, so we have chosen not to talk about it. Instead, we must ponder how to negotiate the stretch of *café-con-leche*-coloured water that stretches out before us. We have arrived at the river Zújar, a stream made into something more substantial by the digger that worked on it yesterday. I find a place to stand on the riverbank. The water is muddy, deep and unappetising, but, heaven be praised, it's only the Brotherhood and other truly impassioned devotees of Our Lady who are required to make the crossing. The air rings with laughter and expectation. This is the high point of the most important weekend of the year for these people, a moment highly charged with solemn happiness. Most of them have been up all night drinking *fino* and smoking, yet their faces are lit up with well-being. Once again I'm amazed, moved even, by the Spanish lust for life, the fierce Spanish love of pleasure and feeling.

Someone hands me a leather bottle of red wine and I swig from it without letting it touch my lips, the wine squirting down my front and making everyone laugh. A woman next to me in a green puffer-jacket and thigh-high brown leather boots – the typical uniform of the *campera* (Spanish for Sloane ranger, female version) at events like these – jokes about the excessive hedonism of the last twenty-four hours. 'I've made a promise to the Virgin to come next year, and next time I'm not eating, not sleeping, and I'm coming without kids or husband. Well, I might bring the husband at the last minute.'

Tractors and lorries that have made the journey from the Hermitage by road have gathered by the water's edge. If they make it across, the coast will be clear for Our Lady. The first tractor ploughs determinedly into the murk, keeping up speed as the water inches up the side of the engine, perilously near to the spluttering exhaust-pipe. It almost grinds to a waterlogged halt before hauling itself out at the other side. The second tractor takes it too slowly. To roars of mirth from the crowd, the engine stalls and the tractor is marooned. The two young guys in the cockpit climb up on the roof and sit there swigging from a bottle of Marieta's friend's evil coffee liquor, pissing themselves laughing. The cry goes up: '*Salta, salta, salta, salta!*' Jump!

Now all eyes are on the Virgin and Her retinue of ecstatic devotees. There is Serafín Vergara, The Monster, taking up the lead, his silver-topped staff of the Brotherhood still in his hand. And there are Marieta and her friends, up to their waists in the murky river, cheering maniacally. They and a small crowd of fanatical pilgrims are clutching the ends of the multicoloured ribbons that flutter from the roof of the Virgin's palanquin. Slowly the procession sinks into the water. The crowd on the bank is singing. It is nine o'clock on a Sunday morning, and we are all quietly singing. 'The holy waters of Your love . . .'

Tonight at ten, under a cold spring rain that makes The Monster loll his tired white-haired head and say, 'You see, now it's started. Now the water's started,' as if to say 'Our Lady is working Her miracles again'. She'll be taken into the town square, past the town hall, where they'll rock Her lovingly to and fro like they do to the big Virgins in Seville. There'll be bangers that whizz dangerously close to our faces and a sign in fireworks above the door of the church that reads: Long Live Our Patroness. Virtudes will hug and kiss me under her umbrella and make me promise to come again in

October, when the Virgin is taken out again and installed on Her lonely hill. 'I'm going back to Córdoba,' she says. 'I've got a busy month ahead. It's the Crosses of May next week, you know, the decorated crosses in the streets, and then the *feria*. It's a great party – why don't you come?'

I might well take up her offer, but for now I'd rather drink in this scene, the sight of the coloured ribbons flying and the people, now up to their shoulders in the river, and quietly savour the feeling of being here, of having arrived at the mysterious deep heart of something, the pulsing heart of deep Spain.

We walk away in silence, through the improbable spring flowers.

Short Stories

IN BED WITH THE BAKER
(after Manuel Vicent)

One autumn day a few years ago, the Intercity rail service from Madrid to Valencia was chuntering peacefully across the flatlands of central Spain. The view from the window was a dreary landscape of leafless vineyards and fallow fields, broken only by the occasional abandoned farmhouse or the occasional empty silo waiting to be filled by the next spring harvest. From time to time the train tore impatiently through village stations, flashing by so fast you couldn't even read the place-names before the vines and fallow fields began again.

Suddenly there was a terrible screech of brakes and the passengers were thrown forward against the seats in front of them, their bags flying from the luggage racks. The driver had seen something on the line and ground to a halt a few feet in front of the obstruction, which turned out to be a man in a beret, kneeling on the ground with his neck stretched across the track. The driver jumped out of the train and tried to talk to the suicide. At first he refused to move. Then he agreed to sit on a bank beside the train and before long a crowd of curious passengers had gathered around them, standing quietly in the thin sunlight.

The man in the beret came from one of the forgotten villages nearby, where no trains stopped and nothing disturbed the trance-like monotony of village life, unless it were the annual *fiesta mayor* or the arrival of someone's son or grandson on a weekend visit from Barcelona. The man began to cry. His wife had just left him, he told the driver between sobs. Some of the passengers giggled at this, thinking it might cheer him up. '*Hombre*, what are you worrying about? You're a lucky man!' But this was no laughing matter. It transpired that his wife had left him after he found her in bed with the village baker — a woman — wearing a false moustache and a large plastic dildo strapped to her waist. The two of them had been lovers for years.

The train driver shrugged his shoulders. These things happen in the modern world, he said. The passengers nodded their heads: they had heard such stories before, in the fleshpots of Valencia and Madrid.

The man in the beret wasn't convinced, but he promised to reconsider the matter. He stood up, wiped his eyes with the back of his hand and walked away slowly through the rows of vines. The driver climbed back into his seat, the passengers into theirs, and the train continued on its way. For once the Intercity service, so admirably punctual these days, would be arriving a little late.

Epilogue

'*Bueno es recordar*
Las palabras viejas
Que han de volver a sonar.'

'It is good to remember
The old words
That must sound again'
(Antonio Machado, *Nuevas*
Canciones)

They've been fixing up the old well down the road. For months I walked past with the dogs every day and never even knew it was there, between a dirt track through the woods and a stony *torrentera* where the water rushes down from the hills during the rainy season. All that was left of the original well was a shallow basin with a rudimentary plug-hole, picked out of a great rock. I remember once thinking of stealing this rock and installing it at home as a spectacular garden ornament. That would have been a terrible act of vandalism, I understand now, because basin and well together form part of the scant cultural heritage of what has become my village, my community, my story.

Between an unknown, unrecorded moment in the distant past and a particular moment almost half a century ago there used to be an annual dance around this well, clearly rooted in pre-Christian rituals of fertility and water-worship. The last dance was in August

1952. Nobody knows why the tradition died. The first foreigners for thirty years were being seen on the island, presaging the tourist boom of the 1960s. The TV was to arrive a few years later. Perhaps there was a general mood of self-consciousness about, a feeling that dancing in praise of water was somehow an embarrassing thing to be seen doing in the formica-crazed 1950s. Certainly there was a strange moment at about that time when large numbers of peasant women decided to cut off the long tresses that hung down their backs, which had never been cut since birth. Could anything be more perfectly symbolic of the idea of rupture, breaking with tradition, cutting links with the past, than that grand, reckless gesture? In any case, the Pou des Baladre – *pou* meaning 'well', *baladre* 'olean-der', the bed of the stream being a jungle of them, their flowers coming dayglo pink in early summer – has just been rebuilt. There is now a dome-like stone structure over the well, a little cross on top, a stone floor spreading around it, and a simple door in the side of the dome made of naturally curving sticks of pine. This winter it has rained more than over any winter in the past decade, putting paid to seven years of drought, and the *torrentera* now trickles quietly from pool to pool. Peer into the well, and you'll see that it's full. Elderly people, light in their eyes, will tell you these days the countryside looks like it did when they were young; even *sounds* the way it did, criss-crossed with streams and waterfalls, with water seeping from under stone walls and springs bursting out of rocks . . .

When we moved into this house two years ago it was a time capsule; it was a museum of local life; it was a mess. The house had, has, a few years on its back, you could tell that by the thickness of the walls – more than a metre in places – and their uneven, curvaceous surfaces, suggesting various hundred years of whitewash, layer upon layer forming organic shapes. The house had been carved out of a rocky escarpment on the side of a hill. The back part of it is actually buried in the rock, with its little fortress windows peering out at ground level. It faces south, so that in high summer the heat batters on the front door. But the windows have wooden shutters, the heavy door is kept firmly shut, and the interior of the house becomes a dark refuge, twenty degrees cooler than the inferno of the patio.

The house on the hill had been shoved out of the way and left behind by the twentieth century. It had no running water, no telephone, no E-mail and no Internet, no speed-of-light connection with the brains of 50 million, or 200 million, or a billion people. It had never been seen by artificial light, though the landlord's father had once tried rigging up a Heath Robinson system of snaking wires connecting a series of low-watt light bulbs to the battery of his tractor. This was still in place, though fouled up with grime.

The house hadn't been lived in full-time since the landlord's mother died twenty years before, and had not been properly cleaned for even longer. Prints of virgins and martyrs in dark frames hung on the walls, almost invisible with dirt. A mysterious brown bulk in a corner, covered with what looked like a brown woollen blanket, turned out to be a neolithic Singer sewing machine, with a scrap of cotton still under the needle and a coat of dust lying thickly over it. The place was a living refutation of Quentin Crisp's theory that after four years of non-dusting, the dust doesn't get any worse. I walked through it in the grip of a strange emotion, somewhere between wonder and trepidation. Recep, three beds, no bathroom, fully carpeted throughout – with dust.

In the kitchen, a great black cathedral of a room with a false wall and door half-way along and half-way up, the trepidation turned to horror. For centuries there had been no fireplace here; the farmer and his family had simply made their fire in the middle of the earth floor. The result was that the stone walls and the beamed ceiling were indistinguishable under a black miasma of soot and animal fat, hanging in dense, clinging webs. Beyond the false wall lay piles of rotting farm equipment, baskets, barrels, objects whose function would never again be clear, piles of decomposing almonds in their shells, and mummified rats with parchment skins, strewn around plates of the poison that killed them. In the corner of the room was a terracotta basin, plastered into the wall, in which clothes would have been washed with an alkaline substance made from burned almond husks. On a plank jutting out from the wall in what had latterly become the food-preparation area were the remains of a widower's sad fried meal, blackened and stuck like glue to the base of a handsome iron frying-pan.

The house stood in a landscape of steep terraces planted mostly with almond trees, which were about the only things still thriving after the almost total abandonment of the land for two decades. Hundreds of yards of stone wall, a major feat of civil engineering in itself, were crumbling yard by yard through lack of maintenance. A tiny lemon tree had clung to life, a fig tree had gone into a dried-up coma, and a pomegranate was hemmed in by thorns. One of the first things we did was to prune the lemon savagely, lavishly manure the fig and free the sleeping beauty from its prison of spines. It was said to be a dry house, built on rock and high enough to catch the east wind that blows in from the sea along the valley. The water supply was rainfall, gathered in a deep cistern with a whitewashed dome over the mouth, and there hadn't been much of that during the long and terrible drought of the early 1990s. With no irrigation, it was also a dry house in another sense. The land around it might once have produced beans, peas, potatoes, tomatoes, but now it seemed condemned to a future as *secano* land, good only for hardy almond, carob, olive trees. The dust blew in gusts around the house, carried on the spring wind. It had scarcely rained at all this last winter, and the countryside looked stressed and sickly, as though it were wasting away. Even the weeds were droopily undernourished. Stories had been appearing in the Spanish press about the creeping desert, the barrenness moving slowly north through Spain from the Sahara, and it made me uneasy. In my mind's eye I pictured a yellow sea of sand-dunes billowing wildly across the country, breaking incessantly upon a crumbling fortress of green.

We dumped our possessions in piles outside the front door and wondered where to start. For the first few months we washed and washed up with cold water in a metal bucket from the well, learning how to value and be grateful for every drop, as Spanish country people had always done before the days of mains water and PVC plumbing. Our lives were lit by candles and glass oil-lamps with thick woven wicks. In one of the cave-like stables that clustered around the central patio like houses around the village square lay a rusty carriage-lamp with a curved glass eye that concentrated the light of a single candle into a powerful beam like that of a torch. We found baskets woven out of olive shoots or the fibre of the agave cactus, far more durable and better-looking than plastic shopping-bags; a Flintstones-style knife-sharpener with a granite wheel that you turned with a handle; fat-bellied clay cooking-pots that magically transformed even the simplest chickpea *cocido* into a complex, richly-flavoured thing; and a little wooden wash-stand with a mirror and bowl and shelf for the soap, which had once stood by the front door. We were delighted by the practicality and beauty of these requisitioned objects, and it disturbed us to think that they had been cared for so well for generations, and then been cast off and dumped in outhouses, a prey to rats and rot.

The banging and crashing, the piles of rubble, the sweat and tears of that summer almost destroyed my sanity, but the discoveries we made were a source of wonder. An unaccountable skin of green bathroom tiles was torn away from an inner wall, and from behind the cloud of dust emerged the rocks of the original wall, coloured manganese and ochre like the ones on the sea-shore, reached along a forest path from the house – where they had surely been gathered. In the midst of the multicoloured rocks was a plastered, white-washed niche, a tiny room with its own beamed ceiling, possibly a hiding-place for jewellery or other precious things.

Pulling at the drought-starved weeds on the patio, I saw that under a thin crust of earth lay a magnificent stone paving, the individual stones each picked into shape with a chisel. It would have been an ideal surface for anything that required a flattish surface and plenty of open space, such as the killing of the pig. The pig would have lived a few steps away in its own stone *corral*, and the things it became were stored in a cool chamber at the back of the house. Between the low beams of this room and the ceiling of the house itself, it dawned on us, there was another space which for some reason must have been shut off. This often happened when the room in question had witnessed a death, or some other disagreeable event. A mark of respect, or a mark of revulsion. We made a hole big enough for a head, and peered through. The room contained a pile of old handmade tiles and the mummified body of a cat.

More spooks were to come in the kitchen, and not just because of its Stygian condition. A local witch-woman came visiting and, raising her eyes to the blackened rafters, promptly went into a sort of trance, mumbling something about a *presencia negra* and the need to cleanse the room thoroughly of spiritual, as well as material, nastiness. A few days later she rushed back in glee to tell us that, according to her researches, a whole family had once been hacked to death in that very room. She gave us incense and white candles. We dutifully burned both and have never been troubled with ghosts or bad vibes ever since.

Week by week and month by month, the house seemed to be offering us clues about the way life was once lived in it and might perhaps be lived again. From one of the stables came a basketful of traditional clothes, once apparently the property of the farmer's wife. There was a thick pleated long black bodice dress – exquisitely made, probably on the old Singer in the porch; a Sunday-best hat with a black ribbon round the crown, tightly woven in cactus fibre and painted with whitewash; and a pair of esparto-grass *alpargatas*, perfectly tiny and delicate. From the cactus patch below the house came a collection of bottles: fat little old pink glass medicine-bottles with the names of Barcelona pharmacists along the side; fine blue blown glass jars with a Roman look; a beer-bottle with a ceramic stopper that read 'La Fourmilière, Alger'. In times of poverty, after the Civil War, or when the wheat harvest failed and whole families were reduced to living on carob pods, the young and able-bodied and adventurous would often look for work abroad, particularly in Algeria. The beer-bottle must have been brought back as a souvenir.

In a corner of the kitchen stood a four-legged wooden object. So much of pre-modern culture is as foreign to us now as alien space-craft from another galaxy. It took me a few minutes of examining it from various angles to realise that it was some sort of receptacle for treading grapes. It would be placed on top of a barrel and one of the smaller members of the family would cavort barefoot inside the high-sided square wooden treader, while the juice dripped into the barrel below. There were no vines left alive on the property except the great over-arching Muscat beside the front door which gives such a wonderful crop of sweet and fragrant white grapes. Impossible to know when the last wine was made, but an old brandy-bottle with the word 'Moscatel' scratched on the label in pencil contained a sticky golden liquid that could have been a couple of decades old.

During those first few months we cleaned everything in the house, and I use the word 'cleaned' in its broadest sense. Doors and shutters slathered in grey and brown and green paint were taken off their hinges and treated with caustic soda and sawdust, revealing dark wood surfaces covered with chisel-marks – the planks had been pried away from the trunk with a chisel, not cut with a saw. The few bits of rustic furniture belonging to the house – ranks of tiny antique chairs with rush-woven seats, a wooden-framed meat-safe with sliding doors, the sturdy splay-legged table for the *matanza* (Table of Death), three or four home-made trunks for clothes, the squat little table I'm writing on at this moment – were treated with beeswax and linseed oil. Anything with varnish on it was ruthlessly stripped. The beams were painted with cheap motor oil thinned with turpentine, which turned us into glue-sniffers for a couple of days but brought out the shine and rich russet colour of the local pine. I became an expert in the use of cleaning fluids now thought hopelessly antiquated. Vinegar and newspaper for windows – surely the most efficient method there is. Bleach; ammonia; *sal fumant*, 'smoking salt', aka hydrochloric acid, still sold over the counter in Spanish hardware stores, for bathrooms and begrimed kitchens. To disinfect our drinking water, we lobbed a lump of quicklime in the well. When we had finished, the house smelled the way cleanness used to smell, raw and pungently chemical, before the word 'natural' became a touchstone of modern life and everything had to reek of 'forest pine' or 'alpine flowers' and other artificial pongs.

I set to painting the house inside and out, mixing up the whitewash in the big terracotta lime-encrusted whitewash pot that stood in the hall. The rocks boiled and rumbled in the water, then resolved themselves into a liquid with the consistency of milk that slopped wetly on to walls and seemed at first pathetically ineffectual as paint, but then dried suddenly to a miraculous, unearthly whiter-than-white that dazzled in the summer sun and glowed ultraviolet under the moon. Plastic paint is much easier to use and you have to apply it only once in a lifetime, but the colour has a dull, empty sheen. Deep Spain knows that whitewash is better, that it is naturally disinfectant, that it allows the wall to breathe. I felt the curious ritual undertow that whitewashing brings with it, the way it takes its place among the universe of activities peculiar to springtime, when the spirit wants things to be light and bright and sparkling.

The downside of whitewashing is that it leaves your hands feeling like dried-up bits of leather. But for this, too, deep Spain has a solution. A leaf of the aloe cactus, which grows wild all over the south, is broken and the jelly inside is smeared on the skin, for near-instant healing of burns, minor cuts and dryness. Our neighbour showed me this when she clambered up the terraces one day to see how the work was progressing. She showed me other tricks, too, though she wouldn't have thought of them as anything special. The dog barked and bared its teeth at her. Rattled by this unfriendly treatment, she reached inside her dress and discreetly rubbed her right hand under her left arm, holding out this hand for the dog to sniff.

Instant recognition, instant respect, if not quite instant friendship.

For as long as she could remember until a few months previously, the neighbour had brought her sheep up to graze around the house. She approved of the changes we were making, but regretted the imminent conversion of the old *cuarto de matanzas*, the pig-product store, into a bathroom. Where would we store all our sausages and bacon and lard from now on? Remembering that we didn't have a pig, and would therefore have no pig products that needed storing, she shook her head a little sadly. The house had been without a pig too long and, without one, a house is not a real house. 'The pig is its soul,' she said.

The house had no pig, but it also had no telephone. So, early one morning, a gang of workmen came up from the town with a mechanical digger, planning to lay a length of cable along the dirt track from the house to the main road. Everything went smoothly until they reached a point some ten metres from the road, when one of the workmen called me over. The path of Progress is fraught with perils. A little old man with a hunched back, wearing a jacket and beret and clutching a stick, had appeared as if from nowhere and stood in the path of the digger, shouting imprecations and refusing to move. His hunch was so extreme that his swearing appeared to be directed mostly at the ground. This part of the track was his property, and nobody and nothing would be allowed to touch it. I noticed that in his fury he had bitten his lower lip, which was now seeping blood.

Little by little the whole truth emerged. The old man was a neighbour on the other side of the farm, and his objection to the digger sprang from a poisonous century-old feud between his great-grandfather and the great-grandfather of my landlord. Nothing personal, we were to understand, but he would never do anything to oblige our landlord, who was just as wicked and untrustworthy a man as his ancestors before him.

In the café next to the village church, a dark and silent place except on Sunday evenings when the old men gather to play *mus* (the deep Spanish card game *por excelencia*), they told me the story of the quarrel. It involved a father's emigration to Argentina at the turn of the century, a piece of land lost by his son in a card game – *mus*, on a Sunday evening at the village café – and the father's vain attempts to claim back the land on his return. The general opinion in the village was that my neighbour was so cantankerous and stubborn that the only way the phone would ever be installed would be if he keeled over and died. The carpenter's wife even remarked, with a certain brutal but none the less admirable realism, that it might be an idea to go ahead with the digging, because then the old man might have a heart-attack and our problems would be over.

Spring turned to summer, and the saga of the feud and the phone dragged on. There seemed to be no solution. Then we realised that there was a point, just between the neighbour's track and the field above it, where the cable could pass without awaking any more ancient enmities. The only thing that stood in the way was a great carob tree with twisted roots that tentacled out and down into the rust-red earth. When the phone company suddenly announced on a Friday that they were coming to connect on the Monday, and there was still no cable laid, we spent the weekend digging a trench along the only viable course for it, and when the trench reached the carob tree, simply threaded the cable among its roots. It felt as though we had built a spindly, precarious, pioneering bridge between the old ways and the new; between doing things that had always been done, for no other reason than that they had always been done, and doing things that have never been done in the whole history of man; between the way to 'before' and the motorway of modern times.

The rhythm of deep Spain is something you feel with increasing clarity as you open your ears to it. You fall into step with it, like a soldier joining a bedraggled and battle-weary but still tramping army. Civilisation has become progressively more alienated from the rhythm of the natural world, and the process of readjustment, reacquaintance and remembering is not always an easy one.

'To every thing there is a season.' It's a notion the Europeans have all but forgotten, now that supermarkets sell tomatoes and apples and red peppers and green beans all year round, riding roughshod over the concept of seasonality, and now that the old cycles of the religious year with their complex ritual machinery are ever more and more remote from us.

In what remains of all the old societies of Europe, early summer is the season of the wheat harvest. At a nearby farm the corn was ready, the grains bursting with ripeness in the heats of June. But labour was in short supply. The farmer's sons have sensible jobs in offices and hotels and are supremely uninterested in the ways of the country. When the old man retires, there'll be no one to take over the farm. So, *faute de mieux*, we were taken on as harvest hands. We reported for work at five am, wearing straw hats from the house and pitchforks made from tree-branches, and drank coffee in the farmer's kitchen. If we started at first light, we'd have a clear six hours before the heat kicked in at midday.

At first we were clumsy and incompetent: the farmer's wife laughed at our ignorance. But as dawn brightened into morning we learned how to rake the newly-cut corn into neat sheaves and to pile them cleanly on the back of the truck without dropping a single stem. The work was agonising. As the lorry filled up with corn, the sheaves had to be lifted higher and higher on the fork, putting the shoulder muscles through a gruelling punishment. The morning sun found its way under my hat and dazzled me. Grain-dust worked its way under my T-shirt and into my lungs. By ten o'clock I was sweaty and dust-choked, but more than two-thirds of the field was still carpeted with cut corn. It was a revelation and a shock, to think that wheat would have been collected this way, more or less, from the very dawn of agriculture until the invention of the combine harvester.

The grain was threshed in an old wooden contraption that

rumbled and creaked and shook and spat stray husks into the air. It was ground into flour in an old stone mill. Staying true for once to the age-old process, we fired up the domed bread-oven on the terrace at home – it had lain unused for decades – and made great roundels of country bread (*pa pageés*), so wide you could carry them in the circle of your linked arms.

The turning year brought in other harvests from the land: almonds in late August, figs and prickly pears in September, olives in December. The land's wild produce came in alternative waves: capers in May, blackberries in July, wild mushrooms in November. At the turn of the New Year we began to pick wild asparagus, which everyone who has tried it knows is one of the sublimest vegetables known to man or woman: tender and crunchy at the same time, and with a bitter tang long since bred out of modern commercial varieties. It flourishes wherever ploughed fields have been abandoned, wherever cultivated land is reverting inevitably to fallow. It is creeping and insidious, with its long tap roots and fiendish spines; you can hinder its growth, but you can't entirely halt it. It could almost be a metaphor for the decline and decay of the Spanish countryside, and its bittersweet flavour for the hard-won rewards of traditional life.

One winter morning the silence was broken by a high-pitched shriek from across the valley. The *matanza* season had begun, and there was more demand that year for the skills of the pig-killer, with his terrifying knife, than there had been for years. When a family in a neighbouring farm decided the time was ripe, we were drafted in to help, along with a handful of elderly neighbours who smiled inquisitively at us, clearly wondering which planet we had descended from.

An early start; coffee in the kitchen, again, in nervous contemplation of the bloody ceremony to follow. The sow had been starved for a day, and was already restlessly snuffling in her stone hut a few steps away from where we sat. The winter sun broke through the dawn mist. The party put down its coffee cups, scraped back its chairs and split into the two primal, equal-but-opposing, elements of pre-modern society. The women fetched the pots and pans, picked oranges and rue branches for cleaning, and set up tables and chairs in the shade of a rock. And the men went to kill the pig.

We led the animal out of its house to a low, sturdy table on a flat piece of ground nearby. So far she seemed calm of spirit. She seemed far more interested in the lush green world that lay beyond her front door than worried by intimations of mortality. But then we bound her feet with rope, flipped her on her back and hoisted her on to the table, all 150 kilos of reluctant pig. Then she knew the story. She fought to get free and we fought back, pulling her feet, tail and ears with all our strength. She launched into an ear-splitting scream of fear, shock, but mostly of outrage, that echoed the length and breadth of the valley. The peasant women cackled to each other by the kitchen door. '*Ay, ay!* What a racket! Someone stop that noise! You'll wake up the neighbours!' they joked.

But they had been here many times before, and knew the noise wouldn't last long. The moment of the sacrifice had come. The farmer, with the clear head acquired from a lifetime of *matanzas*, poised his shining knife above the neck of the beast and plunged it in as far as it would go, stirring it about inside, searching with its point for the jugular vein and, beyond it, the heart. The blood gushed in a thick hot torrent, splashing steaming into a washing-up bowl, while the pig hurled its last insults at the world. It was a terrible moment of heightened, sickening emotion: horror and pity, fear and fascination curdled inside me. No, it didn't last long. Within a minute the pig's body began to grow faint and loose, her blood-gush slowed to a drip, and her scream gradually weakened and grew sluggish like a 78 record on a wind-up gramophone. Within another minute she lay still on the table, ready to embark on her miraculous journey from pig to pork. And we stood back dry-mouthed and gasping, in a moment of awestruck silence, shot through with gratitude, that felt very like a prayer.

We lived through the rest of the day in the wake of that moment, learning how to burn the hairs off the animal and scrape the bristle away with rough stones from the beach, watching the carcass open up like a deep freeze under the butcher's knife and the way the women rinsed the entrails clean with sweet well water and the juice of bitter oranges. The old people showed us how to sort the meat into various classes, how to grind it and spice it and salt it and preserve it, and what to do with the feet, ears and tail that we'd gripped with all our might a few hours before.

We left in the evening with our arms full of sausages stained vibrant orange with paprika and black blood-sausages made from the foaming contents of the blue washing-up bowl. And we felt that the day had brought us closer to the mysterious knot of ecology and metaphysics and pure human ingenuity that lies at the heart of Spain than we had ever come before.

Closer than we'd come, that is, until we had a pig of our own, and our house, which had languished for so many years on the brink of death, was finally rewarded with a soul.

Sant Vicent de sa Cala
February 1997

Glossary of Spanish Terms

aceituna: olive.
acequia: irrigation channel.
alameda: tree-lined promenade.
alcantarilla: sewer.
alpargatas: rope sandals.
aquelarre: witches' moot.
azulejo: glazed tile.

barranco: ravine, gully.
bocadillo: Spanish sandwich.
bonita: pretty.
bota: leather container for wine.
bruja: witch.
brujo: sorcerer, wizard.
buenas: hello (short for good morning, good afternoon).
buenas tardes: good afternoon.
buenos días: good morning.
butifarra: Catalan sausage.

cabildo: local island government.

café con leche: coffee with milk.

café solo: black coffee.

calabaza: pumpkin.

caldo: broth, soup.

calle: street.

campanillas: convolvulus (lit. little bells).

campo: countryside.

cañada: sheep track.

¡caramba!: good gracious!

cármen: a villa with a garden in Granada.

casa: house.

castro: Iron age fortress/settlement.

cementerio: cemetery.

cerdo: pig.

cerveza: beer.

chino: pig (in Murcia region).

chorizo: spicy, cured Spanish sausage.

churros: fried dough.

cochinilla: prickly pear beetle, bred for red pigment.

cochino: pig.

cocido: stew.

comida: food, lunch.

coplas: folk songs.

costalero: float-carrier in Holy Week processions.

costillas: ribs.

cuadrilla: bunch of friends.

cuarto: room.

curandeiro: (Galicia) natural healer.

curandero: natural healer.

dehesa: natural Iberian pastureland.

Dios: God.

¡Dios mio!: My God!

envuelto: Murcian pork sausage.
eternidad: eternity.
Euskadi: (Basque) Basque country.
euskaldun: (Basque) Basque.
Euskera: (Basque) Basque language.

favor: favour.
festa: (Galicia) fiesta.
fideos: thin Spanish noodles.
filliño: (Galicia) dear son.
fino: dry sherry.
fonda: lodging house.

ganado: livestock.
gofio: Canary Island cereal mush.
gracias: thank you.
gràcies: (Catalan) thank you.
grande: big.
guapa: good-looking, beautiful.
guapísima: very good-looking, beautiful.
Guardia Civil: Spanish police.

hola: hello.
horno: oven.
hórreo: raised granary.

íbero: Iberian.

jaleo: disorder, fun, hassle.
jamón serrano: mountain ham.
jamón York: boiled ham.

leyenda: legend.

madrugada (madrugá): early hours of the morning.

magdalena: sponge cake.

Mahou: popular brand of beer from Madrid.

maravedí: old Spanish currency.

maravilla: wonder.

maricón: poof.

matanza: pig-killing.

meiga: (Galicia) witch.

Mesta: powerful Castilian shepherd brotherhood.

mierda: shit.

migas: fried crumbs.

mojo: Canary Island sauce.

monasterio: monastery.

Montilla: an Andalusian wine, similar to sherry.

morcilla: blood sausage.

moscatel: muscat grape, the sweet wine it produces.

mozárabe: Spanish Christian under Islamic rule.

muchacha: girl.

mus: a Spanish card game.

nada: nothing.

nazareno: participant in Holy Week procession, normally wears tall conical hat.

niña: young girl.

noche: night.

número: number.

pa: (Catalan) bread.

pagés: (Catalan) farmer, peasant.

pan: bread.

panceta: fat bacon.

papas: potatoes (Canary Islands).

parcela: plot, piece of ground.

parque: park.

pastor: shepherd.

pelo: hair.

pelota vasca: Basque ball game.

pensión: lodging-house.

pequeño: little, small.

pimentón: paprika.

pimiento choricero: dried red pepper.

pipirrana: dish typical of La Mancha.

playa: beach.

por favor: please.

pórtico: door, gate.

posada: country boarding house.

prado: meadow.

Prado (museo): Spanish national gallery.

pueblo: village, people.

puente: bridge.

pulpeira: (Galicia) octopus stall.

pulpo: octopus.

Rastro: Madrid street market

real: old Spanish coin.

regalo: present.

Ribeiro: a Galician wine.

romería: pilgrimage.

romero: pilgrim.

rosado: pink wine.

salchichón: cured sausage analogous to *saucisson*, salami.

secano: unirrigated land.

señorito: Andalusian landowner.

serranía: mountain range.

sevillanas: dance, originated in Seville.

sierra: mountains.

sobrassada: soft sausage cured with paprika,
from the Balearic Islands.
sombrero: hat.

tabaco: tobacco.
tapita: little *tapa*.
tariqa: (Turkish) Sufi group.
terrero: arena for Canarian wrestling.
tocino: pork fat.
tonta: silly girl.
tonto: silly boy.
torrentera: dry river bed.
tortilla de patatas: potato omelette.
treball: (Catalan) work.
trenza: plaited hair.
tunera: prickly pear cactus (Canary Is.).

valle: valley.
vaquero: cowboy.
¡venga!: come on!

Abacus now offers an exciting range of quality titles by both established and new authors. All of the books in this series are available from:

Little, Brown and Company (UK),
P.O. Box 11,
Falmouth,
Cornwall TR10 9EN.

Fax No: 01326 569555
Telephone No: 01326 569777
E-mail: books@barni.avel.co.uk

Payments can be made as follows: cheque, postal order (payable to Little, Brown and Company) or by credit cards, Visa/Access. Do not send cash or currency. UK customers and B.F.P.O. please allow £1.00 for postage and packing for the first book, plus 50p for the second book, plus 30p for each additional book up to a maximum charge of £3.00 (7 books plus).

Overseas customers including Ireland, please allow £2.00 for the first book plus £1.00 for the second book, plus 50p for each additional book.

NAME (Block Letters) ....

....

ADDRESS ....

....

....

☐ I enclose my remittance for ....

☐ I wish to pay by Access/Visa Card

Number ☐☐☐☐☐☐☐☐☐☐☐☐☐☐☐☐

Card Expiry Date ☐☐☐☐